实用英语翻译教学研究

A Study on Practical English Translation Teaching

余胜映 编著

北京理工大学出版社
BEIJING INSTITUTE OF TECHNOLOGY PRESS

版权专有　侵权必究

图书在版编目（CIP）数据

实用英语翻译教学研究 / 余胜映编著. -- 北京：北京理工大学出版社，2024.7.
ISBN 978 - 7 - 5763 - 3538 - 5

Ⅰ. H315.9

中国国家版本馆 CIP 数据核字第 2024VE1991 号

责任编辑：芈　岚	**文案编辑**：芈　岚
责任校对：刘亚男	**责任印制**：施胜娟

出版发行 / 北京理工大学出版社有限责任公司
社　　址 / 北京市丰台区四合庄路 6 号
邮　　编 / 100070
电　　话 / （010）68914026（教材售后服务热线）
　　　　　（010）63726648（课件资源服务热线）
网　　址 / http：//www.bitpress.com.cn

版 印 次 / 2024 年 7 月第 1 版第 1 次印刷
印　　刷 / 保定市中画美凯印刷有限公司
开　　本 / 710 mm×1000 mm　1/16
印　　张 / 17.5
字　　数 / 274 千字
定　　价 / 89.00 元

图书出现印装质量问题，请拨打售后服务热线，负责调换

前　言

英语翻译教学的任务是向学生传授基本的翻译理论和常用方法、技巧、策略等，并通过大量实践和反复练习培养学生的翻译技能，提高其翻译质量。

《实用英语翻译教学研究》共五章。第一章简要介绍了当前翻译教学的现状、目标、原则和翻译教学的本质，以及文化差异与英语翻译教学的关系。第二章介绍了不同视角下的翻译教学。第三章介绍了汉英互译常见的方法和技巧。第四章介绍了不同语境下的汉英互译方法和技巧。第五章对数字化时代英语翻译教学面临的机遇与挑战进行了讨论和思考。

书中例句大部分选自国内外出版的书报、杂志，也有部分例句来自网络。不同译者对同一作品有不同的译法，本书在介绍翻译方法和技巧过程中所采用的译例仅供参考。作者在写作过程中借鉴和参考了许多有关书刊，并从中选用了不少例句。由于编写和排版工作需要，文中译例等大多没有注明出处，而在参考文献部分另列。

由于作者翻译教学经验有限，书中难免有疏漏及不妥之处，希望广大同行和读者批评指正。

余胜映
2024 年 1 月 21 日

Contents

Chapter 1　An Overview of English Translation Teaching ······ 1

　　Section 1　Current Situations of Contemporary English Translation Teaching ······ 3
　　Section 2　Philosophies and Objectives of English Translation Teaching ······ 10
　　Section 3　Modes and Principles of English Translation Teaching ······ 17
　　Section 4　English Translation Teaching from the Perspective of Communication Studies ······ 22
　　Section 5　Cultural Differences and English Translation Teaching ······ 25

Chapter 2　Different Perspectives of English Translation Teaching ······ 37

　　Section 1　English Translation Teaching from the Perspective of Functional Equivalence ······ 39
　　Section 2　English Translation Teaching from the Teleological Perspective ······ 47
　　Section 3　English Translation Teaching from the Cognitive Linguistics Perspective ······ 52
　　Section 4　Translation Teaching from the Perspective of Communication Studies ······ 61
　　Section 5　Translation Teaching from the Perspective of Pragmatics ······ 80

Chapter 3　Translation Techniques and Methods ······ 97

　　Section 1　Approaches to English Translation Teaching ······ 99
　　Section 2　Literal Translation in English Translation ······ 103

Section 3　Techniques and Methods of Vocabulary Translation ·········· 107
Section 4　Techniques and Methods of Sentence Translation ··········· 148
Section 5　Techniques and Methods of Discourse Translation ·········· 160

Chapter 4　Practical Application of English Translation ············· 167

Section 1　Business English Translation ································· 169
Section 2　Translation of College English Test ·························· 175
Section 3　Translation of Subjunctive Mood in Business English Translation
　　　　　·· 179
Section 4　Translation of English Advertisement ························ 185
Section 5　Translation of Chinese Cultural Classics ···················· 190
Section 6　Translation of Chinese Political Documents ················· 213
Section 7　Translation of Chinese Culture ································ 222

Chapter 5　Opportunities and Challenges of English Translation Teaching in the Digital Era ·· 241

Section 1　Opportunities of English Translation Teaching in the Digital Era
　　　　　·· 244
Section 2　Challenges of English Translation Teaching in the Digital Era
　　　　　·· 246
Section 3　Strategies of English Translation Teaching in the Digital Era ···· 248
Section 4　Expectations of English Translation Teaching in the Digital Era
　　　　　·· 250
Section 5　Translation and Technology ··································· 252
Section 6　The Development Trend of Translation Studies in the Digital Era ·· 257

主要参考文献 ·· 268

Chapter 1
An Overview of English Translation Teaching

Section 1

Current Situations of Contemporary English Translation Teaching

The current situation of contemporary English translation teaching is not promising, for it faces several problems. Let's briefly examine these problems below.

Ⅰ. Problems of the Curriculum

Despite the significant role of translation, it has not received adequate attention in English teaching. The reasons are mainly as follows: Firstly, the *Teaching Syllabus for English Majors in Higher Education Institutions* serves as the guiding document for college English teaching, yet it does not place sufficient emphasis on translation instruction. Although the 1999 edition of the syllabus mentioned the cultivation of students' translation abilities in teaching objectives, its primary focus remained on developing students' strong reading skills as well as listening, speaking, reading, writing, and translating abilities. The 2004 edition of the *Teaching Requirements for College English Courses (Trial)* emphasized the development of students' comprehensive application abilities in English, particularly in listening and speaking. Thus, it is evident that translation instruction does not receive much attention in college English teaching. Additionally, college English has traditionally been considered as a foundational course, with most universities offering intensive reading, extensive reading, and audio-visual courses. However, translation instruction has been neglected and often treated as an optional component. Following the introduction of English-to-Chinese translation questions in the 1996 CET-4 (College English Test Band 4) test paper, translation questions only appeared twice in the subsequent 12 exams until

2002. This indicates that translation instruction in college English has not been strongly guided by the exams. The *Reform Plan for the National College English Test Band 4 and 6 (Trial)* issued in 2004 introduced translation as an examination component, transitioning from English-to-Chinese translation to Chinese-to-English translation. Translation questions now appear alternately in the comprehensive test section and the passage-based Q&A section of the exam, accounting for 5% of the total score. Finally, translation has been included in the prestigious CET-4 examination, but the percetage remains minimal.

Ⅱ. Issues in Students' Translation Practice

Translation ability is one of the comprehensive language skills. Based on some widely recognized tests, it can be seen that students currently have many problems with their translation abilities, primarily manifested in the following aspects:

1. Excessive use of "的" (de)

Many students tend to excessively use the word "的" (de) during the translation process. Whenever they encounter an adjective, they mechanically translate it as "的" (de). For example, "It serves little purpose to have continued public discussion of that issue", students may translate it as "继续公开讨论那个问题是不会有什么益处的". (The continuing public discussion of that issue won't have any benefit.) However, a more concise translation would be "继续公开讨论那个问题没有益处". (The continuing public discussion of that issue has no benefits.)

2. Inability to choose and adjust words

Students often choose the word-for-word translation without considering the need for adaptation in the target language. For example, in the sentence "Women screamed, and kids howled, but the men stood silent, watching, interested in the outcome", a literal translation may result in "女人尖叫，小孩欢闹，男人们静静地站着看着，对结果感兴趣". However, a more accurate and concise translation would be "女人们尖叫，孩子们号啕大哭，男人们静静地站在一旁观望，对结果产生浓厚兴趣". The sentence "Her grace was a delight" was originally translated into "她的优雅是一种快乐". However, a more accurate and concise translation would be"她的优美风度,令人欣悦".

3. Overuse of dialects and slang

In China, dialects are widely used in different regions, which sometimes make the translation process awkward. For example:

a. But, Papa, I just can not swallow it, not even with honey.

Original version:可是,爹,我受不了,就是拌了蜜也咽不下呀。

Revised version:可是,爸,我受不了,就是拌了蜜我也受不了啊。

b. The children lived in terror of their stepfather, who had borne down on them so often and so hard that there was little left.

Original version:孩子们对他们的继父怕得要死,继父经常整他们而且整得很重,简直把他们整瘪了。

Revised version:孩子们对他们的继父怕得要死,因为继父时不时就狠狠地教训他们一顿,他们已经无力应对了。

Therefore, in translation, it is preferable to use standard Chinese. As for differences between English source text and Chinese translation in terms of literary or colloquial language, we can selectively use archaic words and dialects or slang that are widely accepted by readers in various dialect regions and have vitality in contemporary Chinese.

4. Incorrect word choices or extension of meaning

Some students may not choose the correct words or extend the meaning based on the context, resulting in difficulties in understanding the translation, or even causing problems. For example:

a. He has developed an interest in gardening.

Original version:他对园艺发展了兴趣。

Revised version:他对园艺产生了兴趣。

b. The aim of this course is to develop students' writing skill.

Original version:这门课的目的是发展学生的写作技巧。

Revised version:这门课的目的是培养学生的写作技巧。

Based on the given examples, it can be seen that the translation fails to determine the meaning of words based on their collocation and combination within the context. English words have a great deal of semantic flexibility, wherein the same word or part of the speech often carries different meanings in different contexts. During translation, it is crucial to consider the interconnection, logical relationship, or sentence structures within the given context to accurately determine the appropriate meaning of a word in a specific scenario. In some cases, it is even necessary to extend or broaden the scope of a word's meaning. Without considering the context, translating a word in isolation makes it difficult to convey the deeper meaning of a sentence.

5. Improper word order processing

In Chinese, logic is highly emphasized, and sentences typically follow a specific order that progresses from cause to effect, hypothesis to conclusion, fact to judgment, and condition to result. This approach ensures a clear and structured narrative. On the other hand, English has a more flexible word order, which often prioritizes directness and provids explanations afterwards. When expressing complex logical thinking, English arranges word order based on the meaning and desired outcome of the sentence. However, when translating, students often adhere too strictly to the word order of the source English text, resulting in errors in sentences or the word order. In situations where Chinese and English expression habits differ, there may be awkward translations. For example:

a. It is simple that they do the same things in different ways.

Original version：只不过是不同的人做同样的事以不同的方法。

Revised version：只不过他们用不同的方式做同样的事情而已。

b. The doctor is not available because he is handling an emergency.

Original version：医生现在没空，因为他在处理急诊。

Revised version：医生在处理急诊，现在没空。

6. Overly fixed patterns

The passive voice is widely used in English, but students often translate it to Chinese as "……被……"(be + past participle) in a rigid and mechanical manner. For example：

It is considered of no use learning a theory without practice.

脱离实践学理论被认为毫无用处。

While this translation isn't technically wrong, it may sound a bit awkward. Since the passive voice is less commonly used in Chinese, many passive structures can be transformed into active voice. Therefore, a smoother and more natural translation of this sentence could be "脱离实践学理论毫无用处". (People believe that learning a theory without practice holds no value.)

7. Mishandling of long sentences

Long sentences are frequently used in English. When translating such lengthy sentences, students often struggle to properly convert prepositions, phrases, and relative clauses into separate clauses. This can result in foreign-style long sentences that deviate from the expected structure in English translations. For example:

a. Think of ways to turn a trying situation into a funny story which will amuse your family and friends.

想办法把令人尴尬的处境变成一件能让你的家人和朋友开心的趣事。

The English sentence contains an attributive clause. Though the grammar is correct, the translation does not conform to Chinese language habits. When the structure of an English attributive clause is complex, the attributive part of the sentence can be translated into a separate clause. This sentence can be translated as: "想办法把令人尴尬的处境变成趣事,让你的家人和朋友开心". (Finding a way to turn an embarrassing situation into a humorous anecdote brings a little joy to your family and friends.)

b. Since hearing her predicament, I have always arranged to meet people where they or I can be reached in case of delay.

听了她的尴尬经历之后,我就总是安排能够联系上的地方与别人会见,以防耽搁的发生。

The sentence is quite long and contains adverbial clauses. The translation of the text gives people a somewhat confused feeling and may not be easily understood after reading. Therefore, the sentence should be translated into "听她说了那次尴尬的经历之后,每每与人约会,我总是要安排在彼此能够互相联系得上的地方,以免误约".

From the regular semester exams and large-scale standardized tests that are recognized as measures of English proficiency for students, it is apparent that there is an urgent need to improve students' actual translation abilities. At the same time, many shortcomings of students have been exposed in translation practice.

During the regular learning process, many students do not carefully analyze and ponder over the translation exercises assigned by teachers; they simply check the answers directly in the textbook. Even when taking mock exams, they skip the translation part or hastily translate without properly checking the answers. These students rely on teachers' explanations, unwilling to put in their own efforts and are heavily dependent, resulting in a state of blind anxiety.

Another group of students, after realizing their shortcomings in translation abilities, attach great importance to their translation learning and practice. However, they have not found suitable learning methods for themselves. Some of them mindlessly do a bunch of exercises without summarizing key knowledge points in a timely manner. Others randomly find a translation theory book to read through without understanding how to connect translation learning with the improvement of other skills. As a result, they feel that their efforts in translation learning yield only half the results, leading to a sense of fear and difficulty.

The mental and emotional conditions of these two kinds of students mentioned above are not conducive to the learning of translation knowledge and the improvement of translation skills.

Ⅲ. Challenges in Translation Teaching

Translation is a critical skill for effective oral and written communication. Therefore, teaching translation is an essential aspect of English instruction. However, there are several issues that teachers encounter in translation teaching, which can impact the quality of instruction.

1. Limited teaching methods

Currently, translation teaching primarily focuses on guiding students to translate from Chinese to English, neglecting the practice of translating English into Chinese. Teachers often follow a single teaching method, which involves assigning translation exercises to students, correcting their work by identifying and rectifying errors, and discussing the exercises by primarily focusing on error correction and analyzing common mistakes. Despite being time-consuming and demanding, this teaching method does not yield satisfactory results.

2. Insufficient emphasis

The current English curriculum does not place enough emphasis on the development of translation skills. Translation has not been given the same importance as other English language skills. Most teachers employ traditional translation methods that only superficially compare and contrast the differences between Chinese and English. Translation is considered a means to comprehend and reinforce language knowledge, which prioritizes language form over language essence and places greater value on translation knowledge rather than translation abilities. The translation exercises in textbooks often focus solely on key words and sentence patterns without providing systematic translation training. The teaching of translation techniques lacks comprehensive planning and is often taught sporadically, depending on the availability of time.

3. Lack of students' participation

Translation classes tend to have a monotonous atmosphere, resulting in poor teaching effectiveness that does not align with the modern educational concept of student-centered learning. In such classrooms, the teacher becomes the center of attention, who delivers lectures while students passively listen, with limited opportunities for active participation. English translation teaching should move away from a teacher-centered and one-way communication approach to encourage students' involvement through activities such as peer editing, group discussions, collective corrections, or class discussions and revisions of individual student's assignments. By implementing these teaching methods, students' critical thinking skills can be enhanced, their active learning abilities can be cultivated, and they can develop the capacity to identify and solve problems independently. Moreover, this approach creates a lively classroom atmosphere, ultimately improving teaching effectiveness.

Section 2

Philosophies and Objectives of English Translation Teaching

Ⅰ. Philosophies of English Translation Teaching

The goal of English translation teaching is to enable students to grasp the necessary translation knowledge and acquire basic translation skills. Its philosophy generally includes the following points.

1. The prelude of translation teaching

The prelude of translation courses is translation theory. The significance of theory lies in its guidance for the curriculum. Currently, there are not only numerous schools of thought in the field of translation theory, but also a wide range of theories. If all the theoretical viewpoints and related content of different schools of thought are incorporated into one translation theory, it would appear vague and lack coherence and specificity. Many translation theories are traditional which originated from religion and literature, thus relatively lacking applicability. According to relevant data statistics, most translation theories can only be applied to literary translation, while more than 90% of practical translation is rarely discussed at the theoretical level. This imbalance between theory and practice leads many people to believe that translation theory lacks practical value.

On the other hand, Functional Equivalence Theory is more relevant to practical translation. This theory holds that the determining factor in the translation process is neither the source text itself, nor the impact or reflection it has on the receptor. The function endowed by the author to the source text (as claimed by the Theory of

Equivalence). Instead, it is the expected purpose and function of the target text. Practical genre translation generally has practical or even utilitarian purposes. Such purposes are largely constrained by the translator, the target text recipients, their cultural background, and the situational context. Purpose and function serve as the basis and criterion for practical genre translation, and the core of Functional Equivalence Theory lies in the mutual confirmation of purpose and function, effectively combining theory and practice. In fact, translation courses offered by schools aim to enable students to apply translation in practice and see its application. Students' choices of this course are largely driven by the desire to achieve high scores in relevant exams or the reason for future practical work considerations. Therefore, guiding translation teaching with the Functional Equivalence Theory of translation serves to stimulate students' creativity and enthusiasm for learning.

2. The foundation of translation teaching

Language comparison serves as the foundation of translation teaching. We all have such experience that once we step out of the English-speaking environment, we instinctively resort to using our native language, especially beginners. However, as our vocabulary expands, we become willing to speak in English. During this process, we tend to compare Chinese and English, meaning that when we encounter phrases that we are unsure how to translate, we rely on thinking in Chinese. For example, in the 1930s, someone translated "the Milky Way" word-for-word as "牛奶路" (milk road), which becomes an interesting tale in the history of translation. Similarly, students might translate "他的英语水平比我高" (His English level is higher than mine.) as "The level of his English is higher than mine", which is an example of Chinese-like English resulting from a lack of understanding of the differences in linguistic forms between English and Chinese. Translation involves the process of comparing and correlating between the two languages. The purpose of translation courses is to guide students to learn various translation techniques and improve their translation skills based on the mastery of the two languages of Chinese and English, so as to deepen their understanding of the similarities and differences between the two languages.

The emphasis of language comparison lies in the aspects of differences and similarities within them. There are many differences, such as differences in word orders, arrangements of information emphasis, and connective expressions. However, there are also similarities within these differences. For instance, both English and Chinese have prepositions, and sometimes their usage is similar. However, most prepositions in Chinese are derived from verb changes, and some are still difficult to be determined whether they are verbs or prepositions. On the other hand, verbs and prepositions in English are entirely different. Due to this distinction, English prepositions often need to be translated to verbs in Chinese. For example, "to go by bus" is translated as "坐公交车去" (go by bus); "a girl in white" is translated as "穿白衣服的女孩" (a girl wearing white clothes). Certainly, similarities amidst differences are not absolute. Through the comparison of numerous cases of similarities within differences and differences within similarities, one can overcome native language interference and achieve the goal of correct understanding and smooth expression.

3. The core of translation teaching

Translation skills are the core of translation teaching. Mastering translation theories and rules of language comparison helps translators understand the essence and principles of translation from a scientific perspective, opening up the path to the correct and comprehensive translation. However, to be truly excellent in translation, diligent study, practice, and attention to translation methods and techniques are also required. Translation courses primarily focus on imparting and inheriting valuable experience accumulated by previous translators, including both understanding and expression, reflected by translation methods and techniques. For example, in terms of word order, in Chinese, we say "我们在教室里学习", which is expressed as "We are studying in the classroom" in English. In Chinese, the adverbial phrase "在教室里 (in the classroom)" comes before the predicate verb "学习 (studying)". However, in English, the adverbial "in the classroom" must come after the predicate verb "study". The word order of the main elements, such as the subject, predicate verb, object, or predicate complement, is basically the same in English and Chinese sentences. However, the position of various attributive words and the order of various adverbs in English and Chinese differ to some extent, resulting in more variability.

Therefore, adjustments in word order are often necessary during translation.

4. Means of translation teaching

The means of translation teaching combine synthesis and analysis. During the translation process, we will find that a sentence can have multiple translation options, all of which have correct grammar, but there will definitely be one that is the best. To translate accurately, it not only requires translators to have sharp, clear, and insightful minds but also requires a deep understanding of languages.

In the translation process, we need to fully utilize both synthesis and analysis. Synthesis refers to observing and contemplating from the perspective of the overall and systematic relationship of elements. We need to grasp the overall structure, connect the parts, and ultimately form a complete system. At the same time, we need to analyze and observe various aspects dynamically or statically, delving into the essence and true nature of things.

In the process of expression, synthesis and analysis are also required. Analysis is the key to achieve synthesis, and synthesis is our goal. We need to analyze each detail, understand its meaning, and then synthesize them to form a complete, accurate, and fluent expression.

Therefore, in translation teaching, we need to cultivate students' ability to use synthesis and analysis. They need to learn to observe, think, and analyze the relationship between words, language, and culture. They also need to synthesize these elements to produce accurate, fluent, and expressive translation work.

Finally, to be excellent in the field of translation, in addition to mastering the skills of synthesis and analysis, one needs to study diligently, practice diligently, and pay attention to translation methods and techniques. By learning from the valuable experience accumulated by predecessors, we can continuously improve our translation skills and achieve the goal of accurate understanding and fluent expression.

5. Carriers of translation teaching

Classroom teaching is an important means and carrier of translation teaching. Through classroom teaching, teachers can explain the content of the text-book in detail, and provide corresponding guidance on knowledge, skills, processes, methods, as well as emotions, attitudes, and values. In classroom teaching, the principle of practice-oriented and student-centered should be actively implemented, including the following five steps: teachers' explanation, appreciation of model translations, comparison of translated texts, students' practice, and practice review.

(1) Teacher's explanation.

In this step, teachers focus on explaining translation analysis based upon the comparison of English and Chinese languages. They also provide some translation techniques to elevate students' understanding of translation from a perceptual level to a rational level. Through explanations, teachers can elucidate important considerations, problem-solving approaches, and methods during the translation process, helping students establish correct translation concepts and modes of thinking.

(2) Translation appreciation.

Translation appreciation means that teachers can select and explain famous translations that are linguistically beautiful and easily understood. This not only helps stimulate students' appreciation for excellent translations but also provides examples for them to learn from and emulate. By appreciating outstanding translation works, students can experience the artistic beauty of translation while acquiring valuable translation techniques and experience.

(3) Comparison of translated versions.

Teachers can choose two or three different translations of the same source text for comparison and analysis, encouraging students to contemplate and reflect. In the process of comparison, students can evaluate the strengths and weaknesses of different translations and explore different translation styles, in order to choose more appropriate and accurate translation methods, and avoid common translation mistakes.

(4) Practice.

Practice is a crucial component of the entire teaching process. Students' practice includes preview before class and review after, in-class questions and discussions, as well as after-class assignments and exercises. Through continuous practice and application, students can consolidate and apply their learned translation knowledge and skills, improving the accuracy and fluency of their translations.

(5) Practice review.

In this step, teachers can provide feedback and guidance on students' practice works, pointing out areas for improvement and offering relevant suggestions. Through feedback on students' works, teachers can help students correct mistakes, enhance their translation abilities, and stimulate their enthusiasm and creativity in learning.

It's worth noting that when providing feedback on practice, it's important to prioritize understanding the characteristics of both Chinese and English. Analyzing the similarities and differences in their structure and expression helps address challenges encountered in translation, rather than getting bogged down in minor details.

In conclusion, classroom teaching, as a carrier of translation teaching, can provide students with a comprehensive, systematic, and effective learning platform through the guidance of teachers and the participation of students. This helps cultivate students' translation abilities and competence, enabling them to produce accurate, fluent, and valuable translation work in practical applications.

Among the five stages mentioned above, while the explanation stage is primarily carried out by the teachers, discussion is a vital form of organizing teaching in the other four stages. Discussions can take various forms, such as teachers' guiding students in discussions, teachers' asking questions and students' responding, or both teachers' and students' participation in discussions together. Through discussions, students' motivation can be further stimulated, enabling effective communication between teachers and students, as well as among students, ultimately enhancing the overall effectiveness of translation teaching.

Ⅱ. **Objectives of English Translation Teaching**

The goals of English translation teaching can be summarized as follows.

1. To help students understand the basic definitions, nature, forms, and cognitive processes of translation

In the early and intermediate stages of learning, teachers should assist students in gaining knowledge about translation, including its basic definitions, main characteristics, various forms, important roles, major standards, fundamental principles, differences between translation and interpretation, basic skills of both translation and interpretation, as well as the process of information conversion between different languages. It is particularly important to make students be aware of the close relationship between language knowledge and language cognition, and the significance of language cognition in translation. The imparting of this knowledge should be integrated into various teaching activities, requiring active interactions between teachers and students, as well as active participation from students.

2. To cultivate students' bilingual thinking ability and enable them to acquire basic translation skills and methods

Chinese students have been growing up in a Chinese-language environment, so they are accustomed to thinking in Chinese. However, translation requires translators to consider problems using both English and Chinese thinking. Therefore, English translation teaching needs to cultivate students' ability to switch between languages, which becomes an important goal of translation teaching. In addition, to successfully carry out translation, it is necessary to master certain translation techniques and methods. Another important goal of English translation teaching is to enable students to acquire as many translation skills and methods as possible.

3. To improve students' bilingual communication skills

In addition to developing students' translation skills, it is also crucial to enhance their bilingual comprehension and communication abilities. Translation involves the use of language in communicative activities, where language meanings can be rich and nuanced. Therefore, thorough preparation both before and after translation is necessary. This includes expanding students' horizons and knowledge base continuously, as well as strengthening their comprehension skills.

Section 3

Modes and Principles of English Translation Teaching

Ⅰ. Models of English Translation Teaching

Here, we focus on two models of English translation teaching: student-centered teaching model and multimedia teaching model.

1. Student-centered teaching

According to modern educational views, the learning process is a cognitive process where students actively receive stimuli and actively participate in constructing meaning. Students are the recipients of teaching services, and the teaching process should be organized with students as the center, fully harnessing their enthusiasm and creativity, while also considering the guiding role of teachers. Thus, the importance of the student-centered teaching model is emphasized.

The student-centered teaching model exhibits significant teaching characteristics, primarily manifested in the following aspects.

(1) The main objective of teaching is to cultivate students' independent translation abilities.

(2) The focus of teaching shifts from being teacher-centered to being student-centered.

(3) Attention is given to students' learning enthusiasm and initiative.

(4) Emphasis is placed on the translation process.

(5) Attention is given to build students' confidence, and teachers are required to maintain a positive and tolerant attitude towards students' assignments.

Speaking of the cognitive process of learning, only when students actively participate in the learning process can they complete learning tasks quickly and efficiently. In the process of learning, subjective attitudes, consciousness, and emotions of students have significant influences on their translation abilities. Therefore, during the implementation of this model, teachers should be skilled in observing and analyzing students' psychological characteristics, and adjust teaching accordingly based on students' traits. They should create a relaxed and pleasant learning atmosphere, motivate students' enthusiasm, stimulate their interest in learning, and encourage them to express their own opinions. At the same time, this teaching model requires teachers to organize classroom discussions based on students' interests, needs, strengths, and weaknesses, in order to cultivate a communicative personality and foster students' creative thinking. It also demands that teachers adopt a tolerant and positive attitude towards students' translations, actively praise excellent translations, and help students build confidence. Therefore, whether in the classroom or in extracurricular practice, teachers should prioritize students as the main participants in teaching and conduct teaching based on students' actual situations.

2. Digital teaching

The limitations and backwardness of traditional teaching methods have prompted more and more schools and teachers to incorporate multimedia as a new teaching tool in classroom instruction. In the specific teaching process, this teaching mode can be divided into the following steps.

(1) In the classroom, the teacher explains knowledge related to the discourse, helping students understand the content, background knowledge, and context of the discourse. These contents are presented through multimedia, which allows students to quickly immerse themselves in the learning context and develop a profound understanding of the basic knowledge being taught.

(2) Students are asked to recapitulate and summarize the background knowledge, while the teacher provides necessary supplements and corrections to help students grasp the necessary information.

(3) Students are supposed to read the source text, independently contemplate, and then begin translation. The teacher assists students in solving difficulties encountered and provides explanations to the whole class.

(4) Students submit their written assignments via E-mails or other means. The teacher divides them into groups, where the assignments are presented, allowing for mutual communication and the expression of different opinions on the translated text. A group member is selected to consolidate the group's opinions. The teacher can participate in the discussion and evaluate students' activities and translations.

From the text above, it is evident that multimedia teaching not only changes the traditional mode of translation teaching, but also makes students active participants rather than passive recipients. Furthermore, through multimedia technology, students can more easily and effortlessly grasp the different styles of English and Chinese language use, as well as comprehend the differences between the two languages. Additionally, multimedia contains rich teaching resources, providing teachers and students with abundant information and opportunities for communica-tion. Lastly, this novel teaching form stimulates students' enthusiasm and autonomy in learning.

Ⅱ. Principles of English Translation Teaching

Enhancing students' translation skills and cultivating their communicative abilities are the ultimate goals of translation teaching. These principles guide and facilitate the process of English translation teaching. Therefore, English translation teaching should adhere to the following five principles: communicative principle, cognitive principle, cultural principle, systematic principle, and affective principle.

Communicative Principle: Communication is one of the essential functions of language and the ultimate goal of learning English. English communicative competence primarily involves the ability to accurately receive and transmit information. For translation teaching and the development of translation skills, communicative competence also includes the ability to accurately convert information. According to Communication Theory, language is a system of expressing meaning, and its main function is communication. The structure of language reflects its function and communicative purposes. Language encompasses not only its grammar and structural features but also the categories that reflect the functions and communicative meanings in discourse. Thus, in the process of English translation teaching, teachers should always follow this principle and cultivate students' translation techniques and abilities based on it.

Cognitive Principle: Students typically learn and acquire new knowledge based on their existing knowledge, and they also adopt different learning methods and strategies based on their cognitive characteristics and existing thinking patterns. Therefore, in the process of translation teaching, teachers should adhere to the cognitive principle, fully consider students' diverse characteristics, and design activity patterns that can stimulate students' interest, mobilize their motivation, encourage active thinking, and develop their own learning methods and strategies. This helps in cultivating students' translation skills and enabling effective communication.

Cultural Principle: Foreign language learning itself is a cross-cultural communicative activity, and this is particularly true for translation learning. It requires students to understand the political systems, economic models, thinking habits, lifestyles, local customs, and expression habits of different countries. Therefore, in translation teaching, teachers should always remember this principle, place students in the context of cross-cultural communication, and focus on cultivating students' ability to convert cross-cultural information. This enables students to truly realize that achieving communicative purposes cannot be solely based on linguistic correspondence without considering the cultural differences between countries.

Systematic Principle: Language is a vast and complete system, of which various components and elements are closely interconnected and follow certain patterns. Translation teaching is also a complex system that has its own rules and methods. Therefore, in the process of translation teaching, teachers should adhere to the systematic principle. They should develop a systematic and scientific curriculum based on the nature of translation, the basic laws of translation teaching, and the needs of students and the society. This curriculum aims to cultivate students' translation skills, enhance their English proficiency, and improve the efficiency of translation teaching.

Affective Principle: In addition to the aforementioned principles, the affective principle should also be considered in the process of English translation teaching. This is because students' learning motivation, attitudes, interest, and individual personalities can all influence their learning outcomes in translation. As a result, teachers should continuously guide and regulate students' learning attitudes and personal emotions during the process of translation learning.

Generally speaking, these principles provide guidance and direction in English translation teaching, ensuring that students could develop their translation abilities, enhance their communicative competence, and appreciate the importance of culture in effective cross-cultural communication.

Section 4

English Translation Teaching from the Perspective of Communication Studies

Language does not develop in isolation, but rather emerges through the interaction and synthesis of various cultural factors. The English language, too, has evolved gradually within a distinct geographical and cultural context, serving a practical role in real-life situations. English translation, therefore, serves as a channel of communication and cultural exchange among different societies, playing a crucial role in bridging cultural differences. The quality and proficiency of English translation significantly impact the extent of cultural communication. In the era of globalization, translation assumes a vital role in facilitating cultural understanding and exchanges. A profound and comprehensive understanding of English translation necessitates acknowledging its cultural function from a linguistic perspective. Additionally, as a tool for communication across diverse cultures, English translation must consider relevant cultural factors. By incorporating these factors into the translation process, we can ensure the quality and effectiveness, ultimately fulfilling the final goal of English translation.

Ⅰ. The Essence of English translation

The essence of translation lies in facilitating communication between different cultures. The ultimate goal of language is to enable individuals to express their thoughts, ideas, and perspectives in real-life situations. In this sense, language also possesses a certain degree of autonomy, as most languages evolve to cater to specific production and everyday needs of particular regions. English, for instance, originates from English-speaking countries to cater to the needs and enhance the productivity and livelihoods of its speakers.

No language, or pair of languages, develops within the same cultural context. English translation, at its core, is a product of cross-cultural communi-cation. Firstly, the generation of English translation stems from the differences in cultural backgrounds. As social beings, humans possess an unceasing curiosity about the real world, and this curiosity deepens as their understanding of the world expands. English, as a language that has evolved within diverse cultural frameworks, embodies the life concepts, lifestyles, and living conditions of English-speaking countries. The disparities arising from these distinct cultural backgrounds necessitate cultural complementation through English translation. Secondly, English translation fundamentally involves the process of cultural exchange among people. Cultural exchange is essential for individuals to truly grasp different aspects of the world, particularly in the context of cultural communication. Philosophically speaking, human reason is limited and confined to what is present. In other words, our understanding of the present represents the highest level that human reason can attain. On the one hand, people need to perceive the real world to guide their actions, but on the other hand, they lack sufficient tools to comprehend the world fully. These limitations inherently restrict our perception of the world. Therefore, cultural exchange and communication among individuals become inevitable, and this is where English translation originates and finds its purpose.

Ⅱ. Contextual Translation

The discussion of language application is always inseparable from interpretation of the context. Undoubtedly, language is always generated within specific linguistic situations and gains vitality in such contexts. One of the key requirements of English translation is to genuinely consider the specific meaning of English sentences within their linguistic contexts. Different linguistic contexts require different language expressions, and even within the same linguistic context, there can be multiple language expressions. In the process of English translation, it is crucial to pay special attention to the influence of linguistic context on English translation. This is also an essential requirement for accurate cultural exchange and communication.

In order to conduct contextual translation of English, the following points should be emphasized. Firstly, placing the source English text within its expressed linguistic context. Restoring the English language to its specific linguistic context is a primary method of understanding the English language and the most urgent way to restore its true meaning. Secondly, contextual translation of English is essentially a form of cultural translation. Different languages have different modes of expression within different linguistic contexts, and this holds true for both English and Chinese. Contextual translation of English is, in fact, a means to concretely embody English culture and a genuine method for readers to comprehend the English language. Giving high regard to contextualization in English translation is synonymous with placing high importance on the quality of English translation.

Section 5

Cultural Differences and English Translation Teaching

English is currently one of the most widely spoken languages in the world, while Chinese is the language with the largest number of users. The influence of these two languages is significant on a global scale. They have different cultural foundations, embodying their respective historical traditions and national cultures. In the process of learning Chinese, although many factors are closely related to cultural background, it does not affect students' understanding of the articles. However, in the process of learning English, even if students know the meaning of all the vocabulary, sometimes it is still challenging to accurately express their true meaning. The main reason for this phenomenon is cultural differences. When a language is formed, it is combined with certain historical background and geographical conditions. Therefore, when learning a language, it is also necessary to fully integrate the corresponding cultural background. It can be said that culture and language are inseparable. A language actually belongs to a specific culture. People live in a specific cultural system, which subconsciously governs their behaviors and activities. Different cultures manifest different cultural forms, cultural traits, and national characteristics. If we reflect these cultural forms on the linguistic level, it is called language differences. Therefore, cultural differences between East and West will inevitably impact translation. In order to eliminate these differences, it is necessary to strengthen the understanding of relevant cultures, such as customs, historical background, and socio-economic background, during the translation process. By doing so, we can grasp the connection between the two cultures and improve the quality of translation.

Ⅰ. The Impact of Cultural Differences Between East and West on English Translation

For both China and Western countries, there are noticeable differences in terms of history, culture, lifestyle, and mode of thinking, all of which inevitably affect the effectiveness of English translation to some extent. In general, the cultural differences in English translation primarily manifest in ideological, historical, customary, and regional aspects.

Ideological Differences: Certain English words possess specific meanings and symbolic implications, which reflect the differences between Chinese and Western cultures to some extent. For example, the word "dragon" represents a spiritual element symbolizing nobility, auspiciousness, and sacredness in the thinking of Chinese people. However, for Westerners, the dragon merely represents a creature, symbolizing fierceness, demons, and monsters. Thus, it can be seen that the meanings of "dragon" in Chinese and Western cultures fundamentally differ. To avoid misunderstanding, it is advisable to minimize the use of such vocabulary during translation. The differences in ideological perspectives will inevitably lead to different understanding, resulting in certain deviations and even significant differences between the source text and the translation. Therefore, extra attention should be paid during the English translation process to avoid difficulties in comprehension.

Historical and Cultural Differences: Factors such as ethnic conflict, assimilation, conquest, and migration have significant impacts on the historical and cultural development of humanity, affecting the process of language evolution to some degree. Expressions like "All roads lead to Rome" "Rome was not built in a day" and "When in Rome do as the Romans do" carry specific meanings that originate from particular historical contexts. Without understanding these historical and cultural backgrounds during translation, deviations may occur. The development histories of different countries and ethnic groups vary considerably, which greatly complicate the task of translation. Historical and cultural dimensions vividly exhibit various allegorical references, displaying distinct national characteristics and historical individuality. For instance, when translating the phrase "项庄舞剑,意在沛公"

(Xiang Zhuang dances with a sword, meaning to target Liu Bang), the mere translation of the literal meaning would fail to convey the essence of this phrase. On the contrary, having knowledge about this historical and cultural reference allows for a translation like "to have an axe to grind".

In conclusion, cultural differences between East and West inevitably impact English translation. Understanding and considering these differences are essential for ensuring accurate and culturally appropriate translations.

Differences in Customs and Habits: In the translation process, fully showcasing the lifestyles and habits of people in a certain region is influenced by various factors such as literature, art, religion, economy, and politics. Therefore, different social environments give rise to unique linguistic habits. For example, the phrase "all at sea" can be literally paraphrased as "每个人都在海边"(everyone is at sea), but considering the linguistic habits of English-speaking countries, it actually means "茫然, 无助"(confused, at a loss). Therefore, during translation, it is necessary to consider the associative meaning, emotional meaning, stylistic meaning, and connotative meaning of the vocabulary.

Differences in Regional Culture: Regional culture refers to a culture that gradually forms in different geographical environment, reflected by the specific expressions and attitudes of people in a particular region about certain events. For example, the term "东风"(the east wind) in Chinese carries the meaning of "lush grass and singing birds" and "warm and gentle". However, in Western culture, it signifies "biting winds", similar to the term "西风"(the west wind) in the Chinese expression "古道西风瘦马"(on the ancient road, the west wind makes horses thin). In Western literature, the west wind is described as "warm" and "gentle". The main cause of this difference lies in the disparities in geographical cultures between China and the West. China is located eastward facing the sea, making the east wind more comfortable, while Western countries are located on the western coast of Atlantic Ocean, making the west wind naturally warmer and pleasant.

Ⅱ. Effective Measures of Eliminating the Influence of Cultural Differences

The differences between Eastern and Western cultures objectively exist. In order to avoid errors in the translation process, it is necessary to take relevant measures to prevent.

Adding Annotations: For certain words with specific meanings, annotations can be directly added during the translation process. This not only completes the translation but also fully explains the meaning of the words. For example, the phrase "东施效颦" cannot be accurately conveyed through direct translation. On the one hand, the unique connotation of the phrase cannot be expressed, and on the other hand, it increases the difficulty for readers to understand. Therefore, annotations can be used in the translation process to explain the identity of "东施" (Dongshi) for readers' better comprehension.

Adding Words for Clarity in Translation: During the translation process, in order to fully preserve the cultural nuances of the source text, a direct translation approach is often used. However, this may increase the difficulty for readers to understand. Therefore, explanatory vocabulary can be appropriately applied on top of the direct translation to help readers better comprehend the meaning.

Substituting Vocabulary: In English translation, to account for cultural differences, it is not always appropriate to directly use conceptually similar words or phrases to express culturally equivalent ones. Instead, culturally similar words can be used as replacements. This approach both preserves the meaning of the source text and aligns with readers' reading habits. For example, the Chinese phrase "不分青红皂白" can be translated as "unable to distinguish black from white" by omitting the characters "青" and "白". Another example is the phrase "as thin as a shadow", which literally means "someone is as thin as a shadow". However, this expression does not exist in Chinese and could lead to misunderstanding. Hence, it can be translated as "瘦得像猴子" (as thin as a monkey), which aligns better with readers' thinking patterns and fully conveys the meaning of the phrase.

Liberal Translation: Some vocabulary carries strong cultural connotations that are difficult to be accurately conveyed through direct translation. Simple word replacements may lead to misunderstanding. In such cases, liberal translation can be used. Liberal translation means using words or phrases similar to the source text to express words or phrases with rich cultural meanings. For example, the term "革命思想" can be translated as "red ideas", which represents pro-gress and revolution. By combining "red" and "ideas", the meaning of "革命思想" is effectively expressed.

In conclusion, although there are many similarities or commonalities in expressions of Chinese and English, there are still differences in practical application, which can cause confusion and misunderstanding, increasing the difficulty for readers to comprehend. Therefore, in the process of English translation, it is necessary to understand from the cultural and ethnic perspective to better comprehend the meaning of the source text, reduce the differences between the translation and the source text, meet readers' reading needs, and enhance cultural exchange.

Ⅲ. Cultivation of Students' Translation Abilities under the Background of Cross-cultural Communication

Translation, as an important tool for cross-cultural communication, is playing an increasingly significant role in the globalization of the world. However, translation is not merely a conversion between languages; it is also a transmission and exchange of cultures. Therefore, there is a critical issue we should pay attention to in translation teaching, namely, how to cultivate students' translation abilities to enable them to convey cultures accurately and appropriately in cross-cultural communication.

1. Cultivation of cross-cultural communication abilities

The cultivation of cross-cultural communication abilities is a multifaceted process that involves developing an understanding of different cultures, acquiring the skills to communicate effectively across cultural boundaries, and developing an attitude of openness and respect towards diverse cultural norms and practices.

(1) Teaching cultural knowledge and practical skills.

Translation is a cross-cultural communicative activity that requires translators to have rich cultural knowledge and practical skills. Hence, translation teaching should focus on imparting cultural knowledge and practicing cultural communication skills. Teachers can help students understand the characteristics and differences of various cultures through lectures, discussions, and case studies, thereby enhancing the students' cultural sensitivity and comprehension.

To cultivate cross-cultural communication abilities, it is essential to integrate cultural knowledge into the curriculum. This includes teaching about different cultural traditions, values, customs, and behaviors that may impact the translation process. For instance, understanding how various cultures conceptualize time, space, and hierarchy can help translators make more accurate and culturally sensitive translation choices. Practical skills such as language proficiency, non-verbal communication, and cultural negotiation should also be developed through various teaching activities, which is helpful for the cultivation of cross-cultural communication abilities as well.

(2) Encouraging critical thinking and reflection.

Critical thinking and reflection are vital components of translation ability. Teachers should encourage students to think critically and reflect on the problems and difficulties encountered during the translation process to improve their problem-solving and self-adjustment abilities. For instance, teachers can guide students to analyze mistakes and shortcomings in translations, identify causes, and propose improvement strategies.

Developing critical thinking skills is crucial for effective cross-cultural communication. Students should be encouraged to question assumptions, analyze cultural biases, and consider multiple perspectives when approaching a translation task. Reflective exercises such as journal writing, case studies, or debriefing sessions after simulations can help students reflect on their own cultural frame of reference and how it influences their translation decisions.

Through guided reflection, students can develop meta-cognitive awareness—the ability to think about their thinking processes. This self-awareness is key to recognizing potential misunderstandings and adapting translation strategies to better suit the cultural context of the target readers.

In conclusion, the cultivation of cross-cultural communication abilities requires a comprehensive approach that addresses both the cognitive aspects of cultural knowledge and the practical skills necessary for effective intercultural exchange. By integrating cultural content, practical training, critical thinking, and reflection on translation pedagogy, teachers can better enable the students get well prepared to become proficient and culturally sensitive translators in the increasingly globalized world.

2. Enhancement of students' cultural adaptability and flexibility

It is a crucial component of translation education for teachers to enhance students' cultural adaptability and flexibility. Since it enables the students to navigate the complexities of diverse cultural contexts with ease and effectiveness. There are some strategies to enhance students' cultural adaptability and flexibility.

(1) Deepening understanding through simulated translation practice.

Simulated translation is an effective teaching method that helps students apply cultural knowledge and skills in real translation settings, enhancing their cultural adaptability and flexibility. Teachers can design various simulated translation tasks according to the teaching content and objectives, allowing students to deepen their understanding of cultural differences and enhance their adaptability during the task completion process. Simulated translation exercises may include:

Role-Play: Students can take on the roles of translators, clients, or members of the target culture, allowing them to experience different perspectives and understand the cultural nuances that impact translation.

Cultural Immersion Exercises: Virtual or in-person experiences that immerse students in a specific cultural setting, requiring them to use their language and communication skills to interact with native speakers or adapt to cultural norms.

Case Studies: Analyzing real-life translation cases where cultural factors played a significant role, discussing the challenges faced by translators, and exploring alternative strategies for dealing with cultural differences.

By engaging in these simulated activities, students can develop a deeper understanding of cultural dynamics and the practical application of translation theory into practice, thereby enhancing their ability to adapt to and navigate different cultural contexts.

(2) Analyzing real translation scenarios through case studies.

Case study is a research method that focuses on actual problems, helping students understand and analyze real translation scenarios and issues so as to improve their practical abilities. Teachers can select representative and educational translation cases to guide students in analysis and discussion, enhancing their abilities to analyze and solve problems. Case studies offer valuable learning experiences by presenting students with detailed accounts of real-world translation situations. They allow students to examine the sociocultural, historical, and linguistic factors that influence translation decisions and learn outcomes. Through case study analysis, students can identify cultural challenges and how they were dealt with in various translation scenarios. Moreover, the students may develop analytical skills to dissect translation choices and evaluate the cultural appropriateness of certain language expressions or terms used in translations. In addition, the students can learn from the successes and failures of professional translators, so the students can gain insights into best practices and avoid common mistakes. More importantly, it will enable the students to apply a critical thinking to propose alternative solutions to translation problems, cultivating a flexible mindset that encourages creativity and innovation in approaching translation tasks.

In summary, enhancing students' cultural adaptability and flexibility requires a combination of experiential learning and critical analysis. By engaging students in simulated translation practice and guiding them through the examination of real-world translation scenarios, the teachers can effectively prepare students to become adaptable and flexible translators capable of navigating the multifaceted world of cross-cultural communication.

3. Establishment of a scientific assessment and feedback mechanism

(1) The establishment of effective assessment standards.

Assessment is a crucial part of teaching, significantly impacting students' learning outcomes and teaching effectiveness. In translation teaching, effective assessment standards should be established, including aspects such as cultural adaptability, linguistic accuracy, and contextual appropriateness, and so on. Moreover, a combination of process evaluation and product evaluation should be used to comprehensively and objectively assess students' learning outcomes. Here are some considerations for the establishment of effective assessment standards in translation teaching.

Cross-cultural Awareness. Since translation involves two different cultures, it is necessary to make assessments on students' ability to understand and deal with cultural differences in translation. This includes recognizing cultural nuances, idiomatic expressions, and context-specific references.

Linguistic Accuracy. Accuracy is critically important in translation, which makes sure the meanings of the target language is the same as those of the source language so as to achieve the goal of communication. Assessments of linguistic accuracy should focus on words, phrases and structures, ensuring that translations are grammatically correct, the vocabularies are appropriately used, and the meanings of the source text are maintained in the target language.

Contextual Appropriateness. Contextual appropriateness refers to the ability to translate in a manner that is suitable or fitting for a particular situation or context. It involves understanding and adapting to the specific circumstances, expectations, and norms of the environment in which one is interacting. Assessments should evaluate whether the translations are appropriate for the given context or not. The factors, such as the target readers, purposes, expression habits and genre of the text should be taken into consideration.

Combination of Process and Production Evaluation. Process evaluation focuses on the process of translation, including planning, researching, and revising. It can involve assessing drafts, peer reviews, and self-evaluations to provide ongoing feedback and guidance. Production Evaluation focuses on the final product, evaluating the quality of the translation based on established criteria such as accuracy, fluency, and coherence. In translation teaching, these two types of assessment are equally important and be used to give a relatively fair evaluation to the students' performances.

Peer and Self-assessment. Peer and self-assessment frequently occurs in teaching. The teachers should encourage students to engage in peer and self-assessment, which can help them develop critical thinking skills and become more reflective learners.

Formative and Summative Assessments. Formative assessments are assessments for learning, designed to provide ongoing feedback and support throughout the learning process. They can include quizzes, exercises, and project drafts. Summative Assessments are assessments of learning, designed to evaluate students' overall achievement at the end of a course or unit. They usually include final exams, comprehensive translation projects, and oral exams.

Incorporating Technology. Nowadays, technologies are widely used in teaching and assessments. Tools for assessment are also used in translation teaching assessments. These tools are online quizzes, automated translation evaluation software, and collaborative platforms for peer review and feedback.

(2) Timely and constructive feedback and communication.

Feedback is an essential means to improve learning outcomes. The teachers should provide timely and accurate feedback to help students understand their strengths and weaknesses and offer suggestions for improvement. At the same time, students should be encouraged to engage in self-assessment and peer assessment to enhance their self-monitoring and self-adjustment abilities.

Feedback and communication are important aspects of the assessment process in translation teaching. Providing constructive feedback to students on their translation work is essential to help them improve their skills and understand the translation process. Feedback can take various forms, such as written comments on translation assignments, verbal feedback during class discussions, or one-on-one feedback sessions with individual students. Constructive feedback should not only point out areas for improvement but also highlight strengths and offer suggestions for further development.

Effective communication between teachers and students also plays a crucial role in clarifying expectations, addressing challenges, and fostering a positive learning environment. Clear and open communication between teachers and students is equally important in the assessment process. Teachers should communicate assessment criteria and expectations clearly to students to help them understand what is required of them. Students, in turn, should feel comfortable communicating their questions, concerns, and feedback to their teachers to ensure a mutual understanding of the assessment process.

Overall, effective feedback and communication are essential elements in the assessment of translation teaching, helping students enhance their translation skills and promoting a supportive and collaborative learning environment. Translation teaching should focus on developing students' cross-cultural communication abilities, enhancing their cultural adaptability and flexibility, and establishing a scientific assessment and feedback mechanism. Only by doing so can we cultivate translators capable of effective cross-cultural communication in the globalized world.

Chapter 2

Different Perspectives of English Translation Teaching

Section 1

English Translation Teaching from the Perspective of Functional Equivalence

1.1 Theory of Functional Equivalence

Functional translation emphasizes the cooperation between the author, the translator, and readers to construct a holistic translation. It strives to ensure effective interaction between the original work and readers, better conveying the author's intentions, and enhancing the value of translation skills to improve the effectiveness of translation.

Based on analyzing the theory of functional translation, this section studies the techniques of functional translation and demonstrates its value, thus improving the effectiveness of functional translation.

Ⅰ. Theoretical Connotation and Value of Functional Translation

1. Definition of functional translation

Functional translation focuses on meeting the readers' needs and emphasizes effective communication between the readers and the original work. It is a practical and operable translation method formed through long-term practice and accumulation. Functional translation emphasizes a thorough understanding of the original work and strives to make readers feel the essence of the source text in the translated text.

2. Main values of functional translation

Functional translation effectively eliminates the drawbacks of traditional word-for-word and sentence-by-sentence translation, improves the efficiency of translation, and helps readers grasp the essence of the original work. Translation work can better coordinate various conditions and factors, thereby achieving effective translation.

Ⅱ. Translation Principles from the Perspective of Functional Translation

1. Clear objectives

Functional translation is a purposeful task that aims to meet readers' expectations of the source text. Based on effective coordination of the differences between Eastern and Western contexts, it strives to make readers better accept the original work. The translated text should be easily understood by readers. Functional translation fundamentally rejects word-for-word and sentence-by-sentence translation, emphasizing the combination of specific grammar and syntactic structures in translation. Translation should not only respect the original work but also serve readers more, in order to realize the value of translation and achieve the goals of translation. In the process of translation, readers' cultural literacy, background, and expectations for the work should be fully considered. Only by taking into account readers' circumstances can the appropriate translation method be chosen to enhance the effectiveness of translation.

2. Faithfulness to the original work

Functional Translation Theory emphasizes the faithfulness to the original work and the ability to better capture the artistic conception of the original work in the context of the integration of Eastern and Western cultures. Based on the original English translation, it comprehensively considers the differences between Eastern and Western cultures, and requires translators to have a deep understanding of both cultures. Translators should be able to flexibly switch based on the specific circumstances of the work, achieving effective coordination between the source text and the translated text. Functional translation focuses on meeting the readers' needs, requiring a good grasp of the context during the translation process, enabling readers to have a clearer understanding of the main ideas of the original work. Faithfulness to

Chapter 2　Different Perspectives of English Translation Teaching

the original work also requires the appropriate use of rhetorical devices to convey the emotional color of the original work and effectively describe the plot, allowing readers to experience the profound meaning of the work through reading.

3. Practicality and effectiveness

Practicality is a fundamental principle followed by Functional Translation Theory. Functional translation emphasizes practicality, advocating for consistency between the source text and the translated text during the translation process, ensuring the coherence of the translation. It not only respects the author of the original work but also respects the recipients of the translated text.

Ⅲ. Methods from the Perspective of Functional Translation

1. Interpreting

The English translation techniques based on Functional Translation Theory emphasize the respect for the cultural and contextual aspects of the work. It is important to understand the meanings of all the vocabulary used in the work and make appropriate inferences based on the context. Interpreting focuses on immediacy and aims to achieve forward-looking translation goals. It requires translating based on specific contexts to achieve the combination of semantics and cultural ideas. From the perspective of Functional Theory, translation does not emphasize reproducing the exact words of both parties but rather requires effective expressions based on the accurate understanding of the original meaning, highlighting the role of language as a tool for effective communication.

2. Liberal translation

The liberal translation method refers to the fact that translation should not solely rely on the literal meaning of the work but should also consider the differences between Chinese and Western cultures. Therefore, translators should be familiar with the differences between Chinese and Western cultures and make use of specific contexts for translation. In liberal translation, it is necessary to make reasonable changes to the word order, as well as to add or delete vocabulary appropriately, in order to fully express the meaning of the source text. For example, the sentence "他

离家非常远,什么都靠自己" can be translated as "He is far away from home and relies on himself". This translation accurately reflects the profound meaning of the text. To achieve the goal of free translation, it is also necessary to use effective rhetorical devices based on the source text, and to master certain translation techniques based on content and form, making full use of the auxiliary value of rhetoric and sentence structures to truly express emotions based on free translation, thus fully embodying the vividness of translation.

3. Flexible translation

Functional translation emphasizes the practicality of translation. Based on the source text, translators should have a certain understanding of the structure and layout of the original work. While staying close to the source text, they should ensure that readers receive information more accurately. Therefore, translators need to organize the content, language habits, and narrative methods of the source text, effectively eliminate the fragmentation problem in translation, and emphasize the hierarchical nature of translation. In this way, the essence of the work can be better showcased in comprehensive translation.

In addition, to improve the effectiveness of functional translation, it is necessary to clarify translation techniques, innovate translation methods, optimize the selection of linguistic materials, and achieve innovation in translated works based on faithfulness to the source text, thereby achieving the goal of high-quality translation.

4. The perspective of Functional Equivalence

In today's increasingly intensified trend of global integration, English, as an important international language, plays an increasingly important role in the development of countries politically, economically, culturally, and educationally. Therefore, English education, talents cultivation, and translation have become widely discussed topics. This section conducts in-depth research and exploration on English translation strategies from the perspective of Functional Equivalence. Building upon a detailed exploration of the concepts and specific application strategies of Functional Equivalence in English translation, this study analyzes the translation techniques and strategies under the framework of Functional Equivalence. It is hoped that this research can further promote the application of Functional Equivalence Theory in English translation.

With the strengthening of internationalization, interpersonal communication and the interaction of information among nations have increased rapidly, and the role of English translation in international communication has become increasingly evident. Functional Equivalence Theory is an important theoretical guide for English translation, which can improve the quality of translation and enhance people's activities and communication. At the same time, following the principles of Functional Equivalence in English translation ensures the unity of translated information and the smooth progress of translation work. In this context, it is necessary to strengthen research on Functional Equivalence Theory and expedite the exploration of English translation from the perspective of Functional Equivalence to ensure high-quality translation and the integrity of information exchange.

Ⅳ. Overview of Relevant Concepts

1. Introduction of Functional Equivalence Theory

The theory of Functional Equivalence emphasizes the analysis and handling of special phenomena in the translation process. It does not solely focus on the surface features and external connotations of the text but explores the relationship between English and Chinese, optimizing the translation effect and making the translation more complete. Functional Equivalence Theory combines the linguistic forms of English and Chinese, forming a diversified and flexible translation system.

2. The role of Functional Equivalence in translation

The main purpose of English translation is to facilitate information exchange between parties. With the increase in information exchange, the demands for English translation in various industries are becoming higher. English translation must ensure professionalism and accuracy. Functional Equivalence Theory strengthens translators' understanding of the field of translation, equipping them with skills in English translation. This enhances the accuracy and efficiency of translation, and fosters interactive communication. Therefore, Functional Equivalence Theory plays a guiding and facilitating role in English translation, promoting the orderly conduct of translation work.

3. The application of Functional Equivalence Theory

The translation of words needs to follow certain translation principles. Specifically, English translation requires a strong sense of professionalism, highlighting a comprehensive understanding of terminology to avoid translation errors that hinder effective communication. Moreover, sentence translation should achieve equivalence between the translated sentence and the original one based on the principles of Functional Equivalence. Depending on the actual translation situation, if the literal translation accurately expresses the meaning of the source text, translators can adopt a literal translation approach. To achieve formal and functional equivalence, translators can adjust the structure of the original sentence before conducting the translation. Within the scope of Functional Equivalence, discourse translation must ensure the functional equivalence of the discourse, comprehensively grasp the content of the discourse, and conduct an overall analysis of sentences and words in the text. Additionally, it is important to maintain the original writing style while translating.

Ⅴ. Techniques of English Translation in the Context of Functional Equivalence

1. Equivalence of linguistic meaning

Equivalence of linguistic meaning is an important goal in English translation within the context of Functional Equivalence. Therefore, in the process of English translation, translators should actively understand the content of the source text and ensure that the translated text accurately conveys the content and meaning of the source text. This helps to avoid translation errors that may affect information exchange. Additionally, within the framework of Functional Equivalence, English translation should achieve equivalence of linguistic meaning. Translators should enhance their understanding of vocabulary, phrases, and discourse to ensure the equivalence of meanings at these levels. Furthermore, when dealing with specialized terminology, translators should have a deep understanding of the meaning of such terms and ensure a reasonable translation, maintaining the original meaning of the specialized terminology.

2. Equivalence of language style

Equivalence of language style is an important goal in English translation within the framework of Functional Equivalence. It plays a significant role in promoting the organized development of English translation. Therefore, English translation should pay attention to the equivalence of language style. Due to the strong professionalism required in English translation, translators need to have a comprehensive understanding of the stylistic features of the source text. They should retain these features while translating, ensuring a reasonable translation of discourses, words, and seatences. Furthermore, during the translation process, translators should strive to be concise and comprehensive, paying attention to details and avoiding changes in language style caused by neglecting minor details.

3. Strategies for translation to achieve Functional Equivalence

(1) Literal translation.

Literal translation is a commonly used method in English translation, characterized by its straightforwardness and convenience. During the translation process, translators should scientifically develop translation strategies based on the translation content to ensure the specificity of the translation, allowing the translated text to accurately convey the meaning of the source text. Literal translation can be used to translate basic vocabulary and sentences while maintaining semantic equivalence. It also achieves functional and formal equivalence, facilitating readers' understanding of the translation. Therefore, translators can employ the strategy of direct translation within the framework of Functional Equivalence to ensure equivalence in meaning, function, and form between the translated and source texts.

(2) Domestication translation.

Various factors, including language itself, language background, and language culture, influence English translation. Word-for-word translation may result in the inability to achieve linguistic equivalence. In such cases, English translators should adopt the strategy of domestication under the guidance of the theory of Functional

Equivalence. It involves a comprehensive grasp of the central idea in the source text, full understanding of professional terminologies, and capturing the language style of the source text. Furthermore, translators, based on comprehension of the main theme of the source text, should strive to reproduce its content in the translation, enhancing the vividness of English translation. Thus, translators need to flexibly utilize vocabulary, professional terms, and sentence structures, avoiding inaccurate translations. Additionally, accurate expression of professional terminolo-gies ensures precise translation of such terms and eliminates the phenomenon of inconsistency between the translated and source texts. The theory of Functional Equivalence is an important guiding principle in English translation. It promotes the organized implementation of translation work and plays a facilitating role. Therefore, we need to emphasize the significance of the theory of Functional Equivalence, actively master the techniques and methods of English translation within the framework of Functional Equivalence, study English culture in conjunction with practical situations, continuously improve the quality of translators, and enhance the efficiency of English translation, thereby promoting the orderly progress of translation.

Section 2

English Translation Teaching from the Teleological Perspective

Translation is not only a skill but also an art. It requires translators to use various translation techniques proficiently and integrate translation artistry into the translation process. Teleological Translation Theory considers both translation artistry and translation techniques equally important. This part elaborates on translation theory from the perspectives of target audience and target language culture, providing comprehensive translation strategies.

1. Overview of Teleological Translation Theory

Teleological Translation Theory emphasizes prioritizing the translation purpose and using it to determine the translation techniques and process. When translating from a teleological perspective, translators must clearly define their translation purpose since the translation approach and outcome can vary based on different purposes. Teleological Theory greatly changes the traditional emphasis on translation accuracy and effectiveness in the translation process.

2. Principles of translation from the teleological perspective

(1) Principle of purposefulness.

English translation, like other types of work, has specific purposes, which mainly aim at achieving certain translation effects. Due to significant cultural differences between East and West, professional English vocabulary and grammar vary across different industries. Therefore, during the translation process, it is necessary to consider the target audience's cultural background, level of comprehension, and language habits comprehensively. This allows the audience to quickly adapt to the language environment created by the text and understand the framework and content in the shortest possible time. Moreover, appropriate translation techniques should be selected depending on the specific audience. For example, for business and technical English literature, a word-for-word translation should be done meticulously to ensure completeness. For everyday English communication, using locally common expressions should be encouraged to avoid a rigid feeling caused by literal translation. As international communication increases, access to outstanding cultural achievements from abroad through the Internet has become available. Therefore, translation plays an extremely important role. Only by ensuring good translation effects can cultural works be perpetuated.

(2) Principle of fidelity.

Fidelity in English translation refers to faithfully translating the source content into the target language as comprehensively as possible by using language that the audience is proficient in. However, effectively blending two cultures and expressing them coherently in the same language is relatively challenging. Translators need to have a comprehensive understanding of both cultures and be proficient in the conversion techniques between the two languages. In the process of English translation, it is essential to ensure consistency and integrity of the translation while maintaining the original structure. If the translation contains serious errors or significantly alters the original meaning, it becomes meaningless. Therefore, fidelity is a fundamental principle that English translation must adhere to.

(3) Principle of coherence.

The essence of English translation is to convey the source text to readers with the target language. However, language requires specific expressive techniques. Both the translated text and the source text have complete systems, constructed by certain grammar and language structures. Therefore, during the translation process, translators need to analyze and grasp the micro and macro structures of language, attaching importance to the coherence between different sections and the internal knowledge structure. This ensures that the translated work aligns with the language habits of the audience.

3. Translation strategy from the perspective of Teleological Theory

(1) Understanding target readers' needs and defining translation purposes.

From the perspective of Teleological Theory, it is important to first define the translation purpose and then choose the most suitable translation methods and techniques accordingly. This ensures that the translation aligns with the audience's requirements. Since translation activities vary and audiences differ when translating English, it is crucial for translators to appropriately divide the audience into different levels and categories. Accordingly, purposeful translation should be carried out based on the specific circumstances of each level and category.

(2) Respecting the cultural aspects of the target language.

Translators should consider the specific translation purpose and characteristics of the text recipients when translating texts. For literary texts, the focus should be placed on capturing the emotional impact and artistic qualities of sentences. For scientific or technical texts, emphasis should be placed on logical and scientific language structure to ensure the technical content is well-preserved. For official documents, precision and meticulousness in the sentence structure should be highlighted. In general, it is necessary to translate purposefully based on a thorough understanding of the specific text, while considering the target language context and audience. Additionally, the respect for cultural aspects of the target language is crucial. A comprehensive understanding of the target language culture helps translators accurately convey the source texts in a way that is easily understandable and suitable for communication. Failure to respect or accurately comprehend the target language culture during the translation process may hinder the accomplishment of the specific translation or communicative purposes. For example, "three-day weekend" should not be directly translated as "三天的周末" but rather requires a comprehensive understanding of American culture, where people refer to the combination of Saturday, Sunday, and Monday as "Presidents' Day" (总统日).

(3) Strict adherence to the original language style in translation to ensure that the meaning of the translated text remains intact.

In English, it is important to strictly adhere to the original language style, including grammar and sentence structure, when determining the translation order. Taking the passive voice in English as an example: the author's research suggests that in order to translate the English passive voice into a structure that corresponds to Chinese usage, the technique employed is to translate the sentence into an active voice. For instance, in the sentence "Since desire and will are damaged by the presence of thoughts that do not accord with desire, he concludes: ' We do attract what we want, but what we are'", the passive voice is used. In order to adhere to Chinese usage, it can be translated into an active voice "和欲望不匹配的想法会使我们毁灭，因此他得出一个结论：'我们不能过分地期望更多，最重要的是要做好我们自己'". In long sentence translation, the key lies in accurately identifying the order of the main elements of the sentence, namely the subject, the verb, and the object.

(4) Emphasis on the use of specialized terminology.

In general, English articles come in various types, and translation often involves a considerable number of specialized terms. Therefore, it is essential to accurately grasp the professional language when translating into English to avoid any errors. For example: At present the foreign exchange market in New York is very weak while the stock market is very strong. In business English, it can be translated by using relevant specialized terms as "当前纽约外汇市场较为疲软，但股市仍旧非常坚挺".

(5) Determination of the sequence of sentence translation based on language style.

Chinese grammar and English grammar differ significantly, not only in terms of sentence structure but also word order. When translating long sentences, it is necessary to consider the characteristics of sentence order comprehensively and determine the positions of the subject, verb, and object. When translating passive voice, it is also possible to use words like "by" or "from" to convert passive voice into active voice, thus ensuring the accuracy of the translation and enhancing its rationality and scientific nature.

(6) Strict adherence to the style of the target language.

Currently, the translation styles in China mainly involve business, technology, culture, art, and literature. However, in practice, due to factors such as precision of expression and language style, these styles exhibit significant differences in translation. For example, in business translation within international trade, emphasis is placed on rigorous accuracy based on relevant standards. In the translation of cultural arts, such as films, the translation requirements may vary, highlighting the original artistic style or popular humor. For instance, in the animation film *The Lion King*, the sentence "Everything you see exists together in a delicate balance" needs to be translated by considering the scene where Simba's father tells him the reminder to Simba of his true identity and responsibilities as a future leader, being part of the majestic lion lineage in the vast Savannah. It can be translated as "世界上所有的生命都在微妙的平衡中生存", which not only reflects the father's teaching to Simba but also sets the stage for Simba's character development in the subsequent plot.

A purposive approach to English translation holds significant importance as it effectively compensates for the shortcomings of traditional translation and significantly enhances the accuracy and scientific nature of English translation. Therefore, during the process of English translation, translators should clearly understand the actual needs of the audience and determine the translation purpose based on these requirements, thereby guiding the translation process. Moreover, translators should fully understand and master the target language culture, strictly follow the corresponding translation principles, continuously meet the reading needs of the audience, and improve the accuracy of English translation.

Section 3

English Translation Teaching from the Cognitive Linguistics Perspective

Cognitive Linguistics refers to the field of study that examines language from a cognitive perspective. It focuses on how humans understand and express thoughts through language, as well as the impact of language on cognition. By exploring phenomena such as language acquisition, semantic understanding, language generation, and language processing, Cognitive Linguistics aims to uncover the relationship between language and cognition.

Ⅰ. The Theoretical Foundation of Cognitive Linguistics in English Translation Teaching

1. Overview of Cognitive Linguistics

Cognitive Linguistics is a branch of linguistics that investigates language from a cognitive perspective. It explores how language is processed, represented, and used in the human mind. Unlike traditional linguistic theories that focus on formal structures, Cognitive Linguistics emphasizes the role of cognition, meaning, and conceptual systems in shaping language.

One key aspect of Cognitive Linguistics is the emphasis on the meaning of language. It views meaning as being shaped by cognitive processes, such as categorization, conceptual metaphor, and image schema. Cognitive Linguistics also highlights the role of embodiment in language, arguing that our physical experience and sensory perceptions influence the way we conceptualize and express meaning.

Chapter 2　Different Perspectives of English Translation Teaching

Another important concept in Cognitive Linguistics is the notion of construction. It posits that language is not solely composed of individual words or grammar rules, but rather that language is built through the use of constructions. Constructions can be seen as templates or patterns that speakers use to convey meaning in specific contexts. These constructions can range from simple phrases to more complex syntactic structures.

Furthermore, Cognitive Linguistics takes into account cultural and social factors in language use. It recognizes that language is not isolated from its cultural context but is influenced by social norms, cultural practices, and communicative conventions.

Overall, Cognitive Linguistics offers a comprehensive framework to study language by examining the cognitive processes involved in language production and understanding, the role of meaning, the use of constructions, and the influence of culture and embodiment.

2. Connection between Cognitive Linguistics and English translation teaching

Cognitive Linguistics and translation teaching are closely related as both share an interest in the cognitive processes involved in language comprehension and production. Cognitive Linguistics provides valuable insights into how language users perceive and understand meaning, which is crucial in translation. By understanding the cognitive aspects of language, translators can better analyze source texts and produce more accurate and natural target language translations.

3. Impacts of Cognitive Linguistics on English translation teaching

(1) Understanding meaning and structure.

Cognitive Linguistics highlights the importance of understanding the conceptual structures and underlying meanings behind language expressions. In translation teaching, this perspective helps students to grasp the essence of the source text and convey it appropriately in the target language.

(2) Enhancing translation skills and proficiency.

Cognitive Linguistics offers various cognitive strategies and techniques that enhance translation skills. This includes techniques like parallel processing, chunking, and cognitive load management, which help translators handle complex translation tasks more efficiently.

(3) Considering context and communication.

Cognitive Linguistics emphasizes the significance of contextual factors and the influence of social and cultural aspects on language use. In translation teaching, this perspective encourages students to consider the situational and cultural context of the source text, ensuring effective communication in the target language.

(4) Individual cognitive differences.

Cognitive Linguistics recognizes that individuals have different cognitive capacities and preferences. In translation teaching, this perspective allows for tailored teaching methods that accommodate individual cognitive differences. It helps instructors identify students' strengths and weaknesses, allowing for personalized training and the development of each student's unique translation style.

In summary, Cognitive Linguistics provides a theoretical foundation for understanding language processing and offers valuable insights for English translation teaching. It enhances students' understanding of meaning, improves their translation skills, emphasizes context and communication, and acknowledges individual cognitive differences, ultimately contributing to more effective and proficient translation practice.

Ⅱ. The Application of Cognitive Linguistics in English Translation Teaching

Cognitive Linguistics, applied in English translation teaching, encompasses various strategies to enhance students' translation skills and proficiency, which can be seen from the following aspects.

1. Emphasis on the cognitive process of language

Cognitive Linguistics emphasizes the understanding of language meaning and structure. Cognitive Linguistics focuses on comprehending the meaning and structure of language in translation. This involves going beyond a literal translation by understanding conceptual connections and cultural connotations of words and phrases. Besides, Cognitive Linguistics enhances learners' translation abilities and proficiency. By incorporating Cognitive Linguistics, English translation teaching aims to improve translation skills. Students are encouraged to analyze cognitive processes such as conceptualization, categorization, and inference to produce accurate and effective translations.

2. Emphasis on context and communication

On the one hand, Cognitive Linguistics takes into consideration translations in different backgrounds and contexts. Cognitive Linguistics emphasizes the importance of cultural contexts in translation. English translation teaching takes into account the target audience and the intended message in a specific socio-cultural setting. This ensures translations are appropriate and culturally sensitive.

On the other hand, Cognitive Linguistics promotes effective information transfer and communication. Cognitive Linguistics recognizes the need for effective communication in translation. Translators not only convey information accurately but also consider the pragmatic and communicative goals of the target audience. This approach focuses on producing translations that are linguistically accurate, contextually suitable, and functionally appropriate.

3. Emphasis on individual cognitive differences

Cognitive Linguistics respects learners' individual differences and learning strategies. Based on Cognitive Linguistics, English translation teaching acknowledges cognitive variations among students. It caters to diverse learning needs and preferences by offering personalized instructions, adaptive learning methods, and utilizing various cognitive strategies to enhance translation skills based on individual cognitive profiles.

Besides, Cognitive Linguistics emphasizes the cultivation of personalized translation techniques and styles. Cognitive Linguistics takes into account individual cognitive differences. English translation teaching encourages students to develop their own translation techniques and styles, allowing them to showcase their strengths of and unique approaches to translation.

4. Emphasis on fostering autonomy and reflective abilities in students.

Cognitive Linguistics encourages active learners' participation. English translation teaching should motivate students to actively engage in the learning process. This may include interactive exercises, group discussions, and hands-on translation projects, enabling students to take charge of their learning.

What's more, Cognitive Linguistics emphasizes prompting self-discovery and reflection to improve translation skills. Cognitive Linguistics encourages students to engage in self-discovery and critical reflection on their translation work. Through self-evaluation and reflection, students identify areas for improvement, leading to self-directed growth and enhanced translation abilities.

In summary, Cognitive Linguistics in English translation teaching emphasizes the cognitive process of language, enhances translation abilities, considers context and communication, addresses individual cognitive differences, and fosters autonomy and reflective abilities in students. These strategies aim to develop proficient translators who can produce culturally appropriate and effective translations.

Ⅲ. The Analysis of English Translation Teaching Practice from the Perspective of Cognitive Linguistics

English translation teaching practice from the perspective of Cognitive Linguistics aims to enhance students' translation skills and their understanding of language meaning and structure. This practice has been carried out in a university-level English translation course. The approach encourages students to apply cognitive processes, such as conceptualization and categorization, to the translation process.

1. Methods and teaching strategies

Emphasizing conceptual understanding. Students are encouraged to delve into the conceptual meaning of words and phrases in both the source and target languages. For example, when translating the word "apple" into another language, students are guided to consider the underlying concept of "a round fruit", rather than focusing solely on the literal translation.

(1) Promoting context-based translation.

Students are trained to consider the cultural and situational contexts of the source text to produce contextually appropriate translations. For instance, idiomatic expressions or cultural-specific references are translated in a way that preserves the

Chapter 2 Different Perspectives of English Translation Teaching

intended meaning in the target language.

(2) Providing explicit cognitive instruction.

Students are introduced to cognitive strategies such as metaphor analysis, frame semantics, and conceptual blending. These strategies help students develop a deeper understanding of the cognitive processes at play during the translation process.

2. Analysis of English translation teaching process and effectiveness

(1) Preparation.

Before the class, teachers need to use simple techniques to reinforce students' experience and impressions of English translation in their minds. Firstly, teachers can utilize resources on the Internet by posting basic content and teaching outlines for the upcoming class on the school's resource platform or class-based social media platforms. Secondly, before the classroom session, students should read and understand the published content thoroughly. If students have questions or difficulties in understanding certain knowledge points, they can search for information online or consult reference materials to analyze those points. Through this process, students with a strong foundation in English translation can develop a proficient and detailed understanding. As students comprehend new translation knowledge, they retrieve relevant experiences in their minds to explore grammar and translation knowledge they have learned in high schools, thereby experiencing the process of cognitive language acquisition.

(2) Teaching.

During this process, teachers must grasp the advantage of the teaching "process". Teachers can divide their approaches into two categories: seeking similarities and noting differences. Seeking similarities means that teachers should clarify the "similar" thinking process of Chinese-English translation by comparing and displaying the characteristics of Chinese and English translations through whiteboards or PowerPoint presentations. For example, the "subject-verb-object" structure that exists in both Chinese and English thinking can leverage students' linguistic learning experience to memorize vocabulary attributes in English. Conversely, noting differences also utilizes a comparative and three-dimensional approach, highlighting "unusable" translation phrases and grammatical content. In this case, teachers should use content comparisons that are close to students' experience, extract experience from Chinese language contexts in students' translation thinking, and then use a contrasting method to associate new translation knowledge with experiential knowledge, making the memorization process simpler within students' minds and English translation thinking logic.

(3) Practice.

Classroom practice is a crucial component of the "Five-Step Teaching Method" as it enables students to apply their English translation knowledge and move beyond mere memorization to the practical application level. All assessments and exercises used in the classroom practice session should be scientifically and systematically designed based on the scope and difficulty of the learned knowledge. During the actual practice, teachers should use relatively simple translation content to pave the way, following the point in Cognitive Linguistics that "the acquisition of language ability must progress from simple cognition to conceptual knowledge". Therefore, teachers need to consider students' cognitive processes, language structures, and gradually enhance students' mastery of English translation in a progressive manner, fundamentally changing their study habits from rote learning.

(4) Extracurricular learning.

In the process of English translation, factors like cultural acquisition and skill acquisition undoubtedly play important roles. However, vocabulary is the fundamental element for constructing English sentences. Therefore, teachers should deepen students' associative memory of vocabulary outside the classroom. Firstly, teachers can reinforce students' impression of small-scale vocabulary through reading exercises, such as repeating unfamiliar words from the reading and translation materials learned in class. Secondly, teachers can utilize informational teaching aids, such as vocabulary memorization software that focuses on visual memory, to enhance students' deep impressions of words within a specific range through visual imagery.

Besides, teachers should pay more attention to improve students' awareness of English cultural background. In the realm of Cognitive Linguistics, when it comes to cross-cultural acquisition, learners not only need to leverage their language experience in Chinese but also acquire a comprehensive understanding of English culture and context. This will enable students to enhance their translation skills in cross-cultural contexts by establishing a bilingual thinking environment. To achieve this, teachers can guide students to watch films and TV shows related to English history and culture. When students have an in-depth understanding of English and Chinese culture, they will naturally develop relevant thinking in translation contexts within the classroom, eliminating cognitive biases during the English translation teaching process.

3. Learners' feedback and evaluation

Learners' feedback has been collected through surveys and interviews. Generally, learners express positive attitudes towards the practice. They appreciate the emphasis on conceptual understanding and its role in producing effective translations. Students also report an increased awareness of the importance of cultural context and accurate communication in translation.

Formative and summative assessments have been conducted to evaluate learners' progress. These assessments include translation tasks, oral presentations, and written reflections. Based on these evaluations, students have demonstrated significant improvement in their translation abilities and displayed a deeper understanding of the cognitive aspects involved in translation.

The practice has been implemented over a semester and involved a combination of theoretical explanations, practical translation tasks, and group discussions. The effectiveness of the practice has been assessed through various means, including evaluation of translation quality and comparisons to students' previous translation performance.

Analysis of the effectiveness of such practice has revealed several positive outcomes. Firstly, students have demonstrated improved translation skills as evidenced by their ability to produce translations that are more accurate and coherent. Secondly, by incorporating cognitive strategies, students have showed a heightened awareness of the conceptual aspects of the source text, leading to more nuanced and contextually appropriate translations.

In conclusion, the English translation teaching practice from the perspective of Cognitive Linguistics has been proved to be effective in enhancing students' translation skills and their understanding of language meaning and structure. By emphasizing conceptual understanding, promoting context-based translation, providing explicit cognitive instruction, and incorporating students' feedback and evaluations, the practice has fostered a more comprehensive and proficient approach to English translation.

Section 4

Translation Teaching from the Perspective of Communication Studies

Communication is the activity of exchanging information by using various symbols and mediums, while translation is the cross-linguistic, cross-cultural, and cross-regional publicity of information and ideas. Therefore, to a certain extent, translation activities can be considered as a form of communication. Translation and communication are gradually combined with the increasing frequency of international communication all over the world. However, as a form of communication, translation differs from communication practices. Translation is not only influenced by the cultural differences between the source and target languages but also restricted by factors such as ideologies, social systems, public sentiment, and communication tools of both parties. These factors significantly interfere with the effectiveness of translation communication. Successful translation activities can overcome language barriers, publicize cultural information, and facilitate exchanges between countries and ethnic groups with different cultural backgrounds. In summary, translation as a form of communication is distinguished by its intercultural complexity, the need for linguistic accuracy, and the necessity for cultural sensitivity and adaptation. These factors make translation a unique and specialized form of communication.

From the perspective of communication studies, translation teaching is not merely the conversion of language but also the publicity of culture, information, and meanings. Some related questions are to be discussed in this section, such as the relationship between translation and communication, an initial introduction to theoretical system construction of translation and communication studies, the reflections on the quality of translators in translation teaching, and the future development of translation and communication research. The aim is to clarify, summarize, and synthesize the deep connections, interactions, and development trends between translation and communication research.

Ⅰ. The Relationship between Translation and Communication

Translation and communication are closely related. The phenomenon of translation and communication spans various periods of the development of human beings and exists in all aspects of social life. In the streets and scenic spots, there are often signs or introductions written in multiple languages; at important conferences, airports, seaports, and exhibition venues, people speaking different languages engage in effective communication with the help of interpreters; those who are not proficient in foreign languages can read translated versions of various foreign classics, watch blockbuster films with Chinese subtitles, browse popular foreign websites, and absorb elements from all over the world. All information exchange activities facilitated by translation are translation communication activities. So, what is the relationship between translation and communication? Is translation equivalent to communication? Is translation inseparable from communication? A better understanding of the relationship between translation and communication is the basis for further research on translation communication.

1. Close connections between translation and communication

Translation and communication are closely related activities with strong purposes. Communication is the process of interaction between information senders and receivers. Communicators select relevant content in the information based on their intentions and purposes, then transform the content into different symbols according to the characteristics of different media, and send them to recipients. This purpose-oriented communication process is similar to translation. Translation, as a bridge for information exchange between different cultures, is clearly purposeful. The discussion in academia on the purposefulness of translation has a long history. For example, in the functionalist approach, all translations are purpose-oriented, meaning that translations ultimately serve a certain function. That is to say, translation is the

Chapter 2 Different Perspectives of English Translation Teaching

process of transforming the original information into symbols that the target language audience can understand based on a certain purpose. Translation is essentially a cross-cultural information exchange and communication activity conducted to achieve certain demands or goals. For example, the China Foreign Languages Bureau has translated and published classic Chinese works such as *Dream of the Red Chamber* and *Romance of the Three Kingdoms* with the aim of telling Chinese stories and spreading Chinese voices internationally. These translation practices have played an important role in the international communication of Chinese culture and the interaction and connection of different cultural systems.

Translation studies and communication research develop through mutual borrowing and integration. Theories from communication studies have become an indispensable framework for interpretation and theoretical foundation in translation studies. Concepts from translation studies also play a significant role in the study of communication processes. On the one hand, in terms of the history of translation studies, it clearly shows that communication theories is used to describe the translation process. For instance, the term "audience" is closely tied to the study of the translation process and has become an important aspect in explaining the acceptability of translations. This concept originated in communication studies as a general term for the recipient group of social information publicity. However, with its widespread application in translation studies, its connotation and extension have changed, gradually aligning with the meaning of the concept of "receiver", which refers to the information recipient in the communication process. In addition to the related concepts, theories such as mass communication models, research on communication effects, agenda setting, and framing theory have also opened up new perspectives for translation studies. On the other hand, theoretical knowledge from translation studies is widely applied in the field of communication research, which is beneficial to solid the foundation of communication research.

2. Translation and communication cannot be equated

Although translation and communication are closely linked, they cannot be equated; each has its own mechanisms for practical activities. Essentially, communication is the transmission of social information and the operation of the social information system, involving elements such as communicators, content, channels, audiences, and effects. The process of communication requires the communicator to rely on channels to publicize the relevant information to the target audience and then obtain feedback and effects through various means. People use symbols as a medium for information publicity to achieve meaningful exchanges and interactions. Communicators aim to elicit the intended behavior from receivers by successfully conveying messages. This interaction involves both parties constructing and deconstructing the meanings of linguistic symbols. While translation also encompasses many elements such as the source text and the translated version (content), translators (communicators), and recipients (audience), and includes the construction and deconstruction processes of the source text and translated version by the communicators and audience, the difference lies in the general communication process where information is directly sent by the communicator, decoded, encoded, and decoded again through media before reaching the audience. In contrast, during the translation process, the translator is not only the first recipient and responder to the source language message but also the sender of the translated message. Due to the translator's involvement, the information undergoes two periods of decoding: the translator first decodes, translates, and encodes the source language information, then transforms it into a form acceptable to the target language audience. Additionally, as a participant in translation practice, the translator's subjectivity, poetics, ideology, patronage, and other factors also affect the translation process. In order to achieve its intended reception effect, translations must more or less cater to the mainstream of poetic styles and norms of the target language society. Ideological factors mainly restrict or guide translators from political, moral, and ethical perspectives, thereby affecting the initiation and conclusion, climaxes and troughs, as well as breakthroughs and setbacks of translation activities. Various forms of capital from patrons' often overlap, influencing the translator's choice and alteration of translation strategies through their advantages in ideology, economic interests, and status. These factors interact, giving rise to a mechanism of translation practice that differs from communication in its characteristics and connotations.

  Compared to communication, translation is more creative. Translation is not only closely related to communication but also possesses unique traits distinct from general communication practices. More precisely, translation is a creative communicative practice. This creativity is mainly reflected in the following three aspects.

(1) Creativity of the readers or audiences.

First of all, the translated works can be interpreted differently by each reader or member of the audience, based on their unique cultural and personal experiences. Besides, readers may bring forward their own understanding, emotions, and perspectives, which can vary greatly from one individual to another. What's more, the translated text offers multiple layers of meaning that can be explored, questioned, and appreciated in various ways, encouraging a dynamic engagement with the material. In addition, this level of creativity allows for a continuous reinterpretation of the work, keeping it alive and relevant across different contexts and times.

(2) The creativity of the translator's strategic approach.

At the beginning, translators must make strategic decisions about how to translate elements such as metaphors, allusions, humor, irony, and other literary devices that do not have direct equivalents in the target language.

Besides, they may choose to domesticate the text, making it more relatable to the target culture, or to foreignize it, preserving the sense of exoticism or cultural difference of the source languages. Creative strategies also involve considerations of genre, narrative voice, register, and style to ensure the translated work resonates with its new audience while staying true to the source material. Therefore, translators often need to conduct extensive research to understand the cultural references and historical connotations of the source text so as to render the origional meanings of the source text.

(3) The creativity triggered by objective language barriers.

Language barriers such as different grammatical structures and variations in linguistic conventions demand creative solutions to convey the intended meaning effectively. The translators must find equivalent expressions that respect the source culture while being comprehensible and meaningful to the target cultures' audience. They might need to invent new terms, adapt culturally specific references, or use explanatory notes when direct translations are impossible or would lose significance. Overcoming these barriers requires not only linguistic expertise but also a capacity for innovation and an ability to balance the source language author's intention with the audience's expectations.

In essence, translation is an act of bridging cultures and languages through creativity. It is a complex task that goes beyond mere word substitution, involving a deep understanding and a creative approach to communicate the essence of the source materials in a new linguistic and cultural context.

II. An Initial Introduction to Theoretical System Construction of Translation and Communication Studies

Translation and communication have a distinct interdisciplinary nature, thus it is necessary to further integrate multidisciplinary theoretical resources to construct a theoretical research system based on interdisciplinary intersections. As translation and communication activities continue to enrich, it is quite important to accurately grasp the connotations, essence, and laws of translation and communication research, and form a scientific and systematic theoretical research system, which is key for future translation studies.

For a long period in the past, translation and communication were classified into different academic disciplines. Translation studies belonged to foreign language and literature, while communication studies were linked with media and journalism specialties. Translation studies focused on the cross-regional, cross-cultural transformation of linguistic symbols, that is, the process and outcome of translating one type of text into another language text. Communication studies, on the other hand, paid attention to the processes of information migration, diffusion, and change within the global society, as well as its impact on diverse groups, cultures, nations, and even the human community. The categorization of translation studies and communication studies resulted in their separate development and mutual isolation. In reality, with the evolution of globalization and civilization exchanges, translation and communication have become increasingly interwoven, where the quality of translation affects the effectiveness of communication, and the means of communication determine the validity of translation. Together, translation and communication form the primary pathways for cross-cultural exchange. The intersection and integration of these two traditional disciplines possess strong vitality and a distinct sense of the era in the digital era, where "the medium is the message".

The integration of translation and communication is a result of the highly developed media society. Mass media communication encompasses nearly all areas from film, television to news broadcasting, advertising videos, web pages, and electronic billboards, while translation is examined within a broader cultural and social context. Researchers begin to focus on the literary, sociological, and psychological factors contained in translation, as well as the translated work itself as an interlingual and inter-semiotic transference activity, considering its publicity and reception, purposes, and effects in new backgrounds. Therefore, translation and communication have generalized into all areas of cultural life of people. From crowdsourced translations of literature and movie subtitles to the popular participation in translating Internet buzzwords, it reflects the era where "everyone has a microphone". There is a significant enhancement in the subjectivity awareness of both translators and audiences.

In the current international relations system, external translation and communication serve as an important means for a country to safeguard its interests, articulate its governance philosophy, and participate in global governance. Translation and communication, as the representation of linguistic and non-linguistic symbols within another political cultural system, possess strong ideological functions and inherent value orientations. From the perspective of discourse translation, it involves constructing national identity and establish national image through appropriate discourse, achieving international identity recognition. From the viewpoint of communicative power, it leverages traditional and new media platforms to influence the cognition of international audiences, forming an international public opinion favorable to the interests of one's own nation. The way translation is shaped and publicized can either reinforce or erode each other; therefore, they must be treated as a whole. The translator's familiarity with the lexical habits and values of different cultural spheres directly affects the quality and effect of communication. Meanwhile, the platform, method, and capability of communication are the guarantees for discourse to take root in foreign cultures and international public opinion. Therefore, the construction of translation and communication studies holds significant importance for the development of a vibrant national language and the external articulation of national concepts.

However, the integration of translation and communication is not about generalizing translation studies into communication research. Instead, it aims to break the traditional boundaries of linguistic symbol transformation, incorporate the intrinsic laws of communication research, and the changes in media technology into the scope of study. It follows the changes of the times, broadens the research horizon, and expands the research approaches. Firstly, we can update our concept regarding the object of study. The development of new media has infinitely extended people's perception, thereby expanding the objects of translation study. The reading subject is no longer limited to words or texts on paper, but includes composite textual discourses that combine text, images, and audiovisuals. The physical existence of translation research objects is no longer confined to print media but now encompasses various media carriers such as theaters, cinemas, and social media.

Secondly, the integration of translation and communication requires us to re-examine and expand the research approaches in translation. On one hand, the deep integration of technology has brought about significant changes in both the mode of translation production and the ecology of communication. User-generated translations and machine translations have made the traditional research methods and examination paths no longer universally effective. Translation needs to draw on and develop new avenues from emerging communication theories and other related disciplinary theories. On the other hand, the coexistence of various linguistic symbols and semiotic modes has become the new norm for translation communication carriers. The construction of a theoretical framework for translation and communication research not only necessitates mutual borrowing between "translation" and "communication" but also requires drawing inspiration and nourishment from other related disciplines to enhance the explanatory power and guidance over phenomena and practice.

III. The Reflections on the Qualities of Translators in Translation Teaching

Nowadays, translation serves as a vital bridge for cross-cultural communication. Consequently, the requirements for the translator's quality are continuously increasing, especially in the field of translation teaching. Translation is not merely a conversion of language and text but also an exchange of cultural, emotional, and stylistic information. Therefore, nurturing translators with high-quality competencies has become the core mission of translation teaching. This part will discuss the reflections on the quality of translators in translation teaching, including language proficiency, cultural literacy, professional knowledge, basic translation theories and skills, the use of translation tools and reference books, and a sense of responsibility. Through in-depth analysis, this part aims to provide valuable insights and suggestions for enhancing the quality of translation teaching and the competence of translators.

1. The requirements of a qualified translator

(1) Language proficiency.

Language proficiency refers to the level of skill and fluency a person has in a given language. It encompasses various aspects including vocabulary, grammar, pronunciation, comprehension, and the ability to use the language effectively in communication, whether written or spoken. In the context of translation, language proficiency is crucial as it directly affects the quality of the translation. A highly proficient translator is able to accurately convey the meaning, tone, and nuances of the source language into the target language, ensuring that the translated text remains faithful to the original while also being fluent and natural for the new audience. Therefore, continuous learning and practice are essential for translators to maintain and enhance their language proficiency.

The importance of language knowledge and ability to translation is self-evident, as translation fundamentally involves the conversion between two languages. The translator must have a good command of both languages involved in order to achieve effective and high-quality English-Chinese and Chinese-English translation. The more detailed and profound your understanding of phonology, semantics, vocabulary, grammar, pragmatics, rhetoric, style, and other aspects of language, the more assured the quality of your translation will be. For instance, the saying "桂林山水甲天下" can be faithfully and smoothly translated to "Guilin landscape is the best in the world". However, if it is rendered as "East or West, Guilin landscape is best", it may demonstrate a different response from readers due to the English proverb "East or west, home is best". This familiarity can evoke a sense of warmth and closeness for English speakers. How can one improve his language proficiency? Firstly, it can be achieved by extensive reading, and secondly, it can be achieved by thoughtful reflections. As far as the Chinese people are concerned, while translating from Chinese to English, they should not only enhance their proficiency in Chinese but also broaden their reading of English works, especially literature, because literature is the art of language. Through long-term and extensive reading, one can improve his comprehension and appreciation of the words, sentences and texts. Upon encountering an excellent word or sentence, take time to fully appreciate it. Besides, one have to develop the habit of reading and reflecting simultaneously. If a word is used cleverly, what makes it so? What are its phonetic, formal, and semantic features? How does it relate to the context? If a sentence is beautifully crafted, is it due to the novel combination of words, the unique sentence structure, or the use of extraordinary rhetorical devices? All these require careful attention and accumulation in daily practice to cultivate a sensitivity towards language and enhance one's language proficiency.

(2) Cultural literacy.

Cultural literacy refers to an individual's understanding of and familiarity with the cultural contexts, traditions, customs, and values that are expressed through language. It involves knowledge that extends beyond the mere words and includes the ability to interpret and use language within specific cultural frameworks. In translation, cultural literacy is crucial for conveying meaning accurately and appropriately, as well as maintaining nuanced cultural references that may not have direct equivalents in the target language. It is essential in translation. Without an in-depth understanding of culture in the source language, the mastery of a foreign language and the use of dictionaries and reference books are not sufficient to ensure translation quality. Language does not exist independently; it is a carrier of culture, reflecting society and history. A term of color, for instance, does not merely refer to a color but can also carry rich cultural connotations. For example, while the Chinese word "红色" and the English word "red" may seem equivalent, they differ in cultural significance. In Chinese culture, red represents joy and auspiciousness, whereas in Western cultures, red often evokes associations with violence, bloodshed and revolution.

The British translator David Hawkes' translation of 《红楼梦》is a classic translated version. He chose *The Story of the Stone* as the English title, drawing from another name of the novel 《石头记》(*The Tale of the Stone*). It is said that this choice was made to avoid negative associations with the color red among Western readers. In Hawkes' translation, Jia Baoyu's residence "怡红院" was translated by Hawkes as "House of Green Delights", and his sobriquet "怡红公子" became "Green Boy". These translations replace the word "red" with the word "green", because in English green signifies youth, hope, and happiness, echoing the pragmatic effect of red in Chinese.

This demonstrates that culture lies behind language. To excel in translation, one must be well-versed in both languages and their respective cultures. Translation is a cross-cultural communication activity mediated by language, where linguistic ability and cultural knowledge complement each other and must advance hand in hand. A person with high cultural literacy in a particular culture can understand the connotations, allusions, idiomatic expressions, and other cultural elements that are inherent in the use of language. They are able to recognize and adapt to the cultural norms and expectations of communication, which might include aspects such as gestures, social manners, historical references, and more.

In the context of translation, cultural literacy enables translators to make decisions about how to handle cultural concepts and expressions. This might involve finding suitable analogues in the target language, providing additional explanation or footnotes, or making deliberate omissions or substitutions to convey the intended message without misleading the reader. For another example, the Chinese concept of

"关系"(relationship), which relates to the system of social connections and influence in China, does not have an exact counterpart in English. A translator with cultural literacy would be able to choose the most appropriate way to express this concept in English, whether by using existing terms like "relationships", or by providing additional context to explain the meaning of the term.

In summary, cultural literacy is the ability to understand and navigate the cultural dimensions of language, which is essential for effective translation.

(3) Professional knowledge.

Professional knowledge refers to an understanding and proficiency in a specific subject or field related to one's profession. It encompasses specialized skills, information, and expertise that are necessary for effective job performance. In many fields, such as medicine, law, engineering, or finance, professional knowledge is essential for making informed decisions, applying technical skills correctly, and adhering to industry standards.

Professional knowledge is crucial in translation. Translation may involve various sectors such as economics, politics, law, computing, electronics, construction, artificial intelligence and more. Without adequate professional knowledge, it can be challenging to complete translation tasks successfully. For example, a student with a degree in English language and literature might initially struggle with translating scientific and technological materials because their education primarily exposed them to British and American literary works. To engage in technical translation, they would need to catch up by learning and delving into scientific theories and knowledge. If possible, it's best to have a field research. For instance, when translating an installation and operation manual for a foreign-made lathe, it's preferable to have on-site experience in workshops or factories. Otherwise, improper installation or use could lead to economic loss or even casualties. Therefore, veteran translators emphasize that translators should be generalists with diverse interests, extensive reading, and preparations for unexpected demands.

For example, a lawyer must have deep knowledge of legal principles, case law, and legislative frameworks to provide sound counsel and representation to clients. Similarly, a doctor needs comprehensive understanding of human anatomy, disease processes, and treatment modalities to diagnose and treat patients effectively.

In the context of translation, professional knowledge is vital because translators often work with texts from specialized domains such as technology, medicine, law, or finance. A translator with professional knowledge in a particular field can accurately convey complex terminology, concepts, and nuances that are specific to that area. This ensures that the translated document retains its original meaning and serves its intended purpose in the target language.

(4) Basic translation theories and skills.

Basic translation theories and skills of translation refer to the foundational knowledge and practical methods that are essential for anyone engaged in the process of translating texts from one language to another. Some translators disregard translation theories when doing translation, even looking down upon them, believing that one can still translate without understanding these theories. This view is biased. It's undeniable that some translation theories are indeed too abstract and far removed from practical application. However, most translation theories are derived from practice and can guide the process of translation. A proper understanding of basic translation theories, such as principles, methods, objectives, processes, and various factors involved in translation, like the original work, the author, the target readers, and the social and historical background of the publication, helps translators consider all aspects of a translation project and make wise and appropriate choices during the process. Translation techniques are summaries of experiences passed down by generations of translators. By combining theoretical knowledge with practical skills, translators can produce translations that are faithful to the original while also being accessible and meaningful to the target audience.

(5) The use of translation tools and reference books.

A person's knowledge and experience are limited, so it is inevitable to encounter unfamiliar issues during the translation process. When faced with new vocabulary, one often needs to consult a dictionary. A dictionary contains a wealth of information. To fully utilize it, one must study the introductory text carefully, understand its arrangement, the scope and number of entries, and the characteristics of the definitions and example sentences. For instance, when looking up an English verb, it is best to determine whether it is transitive or intransitive, formal or informal, archaic or neologism, and what words it can collocate with. Only by doing so can one fully comprehend and use it accurately and appropriately in future writing or translation. The choice of dictionary also matters. During the comprehension stage, a monolingual dictionary in the source language should be the first choice. When translating from English to Chinese, it is advisable to consult several English-English dictionaries for new words, while an English-Chinese dictionary can be referenced for expression. Dictionary definitions cannot be copied into the translation without any revision; they need to be adjusted and modified according to the context. Nowadays, with highly advanced technology and an abundance of information, there is an endless supply of electronic and online resources available for translators except traditional printed books and dictionaries. The Internet is a vast corpus, much richer than any dictionaries. For example, when translating from Chinese to English, if one is uncertain about English collocations, he can search online to see if anyone has used the phrase and modify it based on the results. When translating contemporary literary works or the latest scientific literature, one may encounter new words or knowledge that existing dictionaries may not yet have entries for, it is essential to search on the Internet. Of course, since online resources are plentiful and varied, they should not be accepted blindly. Discernment is necessary to separate the genuine from the false and make careful selections. Moreover, nowadays there is a wide array of translation software with varying quality, one should neither follow them blindly nor reject them outright. If one can master one or two types of software and leverage their strengths in a human-machine collaboration, translation efficiency can be improved.

(6) A sense of responsibility.

While the above five points are crucial for a qualified translator, a sense of responsibility is also indispensable. With the positive attitude and earnest dedication, even if one's abilities are somewhat lacking, translation skills can be improved step by step. Sloppiness and carelessness are sure to result in poor translation. A sense of responsibility is at the core of a qualified translator's professional morals. Cultivating this sense of responsibility starts with everyday practices and attention to details. In the translation process, one should not easily overlook a single word or even a punctuation mark. Those engaged in translation must strictly follow the translation process, from comprehension to expression, and finally, conduct a thorough review to ensure the accuracy and fluency of the translated text.

2. The cultivation of a qualified translator

To cultivate a qualified translator, translation teaching should encompass a comprehensive curriculum that addresses various aspects of translation competence. Here are some suggestions on how to nurture each quality of translators.

(1) Language proficiency.

The teachers should encourage extensive reading in both source and target languages. Besides it's important to assign exercises that improve language skills, such as grammar, vocabulary, pronunciation and intonation. What's more, the teachers should provide opportunities to speak and write in both languages to gain fluency.

(2) Cultural literacy.

As for cultural literacy, here are some practical suggestions: Offer courses on cross-cultural communication to enhance awareness of cultural differences. Incorporate case studies and examples that illustrate cultural influences on language use. Encourage students to engage with literature, media, and art from different cultures.

(3) Professional knowledge.

In translation teaching, it is necessary to teach some specialized terminologies related to specific fields like law, medicine, technology, and so on. It is highly essential to introduce industry practices and standards related to the professional contexts where translation is used. Organizing workshops or guest lectures by professionals also plays a very important role.

(4) Basic translation theories and skills.

As for this, tips are as follows: teach foundational theories of translation and contrastive linguistics, practice translation techniques through exercises and simulations, analyze and discuss different translation strategies and their applications.

(5) The use of translation tools and reference books.

In translation teaching, the teacher should familiarize students with computer-assisted translation tools (CAT tools), terminology databases, and translation memory systems. It is helpful to teach effective research methods for finding references and verifying facts. It's also important to guide students to use online resources responsibly and efficiently.

(6) Sense of responsibility.

It is essential to prioritize moral considerations in translation, recognizing the importance of maintaining confidentiality and striving for impartiality. It is crucial to have an understanding of legal and copyright implications associated with the translation work. Furthermore, promoting reflection and self-assessment among translators should be encouraged to facilitate ongoing enhancement and advancement in their professional journey.

(7) Practical experience.

It is advisable to offer chances to students with practical translation experiences that replicate real-world scenarios, including offering internships or collaborative projects with actual clients. Additionally, there should be an effort to construct a simulated translation setting that mirrors the conditions found in professional environments.

(8) Assessment and feedback.

It is important to frequently evaluate students' advancement through various assessments, such as quizzes, tests, and hands-on tasks. Additionally, providing valuable feedback on their translations will aid students in recognizing their capabilities and identifying where they can enhance their skills.

(9) Continuous learning.

It is vital to cultivate a perspective of continuous learning among students, given the constant evolution of languages and cultures, as well as the emergence of fresh translation challenges. Additionally, it is essential to keep the curriculum up to date by integrating the latest advancements in translation technology and industry trends.

By integrating these elements into translation teaching, teachers can prepare students to become well-rounded, professional translators who are not only adept at language conversion but also sensitive to cultural nuances, ethically responsible, and adaptable to the ever-changing landscape of global communication.

IV. The Future Development of Translation and Communication Research

1. Research on translation and communication studies driven by technological empowerment

With the rapid development of information technology, the achievements of information technology continue to be transformed and applied across various disciplines. There is no exception to research on translation and communication. Technological empowerment is set to open up new horizons for research on translation and communication. In particular, technologies such as machine translation, databases, text mining, and sentiment analysis are increasingly playing vital roles in both the practical and theoretical research of translation and com-munication. They are leading the way in introducing new topics and methodologies for empirical research in this field.

Firstly, under the influence of technological empowerment, the production model of translation and communication is undergoing significant changes, which in turn are giving rise to a multitude of novel research topics. Take machine translation as an example, it is characterized by low cost and high efficiency. Moreover, with advancements in post-editing technology, the quality of machine translation is continuously improving. At present, numerous international organizations, social groups, and multinational corporations " have already implemented customized machine translation systems, integrating a machine translation plus post-editing model into their product internationalization processes. " As the Internet and information technology rapidly evolve, the production and publicity of target language texts will be increasingly influenced by translation technology. This leads to potential new research areas such as pre-translation and post-editing, technology and standards, ethics, and copyright, all of which could become important subjects for future research on translation and communication.

Secondly, under the empowerment of technology, audience research on translation and communication is poised to embrace entirely new methods of investigation. As one of the important indicators of evaluating the effectiveness of translation and communication, as well as for assessing audience preferences and adjusting translation strategies, audience research has always been a focus and challenge within the field of translation and communication studies. Existing research on audience reception and the effectiveness of communication often relies on surveys based on general reader evaluations in the target language country, book sales, and library holdings to analyze and evaluate the effects of translation and publicity of texts. However, these dimensions are not fully sufficient to represent the true impact and reception of translated works in the target language country. Audience research enabled by technology can significantly shorten the research cycle, especially when dealing with a vast number of recipients. Techniques such as database analysis, text mining, and sentiment analysis allow for the integration, statistics, and analysis of data to comprehensively examine the needs of the target audience, understanding their emotional cognition, attitude tendencies, and preference choices towards a particular translation product. Although there are already a small number of scholars in China combining information technology with audience research, technological methods like data mining, natural language processing, and sentiment analysis still have considerable potential for expansion within the field of translation and communication research, promising to revolutionize the research methods in this area.

Thirdly, under the empowerment of technology, empirical research will become an important direction in translation and communication studies. Empirical research refers to the investigation conducted by researchers who collect and observe primary data to further propose theoretical hypotheses or test existing theoretical frameworks. Empirical research is characterized by its distinct direct experiential features and often yields more scientific and persuasive conclusions.

Technological empowerment is leading translation and communication research into a new phase of development. The production model of translation and communication is becoming more efficient and intelligent, audience research is becoming more precise and comprehensive, and the methods of empirical research are becoming more scientific and systematic.

2. Research on translation and communication talents cultivation

Cultivating specialized talents who meet the needs of international translation and communication in the new era has become one of the important tasks in the research of translation and communication. Specifically, within the overall scope of interdisciplinary research between translation and communication, talent cultivation research can focus on the following aspects.

Firstly, it is essential to conduct research on the integration of translation studies and communication studies for talents cultivation. The integration of translation studies and communication studies is key to training high-level translation and communication talents. From the disciplinary frameworks of translation studies and communication studies, the talent training systems and curriculum designs of the two disciplines still differ significantly when considering the goals of talents cultivation, although there are many areas of knowledge intersection in terms of context, subjects, objects, carriers, receptors, effects, and purposes. Therefore, if we aim to cultivate interdisciplinary international communication talents against the background of the integration of translation and communication studies, it is imperative to achieve a synthesis and crossover between the two disciplines. However, this does not simply mean adding several communication courses to the translation program or merely enhancing students' translation skills in the communication curriculum. In fact, the integration of translation and communication education should aim to cultivate versatile talents who develop comprehensively in multiple aspects such as Chinese and foreign languages, cross-cultural communication, translation, external communication, journalism and more. This will be an important research dimension in the study of translation and communication with a focus on talents cultivation.

Section 5

Translation Teaching from the Perspective of Pragmatics

Language, as a tool for communication, not only carries the transmission of information but also embodies a rich socio-cultural background. As a branch of linguistics, pragmatics focuses on the functions and effects of language in actual use, emphasizing the relationship between language and its users, as well as the context in which language is used. Translation, as a cross-linguistic, cross-cultural communicative activity, is not merely a conversion of words and text but also a conveyance of contextual meanings and cultural connotations. Therefore, applying pragmatic theory to translation teaching is of great significance for cultivating students' translation skills and cross-cultural communicative competence.

Ⅰ. A Brief Introduction to Pragmatics

Pragmatics is the study of how context affects the interpretation and use of language, and how speakers convey meaning beyond the literal words they use. It is a sub-field within linguistics that focuses on the practical use of language in social interaction. Pragmatics has applications in various fields such as second language acquisition, cross-cultural communication, artificial intelligence, and more. In education, understanding pragmatics helps learners to become more effective communicators because they can better adapt their speech to different social settings.

As a distinct academic field, pragmatics primarily focuses on the contextual factors involved in the understanding and use of language. It deals with how meanings of language are comprehended based on context and how language is appropriately used in various social situations.

The concept of pragmatics was first proposed by Charles Morris, who distinguished it from syntax (morphology) and semantics within the framework of semiotics. Pragmatics concentrates on the relationship between signs and interpreta-tions. With the evolution of linguistics, pragmatics has gradually developed its own research methods and theoretical systems.

The key elements of pragmatics include Grice's conversational maxims, implicature, context, and other fundamental concepts and theories. These theories help us understand how people convey intentions through speech in daily communication and how to interpret others' words based on context.

While both semantics and pragmatics study the meaning of language, their focuses differ. While semantics deals with the meaning of words and sentences in isolation, pragmatics looks at how that meaning is affected by the context of use. Semantics is concerned with conventional meaning, whereas pragmatics is concerned with the actual, contextualized meaning in specific situations.

In summary, pragmatics is about how people use and understand language in particular situations, including how they produce and comprehend meaningful expressions, how they manage conversations, and how they adapt their speech based on social norms and conventions. It's an essential aspect of our ability to communicate effectively and appropriately in various contexts.

II. The Evolution of Pragmatics in Translation Studies and Pedagogy

The history of pragmatics as a field is intimately tied to the study of language use in context. From the seminal works of Frege, Peirce, and Morris in the early 20th century to Grice's groundbreaking conversational implicatures and Searle's elaboration of Speech Act Theory, pragmatics has come a long way. This journey has been paralleled by its integration into translation studies, where it has illuminated the complexities of meaning beyond the lexical and syntactic level.

In translation research, the application of pragmatics has moved from being a peripheral concern to a central issue. Initially, translation was viewed primarily as a linguistic exercise focused on word-for-word or even sentence-for-sentence replacement. However, with the advent of pragmatic theories, scholars began to appreciate the multifaceted nature of meaning, which includes not just what is said but also how it is said, why it is said, and under what circumstances it is said.

The current state of pragmatics in translation studies reflects a mature recognition of the role of context, speaker intention, and cultural norms in the translation process. Research now commonly focuses on phenomena such as metaphors, idioms, politeness strategies, and other pragmatic particles that significantly impact the interpretation of texts.

Turning to translation pedagogy, the traditional approach has often been criticized for its lack of focus on practical communicative competence. The classic model of teaching—which emphasizes grammar, vocabulary, and syntax—has been gradually supplemented by more communicative approaches that include pragmatic competence. This change aligns with the growing consensus that effective translation requires not only accuracy but also appropriateness in relation to the target audience's linguistic and cultural expectations.

An analysis of both domestic and international research reveals a pressing need for integrating pragmatics into translation teaching. The benefits are manifold: students can develop a heightened awareness of the dynamic interplay between form and function in language; they can learn to handle different types of texts with greater sensitivity to the nuances of register, dialect, and genre; and they can acquire skills essential for successful cross-cultural communication.

The possibility of combining pragmatics with translation pedagogy is not merely a theoretical construct but has been demonstrated through various instructional models. These models incorporate activities such as role-playing, scenario-based translation, and comparative analyses of original texts and their translations to cultivate pragmatic awareness among learners.

In conclusion, the combination between pragmatics and translation studies has come to stay, enriching our understanding of the translation process and informing pedagogical practices. As we continue to explore this interdisciplinary relationship, it becomes evident that training translators lack of pragmatic insights is similar to preparing them to speak without knowing the listener's language or culture. It is the duty of teachers to ensure that translation teaching evolves in step with the complexities of the real-world communicative demands that translators face.

Ⅲ. The Pragmatic Turn in Translation: Core Concepts and Their Application

The discipline of translation has undergone a significant transformation with the incorporation of pragmatic theory, moving beyond a strict linguistic approach to encompass the dynamic nature of language use in real-world contexts. This part mainly focuses on the core concepts of pragmatics and their impact on translation practice, highlighting the importance of understanding speech acts, the cooperative principle, politeness strategies, and how these contribute to successful cross-cultural communication.

1. Speech Act Theory in translation

The foundation of pragmatic theory is the Speech Act Theory, introduced by J. L. Austin and further developed by John Searle. This theory distinguishes between the locutionary act (the literal utterance), the illocutionary act (the intent or force of the utterance), and the perlocutionary act (the effect the speech has on the listener). Translators must navigate these layers to capture not just what is said but also how it is said and what it is intended to achieve.

2. Cooperative Principle and translation

H. P. Grice's Cooperative Principle posits that conversations are guided by an overarching expectation of cooperation among interlocutors. The maxims of this principle—quantity, quality, relation, and manner—are essential for ensuring effective communication. In translation, adherence to these maxims can be culturally specific, requiring translators to make informed decisions about what information should be included or excluded to maintain relevance and clarity for the target audience.

3. Politeness Principle in translation

Geoffrey Leech's Politeness Principle complements Grice's work, focusing on maintaining harmonious relationships through communication. Strategies such as minimizing imposition, expressing gratitude, and acknowledging shared knowledge are culturally variable and must be sensitively handled in translation. Awareness of these strategies allows translators to convey respectful and socially appropriate performance, even when the source and target languages have different norms of politeness.

4. Contextual influence on translation

Context plays a vital role in shaping the meaning of an utterance. Translators must account for both the physical environment and the socio-cultural setting to correctly interpret and relay messages. Failure to consider context can lead to miscommunication or loss of intended connotations, particularly with idioms, colloquial expressions, and culture-specific references.

5. Dealing with implicature and metaphor in translation

Indirect speech and metaphorical language present unique challenges in translation. They often rely on background knowledge or conceptual frameworks specific to a culture. Translators face the task of conveying underlying meanings without losing the emotive power or rich imaginations that metaphors embody. This requires a blend of literal and creative translation techniques that preserve the essence of the original message while resonating with the target audience.

In short, pragmatics offers a comprehensive lens through which translators can view the complexities of language in use. By applying insights from Speech Act Theory, the Cooperative Principle, and the Politeness Principle, translators can achieve translations that are faithful to the source text while remaining accessible and relevant to the target readership. An awareness of context, implicature, and metaphor is crucial for capturing the full spectrum of communicative intentions and cultural nuances. In this way, pragmatics serves not only as a theoretical framework but as an essential toolkit for those who seek to bridge the gaps between languages and cultures through translation.

Ⅳ. A Pragmatic Approach to English Translation Teaching

In the field of language teaching, the importance of pragmatics cannot be ignored. It is a crucial aspect that contributes to effective communication and understanding between individuals from different cultures. Therefore, it is imperative to integrate pragmatics into English translation teaching in order to develop students' contextual analysis, reasoning, and cultural adaptation abilities. This part aims to explore the implementation of a pragmatic approach to English translation teaching and its benefits.

The pragmatic approach to English translation teaching emphasizes the importance of understanding the context in which language is used. In this regard, teachers should encourage students to analyze the context of a given text or conversation before attempting to translate it. For instance, if a student is translating a text about business negotiations, they should first understand the cultural norms and expectations surrounding such negotiations. By doing so, they can avoid misunderstandings and ensure accurate translations.

Another key aspect of pragmatics is reasoning. In order to effectively translate a text or conversation, students need to be able to think critically and apply their knowledge of language rules and conventions. For example, when translating a sentence that contains idioms or metaphors, students need to understand the underlying meaning and find appropriate equivalents in the target language. This requires them to use their reasoning skills to analyze the context and make informed decisions.

Furthermore, cultural adaptation is another crucial component of pragmatics in translation teaching. Students must be aware of the cultural differences between their native language and the target language. They need to learn how to adapt their translations to fit in with the cultural norms and expectations of the target readers. For instance, when translating a text that contains humor or sarcasm, students need to consider the cultural differences in humor expression and adjust their translation accordingly.

To facilitate the implementation of the pragmatic approach, teachers can employ various teaching activities such as case studies, role-playing, and simulated translation exercises. These activities provide students with practical opportunities to apply their pragmatic skills in real-life situations. For example, through case studies, students can analyze authentic texts or conversations and identify the contextual factors that influence their translation choices. Similarly, role-playing exercises can help students practice their reasoning skills by having them take on different roles in a conversation or negotiation scenario. Finally, simulated translation exercises allow students to apply their cultural adaptation skills by translating texts or conversations that contain cultural elements specific to their target language.

In conclusion, the integration of pragmatics into English translation teaching can greatly enhance students' ability to understand and communicate effectively across different cultures. By focusing on contextual analysis, reasoning, and cultural adaptation, students can develop essential skills that are vital for success in the new era. Therefore, educators should embrace the pragmatic approach as a means to provide students with a comprehensive and practical education in English translation.

Ⅴ. Translation Teaching Strategies Based on Pragmatic Theory

1. Strengthening cultural knowledge learning

English translation is not merely a mutual conversion between two languages; it also requires an understanding of both cultures. Without knowledge of the cultural aspects of both languages, one cannot correctly express or comprehend the language. Therefore, the process of translation is constrained by the cultural contexts associated with the two languages involved. Mastering a language and its culture isn't something that can be achieved overnight; it takes time as it involves accumulating learning over time. This necessitates that in translation teaching, we must facilitate the transmission of linguistic culture, focusing on cultivating students' cultural refinement, and enhancing their cultural awareness. It's important to explain to students the differences between the two cultures, and their different language expression habits. At the same time, students should have some understanding of the basic conditions of the regions where the languages are spoken, such as local customs, geographical environment, historical allusions, religious beliefs, etc. Moreover, students should be encouraged to make full use of their spare time after class. Teachers should recommend classic English works to them, such as newspapers and magazines, and beneficial English-language movies are also excellent choices. These can help students practise their listening skills, grasp the characteristics of language expressions used by characters, and gain some understanding of other countries' cultures.

For example, the phrase "the last straw" is literally translated to "最后的稻草" in Chinese, which might be extended to mean "a last resort" in traditional Chinese culture. However, "the last straw" actually refers to the final burden that breaks the camel's back, which is far from the meaning of "a last resort". If one is unaware of Western culture and translates it literally without understanding, errors may occur. Therefore, in English translation, it is necessary to convey as much of the power of linguistic culture as possible, understand the differences between Chinese and Western cultures, and cultivate students' cross-cultural awareness.

For another example:

—你做得真好!

— 哪里,我做得一点也不好。

—You did a really good job!

—Oh, you're too kind. I did not do well at all.

Before translating this content, the teacher might first discuss the theory of conversational implicature and explain how in Chinese culture, humility is traditionally valued as a virtue, whereas Western countries like the US and the UK generally place a higher emphasis on accepting praise. Once students understand the cultural backgrounds of both English and Chinese, they would be more likely to respond with "Thanks" rather than "I didn't do well at all".

2. Creating optimal learning contexts

Context is the prerequisite for language activities and a core concept in pragmatics. In English translation, context greatly aids in and constrains the understanding and expression of language. In other words, a specific context endows words and sentences with particular meanings. Without context, there would be no speech activities and translation would be meaningless. Therefore, in college English translation teaching, teachers should create contexts that are both relevant to students' lives and close to the use of English, allowing students to experience the impact of different contexts on translation. Only by doing so can we effectively enhance students' English translation skills. For instance, when translating the phrase "你还是老样子" (You haven't changed), common translations might include "You look unchanged" "You are the same as you were" or "You haven't changed much". However, these translations may not suffice when considering the context. If the phrase is used between two elderly friends, it could be interpreted as a compliment or casual greeting. A direct translation like "You are the same as you were" fails to convey this nuance, whereas "You look as young as before" successfully expresses the implied meaning, accurately representing the original scene and achieving the goal of linguistic communication. This further illustrates that in the process of translation, the translator needs to deal with the pragmatic meaning of language within a specific context, which is mainly to reveal the deeper intentions behind people's speech. Therefore, if the role of pragmatic translation knowledge is overlooked in English translation teaching, it will be detrimental to enhancing students' translation abilities. College English teachers should not only strengthen the teaching of translation techniques but also create effective learning contexts for their students.

3. Teaching translation techniques

In the teaching of English, especially in the context of intensive reading courses, it is crucial to impart a substantial amount of translation skills. This approach enables students not only to read but also to enhance their learning of English translation techniques and methods. It moves beyond mere "dead" translation of sentence structures and phrases, which does not contribute to improving students' translation abilities. For instance, in the textbook *College English* (Intensive Reading), published by Shanghai Foreign Language Education Press, there is a sentence in Unit 2 of the first volume: "My wife didn't think I was crazy." Many students might translate this as "我的妻子认为我疯了", which clearly follows a straightforward and literal thinking pattern. Teachers should remind students of being aware of the negative transference used in this sentence structure. By doing so, the teachers should guide students to accurately translate it as "我妻子不认为我疯了", which is correct and more aligned with Chinese logical thinking. Moreover, the phrase "the rough and cold water" appears in the article. Some students often translate it as "汹涌和冰冷的

水", which seems somewhat awkward. After careful analysis of the context, translating it as "海水冰凉, 海浪汹涌" is evidently more appropriate. Therefore, as college English teachers, we must always be mindful to timely impart translation techniques to our students rather than leaving them to interpret texts literally. Only through such intentional instruction can we truly improve students' proficiency of English translation.

Ⅵ. Cultivation of Pragmatic Awareness and Competence in Translation Teaching

It is a vital task to cultivating students' pragmatic awareness and competence in the process of translation teaching. Pragmatic awareness refers to the understanding and sensitivity to context, intention, and effects in the use of language, while pragmatic competence refers to the ability to use language effectively for communication. Here are some key strategies that can help teachers enhance students' pragmatic awareness and competence in translation classes.

1. Integration of theory and practice

Teachers should integrate pragmatics theory into the translation curriculum, using case analysis, translation exercises, and so on to let students understand the impact of different cultural and linguistic habits on translation. For example, by comparing and analyzing the differences in speech acts between Chinese and foreign cultures, students can better understand the socio-cultural factors behind language.

In translation teaching, integrating theory with practice is crucial to cultivate students' pragmatic awareness and competence. Teachers should put pragmatic theory into the translation curriculum through methods such as case analysis and translation exercises. This approach enables students to grasp how diverse cultural and linguistic customs impact the translation process. For instance, teachers can enhance students' understanding of socio-cultural factors in language by comparing and analyzing differences in speech acts between Chinese and foreign cultures. Such activities not only bridge the theoretical knowledge of pragmatics with practical translation skills but also sensitize students to the nuances of cross-cultural communication.

This integration requires a curriculum that balances theoretical input with ample opportunity for practical application. Assignments might include translating authentic materials, such as advertisements, dialogues, or news articles, which entail understanding the implicit meanings and cultural references inherent in such texts. By dealing with real-world materials, students develop the ability to consider pragmatic elements like context, audience, and intent when translating.

Through these integrated and practical approaches, students gain experience in applying pragmatic theories to their translation work. Therefore, their translations are not only linguistically accurate but also culturally appropriate and effective in conveying the intended messages.

2. Critical thinking training

In translation practice, teachers should guide students to critically examine the source and target texts, considering how meaning is transformed between different cultures and languages. Discussing the choices and decision-making processes in translation can lead students to a deeper understanding of the impact of context on translation.

In translation practice, critical thinking training is essential to develop students' ability to analyze and make informed decisions when translating texts between languages and cultures. This training encourages a deep understanding of the complexities involved in conveying meaning across different linguistic and cultural boundaries.

Teachers can guide students to critically examine both the source text and the target text by asking questions that prompt them to consider various aspects of the translation process. For instance, they might discuss how the intended audience, the purpose of the text, and the social-cultural context influence translation choices. By analyzing these factors, students learn to recognize that a word-for-word translation does not always capture the intent or spirit of the original text.

Furthermore, teachers can lead discussions around the decision-making processes in translation. This includes exploring why certain expressions or idioms might be challenging to translate directly and how these challenges can be navigated to maintain the integrity of the source material. Students can be encouraged to evaluate different translation strategies, such as domestication vs. foreignization, and to understand the implications of each strategy for the target language readers' experience.

Critical thinking training also involves teaching students to reflect on their own biases and assumptions. Recognizing personal biases can help students translate more objectively and with greater sensitivity to the source culture. For example, students might be encouraged to consider how their own cultural background affects their interpretation of a text and its translation into another language. To facilitate this kind of training, teachers can use case studies, group projects, and peer review sessions where students criticize and evaluate each other's translations. These activities not only hone students' analytical skills but also foster their capacity for collaborative learning and self-reflection.

Through critical thinking training, students come to appreciate that translation is not merely a technical exercise but a creative and intercultural endeavor that requires profound comprehension of both the explicit and implicit dimensions of communication. As a result, they are better equipped to produce translations that accurately represent the original text while resonating with the target audience, taking into account the multiple layers of context that inform the translation process.

3. Comprehensive understanding of the current state of translation to motivate students' initiative

Cultivating students' pragmatic competence is both the starting point and the ultimate goal of university translation teaching. Students should not only possess a solid knowledge of foreign language vocabulary and translation theory but also have corresponding pragmatic abilities. Teachers should fully understand the current learning background of their students and enhance their initiative, using translation theory as a foundation to develop students' pragmatic competence.

Students is one of the most important participants of translation teaching practice. Therefore, before beginning translation teaching, teachers should first gain a comprehensive understanding of the students' current learning background. Teachers should adopt different teaching methods based on the interests and hobbies of students at different levels, implement hierarchical teaching, and fully trigger students' enthusiasm for learning translation. For example, before starting a translation class, teachers can set some open, social topics such as "What kind of translation talent does current social development and international exchange need?" "What qualities do you need to possess as a translator?" "Where lies your competitiveness in the future industry?" and so on. By discussing these topics, students will have a certain awareness of the translation course. With full preparation, teachers can then explain to students the nature of the course, the basic qualities required of being a translator, the professional knowledge and abilities that need to be mastered, and analyze with cases. Only in this way can students clearly understand that translation is not merely the conversion of text; it demands much from translators. This is why translation talents are highly sought after. On the one hand, the students look forward to their future; on the other hand, the students realize the significant responsibility ahead and will redouble their efforts. Once students' enthusiasm and initiative are stimulated, their interest in learning naturally soars, which is extremely beneficial for the cultivation of pragmatic competence.

4. Enriching students' knowledge reservation

Language ability is the foundation and prerequisite for cultivating students' pragmatic competence. A rich vocabulary, solid grammar knowledge, and standard pronunciation and intonation are necessary conditions for translation teaching. Therefore, mastering basic language knowledge, skills and rules is extremely necessary. Translation theory provides a rational understanding during the translation process, allowing for targeted analysis of the target works, clever application of translation strategies, and flexible use of translation skills, truly achieving twice the result with half the effort. In translation teaching, teachers can guide students to identify common translation techniques, such as re-translation, addition, division and so on, using theories as a support to guide practical activities.

What's more, except for basic translation studies knowledge, the teachers in translation teaching should also focus on teaching geographical knowledge, folk culture, religious culture, and other types of knowledge to reduce non-standard pragmatic errors. As a translator, one must not only master solid translation theories but also understand more extensive knowledge. Translation integrates multiple disciplines. Translators must not only be familiar with grammar knowledge to ensure the accuracy of translation but also combine local history, humanities, customs,

Chapter 2 Different Perspectives of English Translation Teaching

dialects, and so on in translation. As the famous linguist Lv Shuxiang said: "The third barrier to understanding the original text is something that dictionaries cannot help with. " Therefore, it is far from enough for a translator to only master translation theories; they need to know more and have an encyclopedic knowledge reserve.

The purpose of improving students' language abilities is to cultivate their pragmatic competence. From another perspective, possessing language ability does not necessarily mean having communicative competence; communicative competence is an upgrade of language ability. Therefore, in translation teaching, while cultivating students' language abilities, the teachers should also focus on the cultivation of communicative competence. There are cultural differences between Chinese and English, and in translation teaching, the teachers should guide students to stand between the two cultures, treating both cultures from a broader, wider and higher perspective to enhance students' pragmatic awareness. Teachers should make full preparations before classroom teaching, learn more about pragmatics and related theoretical knowledge and use scientific theories as a basis to guide classroom teaching. They should learn more about the cultural backgrounds of different countries, introduce the history, humanities, and customs of different countries to students, reduce pragmatic errors caused by cultural differences and strengthen students' understanding of the target language country's culture. In different cultural and social contexts, the actual situation should be considered to effectively convey the intention and purpose conveyed by the translation.

5. Cultivating cultural awareness

Cultural immersion is a powerful educational strategy that allows students to engage deeply with diverse cultures, enhancing their intercultural communicative competence and pragmatic awareness. This approach moves beyond traditional classroom learning to encompass experiential activities that provide firsthand exposure to different ways of life, value systems, and modes of communication.

One effective method of cultivating cultural awareness is watching foreign films. By watching movies produced in the target culture, students can observe everyday interactions, pick up on non-verbal cues, and gain insight into social norms and cultural mores. Films also expose students to colloquial language and idiomatic expressions, enriching their understanding of the pragmatics of communication within that culture.

Another way for cultural awareness cultivation is to read original literary works. Literature offers a window into the history, psyche, and sociology of a culture. It provides complex narratives that challenge students to interpret meaning not only from the text but also from the cultural context in which it was written. This practice develops their ability to read between the lines and understand implied meanings, nurturing their pragmatic awareness.

Participating in language exchange activities is yet another means of encouraging cultural immersion. These exchanges might involve conversations with native speakers, either face-to-face or through online platforms. Such interactions offer students the chance to practice their language skills in a genuine communication setting and to navigate the nuances of politeness, directness, and other pragmatic elements that vary across cultures.

Finally, cultural awareness can be facilitated through visits to museums, cultural festivals, and other events that celebrate the heritage and contemporary life of different groups. By experiencing these aspects of a culture, students develop a well-rounded appreciation for the diversity of human expression and interaction.

Overall, cultural awareness provides a comprehensive learning experience that empowers students to move from simply understanding another language to truly communicating across cultural boundaries. It prepares them for the complexities of the globalized world by increasing their cultural sensitivity, empathy, and ability to effectively negotiate meaning in an international arena.

Simulated translation projects and interdisciplinary learning are also helpful for the cultivation of pragmatic awareness and competence in translation teaching. By setting up simulated translation projects, such as translating product manuals or marketing materials for real or fictional companies, students can exercise their pragmatic competence in practical operations. Such simulated exercises help students apply their knowledge to solve real-world translation problems. Also, translation involves more than just the conversion of text; it encompasses knowledge from various disciplines. Teachers can introduce knowledge from sociology, psychology, cultural studies, and other fields to help students understand language use and the translation process from a broader perspective.

Ⅶ. Methods for Translation Teaching Evaluation

Teaching evaluation from the perspective of pragmatics in translation involves assessing students' ability to apply pragmatic knowledge and skills when translating texts between languages and cultures. This approach considers not only the accuracy of the translated text but also the appropriateness of language use in the target context, taking into account factors such as audience, purpose, and cultural norms.

To evaluate students' performance in a pragmatics-oriented translation class, teachers can use several methods.

1. Peer reviews

Students can evaluate each other's translations based on pragmatic appropriateness. This peer review process encourages critical thinking and provides an opportunity for students to discuss and learn from each other's approaches to handling pragmatic challenges in translation.

2. Case studies

Teachers can present case studies that highlight specific pragmatic issues in translation. Students would then analyze these cases and propose solutions, which are evaluated based on their sensitivity to pragmatic nuances and effectiveness in resolving cross-cultural communication barriers.

3. Oral presentations

Students might be required to make oral presentations where they discuss the pragmatic considerations involved in their translations. These presentations can be evaluated based on the student's ability to articulate and justify their translation choices in light of pragmatic principles.

4. Objective Tests

While more traditional, objective tests can be designed to include questions that specifically assess students' understanding of pragmatic concepts and their application in translation. These tests might include scenarios where students choose the most appropriate translation based on contextual factors.

5. Real-world tasks

Assignments that simulate real-world translation tasks, such as translating advertisements, legal documents, or dialogues for specific target audiences, can be evaluated based on how well the students consider and implement pragmatic strategies to ensure the effectiveness of the translation.

In evaluating students from a pragmatics perspective, it is essential to provide clear criteria that encompass both the fidelity to the source text and the suitability of the translation for its intended purpose in the target culture. This approach ensures that students are assessed not only on their language proficiency but also on their cultural competence and intercultural communication skills.

In summary, by integrating pragmatic knowledge into translation teaching, we can help students better understand and handle contextual factors and cultural differences in translation, thereby improving the accuracy and appropriateness of their translations. Moreover, for translation teaching to be successful, it is essential to first cultivate students' pragmatic awareness and competence. Only when their pragmatic abilities are enhanced can they combine translation theories and techniques to produce better translations. The cultivation of pragmatic competence requires efforts from multiple aspects. Students should understand the basic qualities required of a translator and be fully mentally prepared to receive education on pragmatic cultivation. While learning translation theories and techniques, they should also fully understand the cultural customs, local conditions and customs, history, geography, and other relevant information of their own country as well as the target language country, enriching their knowledge reserves. They should master the pragmatic norms under different cultural backgrounds so that they can better integrate culture into translation rather than mechanically converting text.

Chapter 3

Translation Techniques and Methods

Section 1

Approaches to English Translation Teaching

In English translation, the mastery of translation methods is particularly important. In this section, we will mainly introduce some common translation methods.

Ⅰ. Schema

Schema is actually fragments of knowledge stored in the brain in a relatively independent form. Understanding language is the process of activating the corresponding schema in the brain. From birth, humans interact with the external world, acquiring knowledge about surrounding objects, situations, and people, and forming different cognitive patterns in their minds. The cognitive patterns formed around different objects and situations create an orderly knowledge system. Schema is the organizational form of knowledge about the external world in the human mind and serves as the foundation for our understanding of surrounding things. When faced with new information, our brains can have a negative impact on comprehension if we haven't formed similar schema. Therefore, introducing "schema" into translation teaching is of great significance since it can successfully stimulate the relevant schema related to the text in students' minds, enabling them to have a correct understanding of the source text.

During translation, teachers can provide students with language materials that require the activation of schema for proper comprehension, and then ask students to translate based on these materials. Additionally, teachers should help students memorize the forms and functions of language, assist them in engaging relevant schema, and correct and enrich their cognitive schema of things.

Ⅱ. Reasoning

Reasoning is the process of deriving conclusions from known or assumed facts. It can be seen as a relatively independent thinking activity that often involves many other cognitive activities. In translation, reasoning is not a random act based on imagination but reflects the inherent features of the text structure. Translators often make a series of inferences based on their existing knowledge and experience. These inferences provide translators with additional information, encouraging them to establish connections between relevant parts in the text and fully understand their meanings. Therefore, in the process of translation teaching, teachers should consciously introduce common reasoning techniques to students, such as using logical words for reasoning, inferring based on the author's implications, and inferring based on the context, to cultivate students' reasoning ability.

Ⅲ. Contextual Method

Context refers to the linguistic environment, including both the macro and micro contexts. The macro context refers to the topic, occasion, and objects, which help fix and specify meanings. The micro context refers to the meaning collocations and semantic combinations of words, which help locate meanings to specific senses. Both of these linguistic environments should be taken into consideration during the translation process because only by combining the two contexts can the meaning of discourse be determined. Translators not only rely on their own language knowledge to understand the meaning of sentences but also need to infer and speculate based on various types of information in the context of source text to grasp the deep intentions of the author and determine the corresponding translation to accurately express the meaning of the source text.

Context plays a crucial role in translation. Understanding and expression in translation occur within specific context. The choice of words, understanding of semantics, and determination of discourse structure are all inseparable from context. Therefore, in the teaching process, teachers should guide students to closely follow the context while understanding the source text, repeatedly pondering, in order to achieve the goal of conveying the meaning of the source text accurately and eloquently.

Ⅳ. Word Guessing

The method of word guessing refers to the ability to elevate fragmentary information in language to concepts during the process of understanding the source text. It involves transforming the perceived input of the original material into the best understanding. Students' ability of word guessing plays an important role in translation. When students lack vocabulary, it becomes difficult for them to form concepts for words, phrases, and paragraphs. Without a proper understanding of the meaning of key words in the source text, they may fail to receive feedback on textual information, leading to random guessing of the content. Therefore, guiding students to use the method of word guessing is necessary.

The word guessing method in translation includes the following approaches.

(1) Guessing the meaning of unfamiliar words based on their composition.

This is a commonly used method that requires students to have a certain knowledge of word-formation rules, especially the meaning of roots, prefixes, and suffixes.

(2) Utilizing signal words.

Signal words are words that act as connections within the context. These words can sometimes play a significant role in guessing the mean-ing of unfamiliar words.

(3) Guessing word meanings based on contextual connections.

Words within a sentence or context often have certain connections in meaning. By understanding these connections, the meaning of unfamiliar words can be inferred.

(4) Inferring the meaning of unfamiliar words by using examples.

Sometimes, examples given in the following text provide explanations for the aforementioned objects in the previous text. The meaning of unfamiliar words related to the object can be guessed by considering the commonly used words in the examples. Conversely, the meaning of unfamiliar words in the examples can also be inferred.

(5) Inferring the meaning of unfamiliar words by substituting with alternative words.

Texts often use different words to express the same meaning, resulting in the phenomenon of the interchange of difficult and easy words. Based on this, the meaning of unfamiliar words can be inferred.

Section 2

Literal Translation in English Translation

This part focuses on different translation principles and controversies in the translation field, emphasizing the importance of literal translation. It traces the historical background of literal translation, explores conditions for its existence and applicable scope, and provides numerous examples to fully demonstrate and analyze the advantages of literal translation as well as aspects to be noted when applying, thus proving the necessity of literal translation.

Translation refers to the activity of transforming information from one language to another while ensuring accuracy and fluency. According to the rules of English translation, it can be categorized as literal translation and paraphrase. Literal translation refers to conveying not only the content but also the stylistic and syntactic forms of the source text as fully as possible, under the condition that the language allows it. The principle we should grasp in translation is to translate literally whenever possible, and only resort to paraphrasing when direct translation is not feasible.

Ⅰ. Historical Background of English Literal Translation

Master Dao'an, one of the main organizers of Buddhist scripture translation, advocated strict literal translation because he couldn't understand Sanskrit and was afraid of distorting the translated text. The Buddhist scripture *Bodhisattva* (《鞞婆沙》) was translated by using this approach. In the history of modern and contemporary Chinese translation, literal translation has been the dominant criterion. Fu Sinian and Zheng Zhenduo both advocated literal translation. Lu Xun and Zhou

Zuoren's work *Outside the Realm of Fiction* (《域外小说集》) is considered the representative of literal translation. Now, literal translation is still widely used.

Ⅱ. Scope of Applicability of Literal Translation in English

There is a possibility of consistency in content and form between the source language and the target language, which is the basis and rationale for literal translation. Literal translation emphasizes the need for the translation to be faithful to the source text. Only in this way can the translation adhere to the principles followed in the translation field: "faithfulness" "expressiveness" and "elegance". However, literal translation is not a mechanical word-for-word translation. It requires the translator to comprehensively and accurately elucidate the meaning of the original work without distorting it. The translator should not arbitrarily add or delete the author's ideas and must maintain the style of the original work. Sometimes, even the emotions or feelings expressed in the original work should not be overlooked, such as joy, excitement, anger, embarrassment, sarcasm, and so on, which should be vividly displayed.

Generally speaking, if the sentence structure of the source text is close to that of the translation, with the same word order and clear meaning, word-for-word translation can be used. For example, the following terms and vocabulary: "dark horse"—"黑马", "software"—"软件", "hardware"—"硬件", "cold war"—"冷战", "to fight to the last man"—"战斗到最后一个人", "to break the record"—"打破纪录", "be armed to the teeth"—"武装到牙齿", and so on.

Some terms and sentences in everyday life can only be translated by using literal translation. In this way, the translation is faithful to the source text, comprehensively and accurately elucidating the meaning expressed in the source text, reflecting the thoughts and emotions the author intends to convey, and meeting the standards of "faithfulness" "expressiveness" and "elegance" emphasized in the translation field. This allows the translator to produce a superb and perfect translation, showcasing the ingenious application of literal translation.

Ⅲ. Advantages of Literal Translation in English Translation

Certainly, compared to liberal translation, literal translation has many advantages.

First, literal translation requires a simpler and more convenient level of technical proficiency. For example, "Six years ago, we ever met there" can be translated as "六年前，我们曾经在那相遇过". This translation can be expressed very clearly without any technical means.

Second, it can be as faithful to the source text as possible. Literal translation does not change the meaning, word order, and style of the source text. It remains completely faithful to the source text, making the translation more appropriate and expressive. For example, "Mike, why don't we go and visit the flower show?" can be translated as "迈克，我们为什么不去看看花展呢?"

Third, literal translation not only preserves the characteristics of the original work but also enables the readers to appreciate the literary style of the original work. It helps readers understand the thoughts and style of the original work more easily. For example, "Hitler was armed to the teeth, but in a few years, he was completely defeated" can be translated as "希特勒武装到了牙齿，可是不过几年，他就被彻底击败了". In this sentence, the literal translation of "armed to the teeth" preserves the original style of the work.

Fourth, literal translation helps us understand the Western culture and, at the same time, contributes to the dissemination of our national culture for Westerners to understand China. For example, "To kill two birds with one stone" is translated as "一石两鸟", and "To shed crocodile tears" is translated as "掉鳄鱼眼泪", "Chain reaction" is translated as "连锁反应", and so on. These are typical examples of literal translation. This kind of translation not only preserves the style of the original words but also introduces some fresh and vivid words, syntactic structures, and expression methods, enriching and improving the expression of the Chinese language.

Ⅳ. Considerations when Using Literal Translation in English Translation

American translation theorist Eugene Nida believes that if readers' reaction to the translation can be basically consistent with their reaction to the source text, then the translation can be considered successful. Nida also advocates that the information conveyed in translation includes not only the content of ideas but also the linguistic form. Therefore, when using literal translation, translators must pay attention to the following issues: first, in literal translation, faithfulness to the content of the original work should take precedence, followed by faithfulness to the form of the original work, and finally, the fluency and accessibility of the translated language. Second, during translation, one must grasp the ideas and style of the original work while regarding them as the ideas and style of the translation. Third, the theories, facts, and logic of the original work should also be considered as the theories, facts, and logic of the translation. We cannot substitute our own ideas, styles, facts, theories, and logic for those of the original work. Fourth, during the translation process, the quantity and form of the target language do not need to be identical to the source language, but they should maintain consistency in terms of content. The addition or deletion of words or meanings should be based on the characteristics of expression and language, and should not be arbitrarily added or omitted in terms of words, meanings, and expressed ideas of the original work. Fifth, in literal translation, efforts should be made to get rid of rigid patterns and strictly adhere to translation principles, which should be applied flexibly. Sixth, literal translation must be readable, meaning that the translation should not cause misunderstanding among readers and should not violate certain requirements of expression. These are some principles we should grasp when using literal translation, which serve as standards for us to accurately gauge the scale during translation, resulting in accurate, vivid, appropriate, and perfect translations that still maintain the style of the source text. Literal translation is a translation technique used by translators during the translation process. Literal translation and free translation are closely connected. Literal translation must have its basis and justification. That is, direct translation can be used only when there is still possibility of consistency in terms of content and form between the source language and the target language; otherwise, the translation may distort the meaning of the source text. Therefore, in translation, one should not stick to literal translation and overlook free translation. In situations where literal translation cannot clearly express the intended meaning, free translation should be adopted. At the same time, it is necessary to continuously summarize experience in practice and flexibly apply translation methods that are suitable to the source language.

Section 3

Techniques and Methods of Vocabulary Translation

The translation techniques mainly involve starting from a subjective understanding and developing towards an objective understanding, and then accurately and completely expressing the ideas of the source text in order to achieve a qualitative leap. It is similar to the art of painting, starting with rough outlines and focusing on the structural shape, then progressing to proportional perspective and emphasizing the portrayal of characters, and finally considering the overall presentation of character traits. In fact, each translation or creative process unconsciously applies these basic techniques. These basic techniques determine the quality of translation or creation, just like the process of creation requiring the correct handling of the relationship between light and dark, reality and vitality, translation should also clearly highlight what needs to be conveyed and what needs to be restrained, in order to reflect the spirit and essence of the original work delicately and on multiple levels.

I. Selection, Extension, and Derogation of Meanings of Words

1. Selection of meanings.

In the translation process, the first challenge encountered is the choice of meanings of words. English words often have multiple meanings, just as Chinese characters do. This is a common linguistic phenomenon. Ferdinand de Saussure, the founder of the London School of Linguistics, pointed out that "Each word when used in a new context is a new word", which fully reflects the flexibility of English vocabulary. Therefore, correctly selecting the appropriate meanings becomes an extremely important step in the translation process. Take the English word "run" as an example, it has different meanings in the following phrases:

run away 跑开   run down 撞倒
run out 用完   run a race 参加赛跑
run a fever 发烧   run a risk 冒险
run to seed 不修边幅   run for presidency 竞选总统
run the streets 流浪街头   run a factory 办工厂
run one's head into a wall   撞南墙，碰壁
The idea runs in his mind.   这个念头萦绕在他的脑海里。
The street runs to north.   大街向北延伸。
The news runs rapidly in the town. 这个消息迅速在镇上传开。

From these examples, it can be seen that the word "run" has a rich variety of meanings, in addition to its literal meaning "move at a speed faster than walk, never having both or all the feet on the ground at the same time", it also has many other connotations.

Let's consider the different meanings of the word "way" in the following sentences:

a. Which **way** do you usually go to town?

你进城一般走哪条**路线**？

b. The arrow is pointing the wrong **way**.

这个箭头指错了**方向**。

c. She showed me the **way** to do it.

她向我示范做这件事的**方法**。

d. 1 don't like the **way** he looks at me.

我不喜欢他那种**样子**看着我。

e. Success is still a long **way** off.

离成功还**远着呢**。

f. We must not **give way to** their demands.

我们决不能对他们的要求**让步**。

There is no exception to Chinese characters. Let's take the character "上" as an example：

上班 go to work 　　上当 be taken in
上课 attend class 　　上学 go to school
上进 make progress 　　上演 perform
上瘾 be addicted to sth. 　　上阵 go into battle

a. 干部要能上能下。

A cadre should be ready to take a lower as well as **a higher pose**.

b. 一连上了好几道菜。

Several courses **were served** in succession.

c. 我来给门上漆。

Let me **paint** the door.

Take the character "轻" as another example:

a. 这件大衣很轻，但非常暖和。

This coat is **light** but very warm.

b. 易碎品！小心轻放。

Fragile! **Handle with care**.

c. 他年纪虽轻,但做事非常负责。

He is **young**, but very responsible in work

d. 不要轻看自己。

Don't **belittle** yourself.

e. 不要轻易做出选择。

Don't make choices so **easily**.

f. 今天我有些轻微的头疼。

I've got a **slight** headache today.

It is evident that there are multiple factors affecting the choice of appropriate meaning for a word in translation. Except for language reference tools that can assist in translation, it is more important to rely on specific language context.

2. Extension of meanings

The so-called extension of meanings of words refers to further extending the basic meaning of a word and selecting more appropriate Chinese characters to express it, making the original ideas more accurate and the translation more fluent. The extension of word meaning is mainly achieved through methods such as transliteration, abstraction, and specification.

①Transliteration of word meanings.

Translating certain words directly from the dictionary can make the translation obscure, ambiguous, or even cause misunderstanding. In such cases, it is necessary to transliterate based on the logical relationship of the sentence or text. For example:

a. The basic meaning of "heavy" is weight. The extension "heavy crop" means a bountiful harvest, "heavy current" means strong electric current, and "heavy traffic" means congested traffic.

b. The basic meaning of "sharp" is having a fine edge or point; capable of cutting or piercing; not blunt or pointed". "Sharp eyes" can be extended to mean keen eyesight. "Sharp image" can be extended to mean a clear image. "Sharp voice" can be extended to mean a piercing voice, and "sharp temper" can be extended to mean a quick-tempered disposition, and so on.

The following are examples of the "green":

a. You cannot expect Mary to do business with such people. She is only eighteen and as **green** as grass.

你不能指望玛丽同这样的人做生意，她只有十八岁，**经验尚浅**。

b. Her friends were **green** with envy when they saw her new dress.

她的朋友们看到她的新裙子时，心中**充满**了嫉妒。

c. In American political elections the candidates that win are usually the ones who have **green power** backing them.

在美国政治竞选中或是的候选人通常都是些有**财团**支持的人物。

②Abstraction of meanings.

In English, it is common to use a concrete word to represent an attribute, object, or concept. When translating such words, it is generally necessary to abstract their meanings for the translation to flow smoothly and naturally. For example:

a. Every life has its **roses and thorns**.

每个人的生活都**有甜有苦**。

(roses and thorns 抽象化后引申为"甜"和"苦")

b. We have to cut through all of **the red tape** to expand to the French market.

我们必须克服所有的**繁文缛节**，开拓法国市场。

(the red tape 抽象化后引申为"繁文缛节")

c. Mary stands **head and shoulder** above classmates in playing tennis.

玛丽打网球的水平在班里可以说是"**鹤立鸡群**"。

(head and shoulder 抽象化后引申为"鹤立鸡群")

③Specification of meanings.

In English, many words have more general and abstract meanings. However, according to Chinese expression habits, these words can be extended to more specific and definite meanings. This allows the translated text to be clear, fluent, and more vivid. For example:

a. The car in front of me stalled and I missed the **green**.

我前头的那辆车停住了,我错过了**绿灯**。

(green 具体化后引申为"绿灯")

b. The big house on the hill is my **ambition**.

山上的那间大屋是我**渴望得到的东西**。

(ambition 具体化后引申为"渴望得到的东西")

3. Derogation of meanings

To faithfully translate the meaning of a text, simply referring to a dictionary is not enough. Translators must also understand the original context, the ideas and even political viewpoints conveyed, and then choose appropriate linguistic means to express them. Some words in the source text carry inherent connotations of praise or criticism, and translators should appropriately convey these nuances in their translations. However, some words may appear derogatory when considered in isolation, but their connotations can be inferred according to the context in which they are used, and translators should express them accordingly.

In English, some words may not inherently carry connotations of praise or criticism, but for the purpose of linguistic expression, translators should translate them in a way that conveys positive or negative implications, thus achieving a more faithful representation of the source text. Look at the following examples:

①Reputation.

a. I'm very lucky to attend this college with an excellent **reputation**.

录取到这所享有**盛誉**的学校,我很幸运。(褒义)

b. He was a man of integrity, but unfortunately he had a certain **reputation**.

他是一个正直的人,但不幸有某种**坏名声**。(贬义)

②Ambition.

a. My sister worked so hard that she achieved her great **ambitions**.

我姐姐如此努力工作,最终实现自己的**抱负**。(褒义)

b. **Ambition** dominated their lives.

他们的生活受**野心**驱使。(贬义)

③Demanding.

a. The project manager's **demanding** standards ensured that every detail of the project was executed flawlessly.

项目经理的**严格**标准确保了项目的每个细节都无懈可击。(褒义)

b. As a **demanding** boss, he expected total loyalty and dedication from his employees.

他是个**苛刻的**老板,要求手下的人对他忠心耿耿,鞠躬尽瘁。(贬义)

Ⅱ. Conversion of Parts of Speech

In translation practice, in order to be faithful to the source text and conform to the language norms of the target language, it is insufficient to mechanically match parts of speech and translate word by word. Therefore, it is necessary to converse words from one class to another in the target language sometimes. This is what we are going to discuss, the conversion.

The conversion of parts of speech is one of the important techniques in both English to Chinese translation and Chinese to English translation. When used properly, it can make the translation smooth and conform to the habits of the target language. The most common conversions in English-to-Chinese and Chinese-to-English translation are as follows:

1. Conversion of nouns

Nouns are more frequently used in English than in Chinese, and their meanings are quite flexible. When translating, it is important to start from their basic meaning, conform to Chinese habits, and make flexible changes through contextual parts of speech conversions. Generally, English nouns can be converted into Chinese verbs, adjectives, or adverbs.

(1) Converting nouns in English into verbs in Chinese.

①Nouns derived from verbs in English are often converted into verbs in Chinese. For example:

Her **decision** to retire surprised us all.

她**决定**退休,我们大为惊讶。

②Nouns with verb meanings in English are often converted into verbs in Chinese. For example:

Every morning, she would go to the park for a **walk**.

每天早晨,她都要去公园**散步**。

③Nouns indicating identity or profession in English are often converted into verbs in Chinese. For example:

She was a **winner** in this competition with her amazing performance.

凭着出色的表演,她**赢得**了这场比赛。

(2) Converting nouns in English into adjectives in Chinese.

Nouns derived from adjectives in English can be converted into adjectives in Chinese. For example:

a. She is a real **beauty**.

她非常**漂亮**。

b. Some nouns in English that function as predicates or attributives with indefinite articles can be converted into adjectives in Chinese. For example:

This promotion was a **success**.

这次促销活动很**成功**。

(3) Converting nouns in English into adverbs in Chinese.

Some abstract nouns in English can be converted into adverbs in Chinese. For example:

It is our **pleasure** to note that China has made great progress in the economy.

我们很**高兴地**看到,中国的经济已经有了很大的发展。

2. Conversion of adjectives

Adjectives in English can be converted into verbs, adverbs, or nouns in Chinese.

(1) Converting adjectives in English into verbs in Chinese.

Some adjectives in English that express perceptions or desires can be converted into verbs in Chinese when used as predicates. For example:

Doctors said that they were not **sure** they could save her life.

医生们说他们不敢**肯定**能否救得了她的命。

(2) Converting adjectives in English into adverbs in Chinese.

Adjectives that modify nouns, when translated into Chinese, can often be converted into adverbs. For example:

I like having **brief** naps in the noon.

我喜欢在中午**短短地**睡上一小会。

(3) Converting adjectives in English into nouns in Chinese.

Adjectives that express characteristics or qualities in English can be converted into nouns in Chinese. For example:

a. The more carbon the steel contains, the **harder** and **stronger** it is.

钢材中含碳越多,其**硬度**和**强度**就越高。

Some adjectives preceded by "the" to indicate a certain group of people in English can be converted into nouns in Chinese. For example:

b. They are going to build a school for **the blind** and **the deaf**.

他们将为**盲人**和**聋人**修建一所学校。

3. Conversion of adverbs

English adverbs can be converted into Chinese nouns, adjectives, or verbs during translation.

(1) Converting adverbs in English into nouns in Chinese.

Some English adverbs can be converted into Chinese nouns. For example:

He is **physically** weak but **mentally** sound.

他**身体**虽弱,但**心理**很健康。

(2) Converting adverbs in English into adjectives in Chinese.

Some English adverbs can be converted into Chinese adjectives. For example:

The film impressed me **deeply**.

这部电影给我留下了**深刻的**印象。

(3) Converting adverbs in English into verbs in Chinese.

Some English adverbs can be converted into Chinese verbs. For example:

Now, I must be **away**.

现在,我该**离开**了。

4. Conversion of verbs

English verbs can be converted into Chinese nouns or adverbs in translation.

(1) Conversion of English verbs into Chinese nouns.

Some verbs in English, especially those derived from or used as nouns, may not have corresponding verbs in Chinese. They can be converted into Chinese nouns. For example:

Most students **behaved** respectfully towards their teachers.

大部分学生对老师的**态度**都很恭敬。

Some verbs in passive sentences in English can be translated into the structures "受到/遭到……+名词" or "予以/加以……+名词" in Chinese. For example:

He **was suffered by** the top-ranking officials there.

他**受到**那边高级官员们的冷遇。

(2) Conversion of English verbs into Chinese adverbs.

Some English verbs have meanings similar to Chinese adverbs and can be translated as such. For example:

When I leave the house, I always **watch out**.

我出门时总是特别**小心**。

5. Conversion of English prepositions

English prepositions have diverse combinations and complex relationships. When translating, one should handle them flexibly based on the context. In general, they can be converted into Chinese verbs. For example:

He caught the ball **with** his left hand.

他**用**左手接住了球。

6. Conversion of Chinese verbs

(1) Conversion of Chinese verbs into English nouns.

Chinese verbs are used frequently and often used in combinations. As mentioned earlier, English tends to use more nouns. When translating from Chinese to English, Chinese verbs can be transformed into English nouns as needed. For example:

每天早上，她都要到公园去**散步**。

Every morning, she goes to the park for **a walk**.

(2) Conversion of Chinese verbs into English adjectives.

Some Chinese verbs can be converted into English adjectives, often expressed as "be + adjective." For example:

他连续24小时上网，这可**说不过去**。

He has been online for 24 hours in a row. This is **inexcusable**.

(3) Conversion of Chinese verbs into English prepositions or prepositional phrases.

The use of prepositions in English is also very flexible. When translating from Chinese to English, Chinese verbs can be converted into English prepositions or prepositional phrases as needed. For example:

如果**遇到火警**，首先要切断电源。

Break the circuit first **in case of fire**.

(4) Conversion of Chinese verbs into English adverbs.

Similarly, some Chinese verbs can be expressed by using English adverbs, which are more concise and precise in meaning. For example:

灯**开着**，但没有人在家。

The light was **on**, but nobody was home.

7. Conversion of Chinese nouns

Some Chinese nouns can be converted into English verbs when translated. However, it's important to note that if there are adjective modifiers preceding the Chinese noun, they should also be transformed into English adverbs. For example:

他的呼吸有大蒜的**味道**。

His breath **smells** of garlic.

8. Conversion of Chinese adjectives or adverbs

Chinese adjectives or adverbs can be converted into English nouns, mainly based on grammatical structure or rhetorical needs. For example:

思想交流是十分**必要的**。

Exchange of ideas is a vital **necessity**.

Ⅲ. Transformation of Word Order

The transformation of word order refers to the technique of rearranging the order of words and organizing the translated text according to the writing conventions of the target language, based on the understanding of the source text. This technique is widely used, especially in the translation of attributive and adverbial phrases. Here, we will focus on the change of order in attributive phrases, adverbial phrases, and other situations.

1. Adjective placement

The position of adjectives in English is relatively flexible and can be placed before or after the noun. In Chinese, however, adjectives are generally placed before the noun. Here are some ways to change the order of adjectives in translation.

(1) Words as adjectives.

①Individual words as adjectives.

In English, indefinite compound pronouns such as "-thing" "-body" "-one", as well as adjectives ending in "-able" "-ible", and certain adverbs or fixed collocations, are usually placed after nouns they modify. In Chinese, they are generally placed before nouns they modify. For example:

<u>something</u> <u>important</u>　<u>重要的</u> <u>事情</u>
　　1　　　　2　　　　　2　　　1

②Multiple words as adjectives.

When there are multiple adjectives before a noun, the word order in English is different from that of Chinese. In English, the order of adjectives goes from small to large, from weak to strong, from less important to more important, from general to specific, with the meaning becoming more specific and tangible as they get closer to the noun. The general order is: determiners + general descriptive adjectives + adjectives of size, height, length + adjectives of colors + adjectives of nationality, regional, origin + adjectives of materials + adjectives of purpose and categories + nouns. However, in Chinese, the order needs to be carefully considered. For example:

<u>practical</u> <u>social</u> activities　<u>社会</u> <u>实践</u> 活动
　　1　　　2　　　　　　　　2　　1

(2) Phrases as adjectives.

In English, phrases used as adjectives are generally placed after the headword, while in Chinese, they are usually placed before the headword. For example:

an article on the ancient Chinese history 关于中国古代史的 文章
　1　　　　　　2　　　　　　　　　　2　　　　1

(3) Relative clauses as adjectives.

Relative clauses used as adjectives are a commonly used sentence structure in English, where the relative clause is placed after the headword. In Chinese, relative clauses are generally placed before the headword instead. For example:

I dislike women who chatter incessantly.
　　　　1　　　　2

我不喜欢整天唧唧喳喳说个不停的 女人。
　　　　　　2　　　　　　　　　1

2. Adverbial modification

The position of adverbial phrases in English is flexible, as they can be placed at the beginning, in the middle, or at the end of a sentence. However, in Chinese, the position of adverbial phrases is not so fixed and they are generally not placed at the end of a sentence. Therefore, in translation, the word order of some adverbial phrases must be adjusted. The following are several ways to change the word order of adverbial phrases.

(1) Words used as adverbs.

①Descriptive adverbs as adverbial modifiers.

When descriptive adverbs modify action verbs, the word order usually needs to be adjusted. For example:

She looked at us suspiciously.
　　　1　　　　　2

她 怀疑地 看着我们。
　　2　　1

②Adverbs of degree as adverbial modifiers.

When adverbs of degree like "nearly" "almost" "hardly" modify linking verbs or action verbs, the word order usually needs to be adjusted. Additionally, when the adverb of degree "enough" modifies an jective or an adverb, the word order also needs to be adjusted. For example:

She $\underset{1}{\text{is}}$ $\underset{2}{\text{really}}$ a good manager.

她 $\underset{2}{\text{的确}}$ $\underset{1}{\text{是}}$ 位好经理。

(2) Phrases as adverbial modifiers.

①Time or place adverbials.

In English, the order of time or place adverbials is usually from smaller to larger, while in Chinese it is often the opposite. For example:

She was born on $\underset{1}{\text{July 13}}$, $\underset{2}{\text{1988}}$.

她是 $\underset{2}{1988\text{年}7\text{月}13\text{日}}$ $\underset{1}{\text{出生的}}$。

②Time adverbials, place adverbials, and manner adverbials.

When time, place, and manner adverbials appear in the same sentence, the typical order in English is: manner adverbial, place adverbial, time adverbial. However, in Chinese, the typical order is: time adverbial, place adverbial, manner adverbial. For example:

She $\underset{1}{\text{reads aloud}}$ $\underset{2}{\text{in the open air}}$ $\underset{3}{\text{every morning}}$.

她 $\underset{3}{\text{每天早晨}}$ $\underset{2}{\text{在室外}}$ $\underset{1}{\text{大声朗读}}$。

3. Reordering in other situations

(1) Fixed expressions.

Both English and Chinese have developed fixed expressions with coordinating words. For example:

a. $\underset{1}{\text{you}}$, $\underset{2}{\text{he}}$ and $\underset{3}{\text{I}}$ $\underset{2}{\text{我}}\underset{1}{\text{你}}\underset{3}{\text{他}}$

b. $\underset{1}{\text{sooner}}$ or $\underset{2}{\text{later}}$ $\underset{2}{\text{迟}}\underset{1}{\text{早}}$

(2) Other sentence elements.

In English, there are also other types of sentences that in certain situations require the use of reordering translation. Such as some post-posed subjects, certain appositives, predicates, parenthetical elements, and certain passive voice sentences. For example:

a. It's nice **to sit quiet here for a little while**.

静静地在这里坐一会真好。(后置主语的换序)

b. Modern science and technology are **developing rapidly**.

现代科学技术正在**迅速发展**。(状语换序)

c. A little, yellow, ragged, lame, unshaven **beggar** came toward me.

一个要饭的,身材矮小,面黄肌瘦,衣衫褴褛,瘸腿,满脸短髭。(主语换序)

Ⅳ. **Translation Techniques of Positive-Negative and Negative-Positive Expressions**

In the realm of any ethnic group, there exists a distinction between affirmation and negation in thinking. However, the ways of expressing affirmation and negation differ among different cultures, including the English and Chinese cultures. For instance, when expressing negation, Chinese does not have strictly defined morphological changes. The expressions are relatively simple and easily recognizable. Almost all words conveying negation contain obvious negative markers such as "不""无""非""莫""勿""未""否""别""没有", and so on.

English, on the other hand, is different. Its negation forms are more complex. In addition to using negation words, there are unique means of expression, such as the abundant usage of negative affixes (e. g. , dis-, il-, in-, non-, un-, -less) and various words, phrases, or constructions that involve affirmative form but negative meaning (e. g. , fail, deny, defy, miss, lack, ignore, but, except, beyond), phrases (e. g. , instead of, in place of), or other structures (e. g. , more. . . than. . . , other than. . . , rather than. . .).

Due to these significant differences in the formal expressions of negation between English and Chinese, it is necessary to adopt the technique of positive-negative and negative-positive translation. This means that certain words or sentences expressed positively in English should be expressed negatively in Chinese, and vice versa. This approach not only makes the language more lively and fluent but also yields better translation results.

(1) Positive-negative expressions.

When English presents in a positive manner, Chinese can convey the opposite meaning. Translating affirmative forms in English into negative forms in Chinese is referred to as the positive-negative expression technique. In English, expressing negation does not always require the use of words like "no" "not" "nor" "neither" or "never" to negate the predicate. Most of the time, negation is achieved through the use of other word classes that already imply negation by negating part of the sentence, resulting in an affirmative form of the predicate. Applying this technique in translation ensures that the target text conforms to Chinese norms and accurately conveys the meaning of the source text. For example, "correct" can be translated as "没有毛病"; "wonder" can be translated as "不知道"; "difficult" can be translated as "不容易"; "exactly" can be translated as "一点不错"; "anything but" can be translated as "一点也不", and so on. For example:

a. **Stop** talking.

不要讲话。(停止说话。)

b. **Wet** paint!

油漆未干!(湿油漆。)

(2) Negative-positive expressions.

English often expresses negation directly, while Chinese tends to express affirmation. When translating a negative sentence into a positive one, it can better convey the original meaning and make the translation clearer and more natural, therefore negative-positive expressions are adopted. Structures in English that contain negation words or double negatives can often be expressed positively in Chinese. For example: "unfasten"—"解开", "dislike as"—"厌恶", "displease as"—"使人生气", "indecisive as"—"优柔寡断的", "fearlessly as"—"大胆地" and so on. Additionally, some expressions in English that convey negation, such as "no" "not" "not...until" "no less than" "no more than" "nothing but" and "cannot... too" can also be translated positively in Chinese. For example:

a. **Never too old to learn**.

活到老,学到老。

b. The problem is still **unsolved** till now.

这个问题至今**尚待解决**。

(3) Positive expressions in Chinese to English.

The technique of translating the affirmative form in Chinese into the negative form in English is called the positive expression in Chinese and the negative translation in English. The difference in expressing positive and negative forms between the Chinese and English languages is due to differences in psychology, culture, and thinking patterns. Therefore, it is not surprising that the affirmative form in Chinese is often translated into the negative form in English. For example:

a. 把鞋带**系上**。

Don't untie your shoes.

b. 他们对此项建议**提出了异议**。

They **signed a disagreement** on this suggestion.

(4) Inverted Chinese-to-English expressions.

Due to the differences in vocabulary, grammatical structures, and even linguistic logic used in expressing negation concepts between Chinese and English, it is not always appropriate to directly translate Chinese negative forms into English negative forms. Sometimes, the translated text may become awkward or inconsistent with English expressive conventions, and in severe cases, it may even lead to errors. In English, negation is not always expressed by using negative words like "no" "not" "nor" "neither" or "never" to negate the predicate. Most of the time, negation is achieved by using other words with negative meanings to negate a component of the sentence, allowing the predicate to appear in affirmative form.

Ⅴ. **Addition and Omission**

As a general principle of translation, translators should avoid arbitrary additions or omissions to the content of the source text. However, due to the significant differences between the English and Chinese languages, it is often difficult to achieve a complete word-for-word correspondence. Therefore, in order to accurately convey the information of the source text, translators often need to make some additions or omissions to the translation, supplementing what is implied in the source text or removing words that are unnecessary or do not conform to the customary expression in the translated language, thereby facilitating readers' comprehension.

1. Addition

The translation method of addition refers to making necessary additions to the translation while preserving the complete consistency of the source text's ideas. This involves adding words, phrases, or even sentences that are not explicitly present in the source text, in order to express the meaning of the source text more faithfully and fluently. In English to Chinese translation, the addition of words primarily caters to the needs of Chinese expression. This method involves adding omitted words from the source text, including necessary conjunctions, quantifiers, plural concepts, words that indicate different tenses or chronological orders, or considering rhetorical coherence, thereby ensuring that the wording and sentence structure of the translation align with the conventions of Chinese expression.

(1) Adding verbs, nouns, adjectives, or adverbs.

a. He **ate and drank**, for he was exhausted.

他**吃点东西，喝点酒**，因为他疲惫不堪。（增加名词）

b. The plane twisted under me, trailing **flame and smoke**.

飞机在下面扭动盘旋，拖着**浓烟烈焰**掉了下去。（增加形容词）

c. He dismissed the meeting **without a closing speech**.

他**没有致闭幕词**就宣布结束会议。（增加动词）

d. He **sank down** with his face in his hand.

他两手蒙着脸，**一屁股坐了下去**。（增加副词）

(2) Adding classifiers.

In English, numbers are often directly used with nouns, while in Chinese, different classifiers are usually needed to modify them. For example：

The students have their class in **a bright classroom**.

学生们在**一间明亮的教室**里上课。

In English, some verbs or action nouns require the addition of certain measure words in Chinese to indicate the action or behavior. For example：

Now that you are tired, **let's have a rest**.

既然你们都累了，我们还是**休息一下吧**。

(3) Adding words to express plural nouns.

In the Chinese language, nouns do not have inflections to indicate plural forms. However, if there is a need to emphasize the concept of plurality, additional words can be used. For example, the word "各" can be added before nouns to refer to people, or "们" can be added after them. Plurality can also be expressed by using reduplication, such as "种种" and so on. For example：

He is the least flamboyant of **the Republican contenders**.

共和党各个角逐者中，他是最不受瞩目的。

(4) Adding modal particles.

Chinese is a language that relies on vocabulary to express meaning, so the strategy of addition translation has become an indispensable method for expressing modality in English. In English-Chinese translation, it is often necessary to add modal particles such as "了""啊""呀""嘛""吧" and "吗" to meet the needs of sentence modality. In addition to these, depending on the context, appropriate function words such as "罢了""而已""究竟""到底" and "才好" are often added. For example：

Let's do it in the way of business.

这件事我们还是按生意场的老规矩办**吧**。

(5) Adding words to express different tenses.

English verbs have different tenses and changes in mood, while Chinese doesn't have equivalent forms to express them. Therefore, when translating, it is often necessary to add some words to indicate tenses and moods. For example：present tense, "现在""目前"; future tense, "将""要""会""就"; past tense, "过去""以前""曾经""那时"; perfect tense, "曾（经）""已（经）""过""了", and so on.

(6) Adding words that indicate voices.

English language has more passive voice sentences, while Chinese language has more active voice sentences. When translating passive voice sentences from English to

Chinese, it is necessary to add some words to indicate the passive voice, such as "被""便""由""受到""得到""遭到", etc. Alternatively, you can add a subject, such as "人们""我们""大家""有人", etc. For example:

At the end of the month he **was fired** for incompetence.

月底,他因不胜任工作而**被解雇**了。

(7) Adding summary words or transitional words.

Both English and Chinese languages have summary words, which are added to the basic translation to indicate "summation". The purpose is to further clarify the concept in the translation and enhance the coherence of the context. For example:

The frequency, wave length and speed of sound are closely related.

频率、波长和声速**三者**是密切相关的。

(8) Adding coordinating words.

Coordinating words are not as commonly used in English as they are in Chinese. In English, certain logical relationships between elements in a sentence can be expressed by using grammar forms such as infinitives, participles, and independent structures. However, when translating into Chinese, it is necessary to choose appropriate coordinating words in order to accurately convey their precise meanings. For example:

Heated, water will change to vapor.

如水受热,就会汽化。

2. Omission

Omission, also known as reduction translation, is a translation method that corresponds to word addition. Generally speaking, Chinese is more concise than English. When translating from English to Chinese, many words that are essential in the source text may become unnecessary wordiness if translated literally, making the translation appear cumbersome. Therefore, omission is widely used in English-to-Chinese translation, with the main purpose of removing words that are optional and not in line with the conventions of expression in the target language. This includes the omission of pronouns in content words, as well as the omission of articles, prepositions, and conjunctions in function words.

(1) Omission of pronouns.

①Omission of personal pronouns.

In English, the subject is usually present in every sentence, so personal pronouns often appear multiple times as subjects. However, in Chinese, if the subject of the previous sentence is the same as the subject of the following sentence, the subject can be omitted. Therefore, when translating English personal pronouns into Chinese, they can often be omitted. For example:

We live and learn.

活到老,学到老。

②Omission of pronouns as objects.

In English, there are certain possessive pronouns used as objects that can be omitted in translation, regardless of whether they have been mentioned before. For example:

I went up to him and held out my hand.

我伸出手,向他走过去。(后半句省略主语"我")

(2) Omitting "it" in non-personal and emphatic sentences.

In non-personal and emphatic sentences, "it" is often omitted in translation.

①Omitting "it" in non-personal usage.

For example:

Outside **it** was pitch dark and **it** was mining cats and dogs.

外面一团漆黑,大雨倾盆。

②Omitting "it" in emphatic sentences.

For example:

It was she who had been wrong.

错的是她。

(3) Omission of conjunctions.

English emphasizes formality and uses appropriate conjunctive words to connect phrases and components in a sentence. Complex sentences are formed by connecting sentences with conjunctive words, resulting in a more structured format. On the other hand, Chinese emphasizes the unity of meaning and relies more on word order to directly combine phrases and connect sentences through logical meaning, allowing for flexible and concise structures. Therefore, in translating from English to Chinese, conjunctive words are often omitted.

①Omission of coordinating conjunctions.

For example:

Early to rise **and** early to bed makes a man healthy.

早睡早起使人身体健康。

②Omission of conjunctions indicating cause.

In English causal sentences, conjunctions are commonly used to indicate causes, while Chinese often expresses cause and effect relationships through word order, with the cause preceding the effect. Therefore, when translating from English to Chinese, it is often possible to omit the conjunctions indicating causes in the source text. For example:

As it is late, you had better go home.

时间已不早了，你最好回家去。

③Omission of conjunctions indicating condition.

The conjunction "if", which typically indicates a condition, can be translated as "假如" or "如果" in Chinese. However, in everyday spoken language or classical Chinese structure, it is often possible to omit this conjunction and not to translate it. For example:

If winter comes, can spring be far behind?

冬天来了，春天还会远吗？

④ Omission of time conjunctions.

Time-related conjunctions such as "when" and "as" can be translated as "当……时" or simply "时" in Chinese. However, if the chronological sequence is evident in the Chinese sentence, for the sake of brevity, "当……时" or "时" can often be omitted. For example:

The day **when** he was born remains unknown.

他出生的日期仍然不知。

(4) Omission of articles.

In English, definite article "the" and indefinite article "a/an" are generally used before nouns to refer to the entirety, unique entities, superlative adjectives, and specific common nouns. However, according to Chinese convention, these articles are not necessary and should not be translated. For example:

A camel is much inferior to **an** elephant in strength.

骆驼的力量不如大象。

(5) Omission of prepositions.

Prepositions in English, such as "in" "on" "at" etc., can have different meanings in various contexts. It is important not to treat these words as synonymous and use them interchangeably. For example:

Suddenly, there came a knock **on** the door.

突然响起了敲门声。

Ⅵ. Techniques and Methods of Translation for Numbers, Quantifiers, and Multiplicative Expressions

1. Techniques for translating numerals in English

Numerals are an essential part of business activities, and there are differences in the way English and Chinese people think. These differences often create difficulties in translating numbers. Moreover, numerals are versatile and can be used as subjects, objects, attributives, and adverbials, so their translation requires flexible handling according to the context. Especially in business activities, negligence or errors in translation can lead to irreparable consequences, so caution is required when translating. Now let's provide an overview of the understanding and translation methods for numerals.

1.1 Translation of numbers above ten thousand

Firstly, there are differences between English and Chinese numerals. Although China has adopted the international standard of grouping digits into sets of three, the reading rules still follow a four-digit grouping system. Each group consists of four counting units: ones, tens, hundreds, and thousands form the first group, while ten thousands, hundred thousands, millions, and ten millions form the second group, and so on. In English, digits are grouped in sets of three, and the reading method is consistent with the writing method. The first group includes ones, tens, and hundreds; the second group includes thousands, ten thousands, and hundred thousands; and the third group includes millions, ten millions, and hundred millions. In terms of place value, the last digit in each Chinese group is always "thousand", while in English, the last digit in each group falls on "hundred".

Secondly, English and Chinese numerals have different counting systems. English does not have separate words for "ten thousand" and "one hundred million", while Chinese does not have distinct words for "million" and "billion". Due to these differences in counting systems, exact one-to-one correspondence is not possible in translation. For example, when Chinese says "32,500", English would express it as "thirty-two thousand and five hundred", Similarly, when Chinese says "860亿", English would express it as "eight hundred and sixty billion".

It is worth noting that, when translating, if the numbers encountered in English materials are directly represented in Arabic numerals, there is no need to convert them to Chinese. They can be used directly for correctness. For example:

a. Foreign funds flowed into China in a spectacular way. The stock of foreign investment grew from under **$5 billion** in 1989 to nearly **$90 billion** by 1994.

外资大量投向中国,外商投资总量由1989年的不足**50亿美元**增长到1994年的近**900亿美元**。

b. Texas' economy is forecast to add more than **191,000 jobs** during 2006—2007. Job growth is expected to accelerate in 2006 and then slow in 2007 as a result of rising interest rates and energy prices hindering the stimulative impacts of increasing levels of population and business spending.

据预测,2006年至2007年得克萨斯州会增加19.1万个就业岗位。如不出预料,2006年就业规模呈现增长趋势,到2007年则会放缓,原因是利率和能源价格提高,将阻碍人口增加和企业开销增长所带来的拉动作用。

c. China has a grassland area of **390 million hectares**, of which about **320 million hectares** can be used, which places China the third in the world in the area of usable grassland.

中国现有草地面积**3.9亿公顷**(1公顷=10 000平方米),其中可利用面积**3.2亿公顷**,居世界第三位。

d. In 1977, the total sum of Chinese imports and exports was less than **$15 billion**, putting China's share of world trade at 0.6 percent.

在1977年，中国进出口总额还不到**150亿美元**，仅占世界贸易总额的0.6%。

e. In 2003, the total national revenue of China reached **1,137.7 billion** yuan, exceeding 1 trillion yuan for the first time.

2003年，中国国家财政收入总额首次突破万亿元，达到11 377亿元。

f. This year's output of wheat reached **41.48 million tons**, about twice that of last year.

今年的小麦产量是**4 148万吨**，是去年的两倍。

1.2 Translation of decreased quantity

(1) General decrease in quantity.

The translation of a general decrease in quantity should be based on the intended meaning of English verbs, adjectives, prepositions, and numerals. Special attention should be paid to the meaning of prepositions.

Firstly, when using verbs such as "reduce" "decrease" "fall" "lower" etc., it is appropriate to use "by n (or $n\%$)" to indicate the net decrease. When using linking verbs, "n less(than)" can be used to express the reduced amount, and the numeric value can be translated accordingly. Tor example:

a. This process used **35%** less fuel.

这种工艺节省了**35%**的燃料。

b. The price of this car is **twice cheaper** than the average, but its quality and reliability are superior to many other cars of the same style.

这台轿车的价格只有一般轿车价格的**一半**，但其质量和可靠性却优于其他同等式样轿车。

Secondly, when using verbs such as "reduce" "decrease" "fall" "lower" etc., to indicate a specific numerical decrease, they can be connected with expressions like "by n times" "n times" "by a factor of n" "n times as + adjective or adverb + as". These can be translated as "reduced by a fraction of $(n-1)$" or "reduced to a fraction of $1/n$". Additionally, in Chinese, fractions in the denominator are not commonly used. If the numerical decrease in English includes decimal points, it should be converted to a fraction. For example:

a. The bandwidth was **reduced by twice**.

带宽**减少了一半**。

b. The automatic assembly line can **shorten** the assembling period (**by**) **ten times**.

这条自动装配线可将装配周期**缩短至原来的十分之一**。

c. The hydrogen atom is nearly **16 times as light as** the oxygen atom.

氢原子的**重量约为**氧原子的十六分之一。

d. The United States' unemployment rate dropped **1.3 percent points** during the year.

美国当年的失业率下降了**1.3 个百分点**。

Thirdly, in English, the verb "reduce" can be connected with "to + n (or n%)" to indicate "to decrease to n (or n%)". For example:

a. By the year 2006, the world's annual oil output is expected to **fall to 33%**.

到2006 年，世界石油年产量预计将**下降到33%**。

b. Owing to natural calamities, the grain output per hectare in that region has **decreased from 500 kg to less than 300 kg**.

由于自然灾害的影响，这个地区每公顷的粮食产量从**500 千克降到300 千克以下**。

(2) Reduce by half.

There are various ways to express "减少一半" (reduce by half) in English. When translating, it is important to be aware of the different idiomatic expressions and use appropriate English phrases to convey the meaning. For example:

The price of this car **is twice cheaper** than the average, but its quality and reliability are superior to many other cars of the same style.

这辆车的价格比平均价格**便宜一半**，但它的质量和可靠性却优于许多其他同款汽车。

1.3 Translation of quantity increase

To express an increase in quantity, we need to use the original quantity as the base. "增加了" (increased), "增长了" (grown), "上升了" (risen) and "提高了" (improved) indicate the net increase, excluding the base quantity. For example, if the quantity increases from ten to fifty, we can say "increased fourfold", but we cannot say "increased fivefold". "增加到" (increased to), "增长到" (grown to) and "上升

到"(risen to) refer to the total quantity after the increase, including the base quantity. For example, if the quantity increases from ten to fifty, we can say "increased to five times", but we cannot say "increased to four times". In English, there are primarily two ways to express this: using the preposition "to" and the preposition "by". The former combines with a quantity to express "increased to" a certain amount or degree, while the latter combines with a quantity to indicate "increased by" a certain amount or degree.

Firstly, we can use copulas or action verbs in combination with words containing the numeral "n". Specific expressions include:

· be n times as + abjective or adverb + as

· be(by)n times + comparative + than

· be + comparative + than + noun + by n times

· be + comparative + by a factor of n

It can be translated into chinese like "是……的n倍""n倍于"or"比……大($n-1$)倍"。For example:

a. Under careful preparation and organization, the productivity of labor has been **three to four times higher** than usual.

在周密的准备和组织下，劳动生产率比平常**高三至四倍**。

b. The output of grain this year is **three times** as great as that of last year.

今年的粮食产量**是**去年的**三倍**。

Secondly, we can combine verbs with the meaning of "increase" (increase, rise, grow, go up, etc.) with the following words containing the numeral "n" (representing numbers, percentages, or multiples). Specific expressions include:

· verb + n times

· verb + by + n times

· verb + to + n times

· verb + n fold

· verb + by a factor of + n

These could be translated as "增加到n倍""增加了($n-1$)倍"。For example:

a. The turnover of the company has **grown five times** over the past three years.

公司的销售额三年来**增加了四倍**。

b. The production of this kind of machine in our plant this year is estimated to **increase to 3 times** compared with 2006.

今年我厂这种机器的产量预计**是** 2006 年的**三倍**。(今年我厂这种机器的产量预计比 2006 年增加两倍。)

c. The small town consumed 32,000 kg of meat in 1975 and 96,000 kg of meat in 1985. The meat consumption of this town **increased three times** in only ten years.

这个小镇 1975 年消费 32 000 千克肉,1985 年消费 96 000 千克肉。只不过十年,这个小镇肉的消费量就**增长了两倍**。

d. From 1978 to 1992, the per capital net income of farmers **rose by six fold**, at an average annual rate of 13.4 percent.

从 1978 年到 1992 年,农民的人均收入以年均 13.4% 的速度**增长了五倍**。

e. Australia is about **25 times larger than** Britain and Ireland, and almost **twice** the combined areas of India and Pakistan.

澳大利亚约**是**英国和爱尔兰面积的**二十五倍**,几乎是印度和巴基斯坦两国面积总和的**两倍**。

Thirdly, we can use linking verbs or action verbs followed by " as + adjective or adverb + as" or "as + adjective or adverb + as". This can be translated as "twice as + adjective or adverb" or "one more time as + adjective or adverb". Additionally, it's important to note that if we add "half" before "again", it indicates "half times more than". For example:

a. In hot, sunny climates, these C4 plants are **half as efficient again as** their C3 counterparts.

在炎热、阳光充足的气候下,这些 C4 植物光合效率比 C3 植物要**高 50%**。

b. The sales of industrial electronic products this month is **twice as many as** that of last month.

本月工业电子产品的销售额**是**上个月的**两倍**。

c. With more than ten years' construction, the area of Shenzhen is **three times as large as** it used to be, or the area of Shenzhen is **twice larger** than before.

经过几十年的建设,深圳的面积比以前**大了两倍**。

Fourthly, use verbs with the meaning of "increase" (increase, up, etc.) to connect "(by) n + units (or n%)", rise, grow, expand, exceed, jump, climb, improve, go indicating a net increase. The numeral n can be translated accordingly. For example:

a. The total volume of state purchase in the first quarter **rose by 5.2 percent**, compared with the same period of last year.

和去年同期相比,国家第一季度的总采购量增加了**5.2 个百分点**。

b. The output **went up** 56,000 tons.

产量增加了 56 000 吨。

c. Kunming Machine Tool was the best performer of the day, **rising** 27.5 cents or **13 percent** per share.

昆明机床(股票)这天的交易最好,每股上涨 27.5 美分或者是 **13%**。

d. Among China's major trade partners, the mainland's exports to Hong Kong SAR and Macao SAR **increased** 63 percent over November 2002 to 3.41 billion Yuan.

在中国的主要贸易伙伴中,大陆向香港和澳门特别行政区的出口总额在 2002 年 11 月增长了 **63%**,达到 34.1 亿元。

Fifthly, use verbs indicating multiplication to express an increase in quantity. "Double" means "to be twice as much" or "to increase by a factor of two". "Triple" means "to be three times as much" or "to increase by a factor of three". "Quadruple" means "to be four times as much" or "to increase by a factor of four". "Quintuple" means "to be five times as much" or "to increase by a factor of five". "Sextuplet" means "to be six times as much". "Septuplet" means "to be seven times as much". "Eight-tuples" means "to be eight times as much". For example:

a. Hunan, China's leading live pig exporting province, expects to export 420,000 lean meat pigs this year, **quadruple** the figure for 2003.

今年,中国主要生猪出口省份湖南可望出口 42 万头瘦肉猪,为 2003 年的**四倍**。

b. The growth rate of GNP (Gross National Product) per capita for China will **be quadrupled** by 2000.

到 2000 年,中国人均国民生产总值将**翻两番**。

c. Our population **is doubled** what it was thirty-five years ago.

我国目前的人口**是**35年前的**两倍**。

d. The efficiency of the machines has been more than **tripled** or **quadrupled**.

这些机器的效率已提高了**两倍或三倍多**。

1.4 Translation of English percentages and fractions

In English, percentages are often used to represent increases or decreases in quantities in economic and trade activities. The expression of English percentage change is generally similar to the word order in Chinese. For example:

Four out of five earned more than 25,000 dollars a year, **two out of five** earned more than 50,000 dollars a year, 3 percent were Jews, 3 percent black, 22 percent Catholic, and **one fifth of 1 percent** union officials.

每五人当中，有四个人的年收入多于25 000美元，**每五人当中**，有两个人的年收入多于50 000美元，其中3%是犹太人，3%是黑人，22%是天主教徒，而**0.2%**是工会负责人。

Here, "onefifth of 1 percent" equals to 1/500, which is 0.2%. We translate it as a percentage to be parallel with the preceding one. Additionally, in English, there is another way to express percentages, which is "out of". For example:

The company's profits have **increased by 20%** this quarter.

该公司本季度的利润**增长了20%**。

Fractions. There are significant differences in how fractions are read in Chinese and English. English has what is called "fraction words", while Chinese does not. In Chinese, fractions are read in the format of "×分之×". For example, 1/2 is read as "二分之一", meaning one out of two. The use of fraction words in English is unfamiliar to those who speak Chinese, as they are identical to ordinal numbers (e.g., 1/2 is read as "one half"). For instance, the word "fifth" indicates "the fifth" when used as an ordinal number, but when used as a fraction word, it means "one fifth". The distinction between it being an ordinal number or a fraction word depends on the context. These fraction words are also used in a unique way, such as 1/5 being read as "one fifth", meaning one out of five, and 3/5 being read as "three fifths", representing three out of five. More examples are as follows:

a. Approximately **75% of the population** voted in the election.

大约**75%**的人口参加了选举。

In Chinese, several words such as "分""成""折""股" are often used to represent percentages.

b. If you pay by cash, we will give you a **30% discount off** the price of goods. 如果现金支付，我们予以**七折优惠**。

Here, "予以七折优惠(providing a discount of 30%)" is equivalent to a 30% price reduction, meaning a deduction of 30% from the original price.

c. The breeding herd in this county this year was just **three fourths** that of last year.

今年这个县的养牛头数仅为去年的**四分之三**。

The expression of English fractions is as follows: the numerator is a cardinal number, and the denominator is an ordinal number. When the numerator is greater than "one", the denominator is in plural form.

1.5 Differences in the Expression of Numbers between British English and American English and Their Translation

For example, in British English, "billion" represents a trillion（万亿）, while in American English, "billion" represents a billion（十亿）. In American English, "万亿" is typically represented as "trillion". Then, there is a difference in the numerical magnitude of "billion" between British English and American English. Therefore, how to determine the meaning of "billion"? The translator should first determine whether the source text is in British English(BrE) or American English(AmE) by utilizing context and logical reasoning, scientific background knowledge and common sense. For example:

The oldest accepted physical remains of life on earth are microscopic fossilized algae behaved **2.3 billion** years old.

人们公认的地球上最古老的生命遗迹，就是据信为**23亿**年前的水藻显微化石标本。

According to the scientific knowledge that "the Earth has only 4.6 billion years of history", billion can only be translated as "十亿(one thousand million)". Understanding the differences between British English and American English is very helpful in determining the meaning of billion in oral and written communication in technical English.

2. Translation techniques for English classifiers

Here, the so-called classifiers are referred to in a broad sense, including both unit nouns and certain quantifiers, which are words or phrases indicating quantity. English and Chinese belong to different language families and have different concepts of classifiers. In Chinese, classifiers are an independent word class, whereas traditional English grammar does not have classifiers. Structures indicating quantity are categorized under nouns in English. These English classifiers have different meanings and usage patterns compared to Chinese classifiers, and they are far less abundant. The specific types of Chinese classifiers listed in the table below give us a glimpse of the complexity of Chinese classifiers.

2.1 Addition of classifiers

In Chinese, classifiers cannot function as syntactic elements. However, when combined with numbers and nouns, they often serve as a bridge to ensure smooth and idiomatic expression. Without classifiers, the expression may sound awkward and deviate from the norms of Chinese language usage. In English, on the other hand, numbers can be directly combined with countable nouns to express quantity clearly without the need for classifiers. Therefore, when translating, it is necessary to apply expansion techniques to add words as needed. For example:

a. The mechanic has repaired three lathes in the workshop.

这个技工在车间里修了三台车床。

In this example, if the translation does not use the classifier "台", the sentence does not resemble Chinese. Of course, it is not necessary to use measure words after Chinese numerals all the time. For example, "one hour"(一小时), "four days"(四天), "six years"(六年), etc. However, the translation of "six months" is "六个月", if translated as "六月", it may be mistaken as "June" in English.

b. Would you please write out a receipt for me?

请给我开一张收据。

In this example, there is no classifier in the English sentence. However, when translated into Chinese, the measure word "张" should be inserted, otherwise the sentence will not sound natural.

c. To our dismay, we find three computer screens got broken in shipment.

令人不快的是,我们发现三**台**电脑显示屏在运输途中破损了。

Here, in English, there is a lack of individual measure word. In the translation process, a unique measure word is added before each noun in Chinese to indicate the shape, type, or other attributes of the item.

In English, certain verbs or gerunds, when translated to Chinese, often require the addition of measure words to indicate the frequency or intensity of the action.

d. I was extremely worried about her, but this was neither the place nor the time for a lecture or an argument.

我真替她万分担忧,但此时此地,既不宜教训她**一通**,也不宜与她争论**一番**。

e. Mr. James toured around our industrial park in the afternoon.

詹姆斯先生下午在我们工业园逛了**一下**。

f. Can you wait for me? I am handling the business for this gentleman.

可以等**一下**吗?我先办理这位先生的业务。

g. He glanced through the document, checking against the Declaration in Chinese on the forms in front of him.

他扫了**一眼**文件,与面前表格上的中文声明核对着。

h. Concerning your complaint, we will have to discuss with one another.

关于你方投诉,我们必须互相商量**一下**。

2.1.1 Choice of classifiers

(1) Polysemy and choice of classifiers.

However, the categories covered by classifiers in Chinese and English are not always the same in many cases. Therefore, the aforementioned corresponding relationship does not always exist, and it is necessary to select appropriate classifiers, such as the dealing of the word "piece" in "He discovered a piece of fossil of an ancient bird". When translated to Chinese, it should be "他发现了一**块**古代鸟类化石". For another example:

I don't know if he has been to London.

我不知道他**是否**去过伦敦。

The word "if" can be used to express both "whether" and "in case", and you write a sentence like "I shall tell you if he will come", the reader won't know if you mean "I will tell you whether he is willing to come" or "If he is willing to come, I will tell you". To avoid ambiguity, when expressing the former, you should replace "if" with "whether", and when expressing the latter, you should use "if".

There are more examples as follows:

a. The old man wore **an** eyeglass attached to **a piece of** ribbon.

那位老人戴了**副**眼镜，眼镜上系了**根**绳。

b. 1 was hurt by **a piece of** falling plaster.

我被一**块**落下的石膏击中。

c. We have met **a piece of** resistance in the construction site.

我们在建筑现场遇到了一**些**阻力。

d. **Another piece of** evidence was presented to support the argument.

另一则证据被提呈出来，支持该论据。

Here, the focus of word selection should be on measure words. The translation of such words in English is both crucial and challenging.

It is important because these words appear frequently, especially in inquiries, offers, and shipping-related business aspects. Moreover, they involve significant unit considerations, and incorrect translation can lead to misunderstanding regarding the terms of commodity transactions, thus affecting smooth cooperation.

The difficulty lies in the fact that, during translation, special attention is required to determine whether these words are metric and whether there are differences in different countries. For example:

The price quoted was for the small lot you named, **5 tons**; we can offer you 10% off for a **150-ton** lot.

这一价格是针对你方小批量订货的，即 5 吨；如果订 150 吨，我们可以降价 10%。

The word "ton" is a commonly used English term that frequently appears as a unit of weight in scientific journals and publications. However, many English-Chinese dictionaries in our country have long had an incorrect definition for the entry of "ton", considering it to be strictly equivalent to the Chinese ton, which is a weight value of 1,000 kilograms (or metric ton). This misconception leads to an error of nearly one hundred kilograms per ton. In fact, as a country that uses the metric system, the Chinese term for "ton" is equivalent to a metric ton (also known as a tonne). Additionally, the situation is more complex in the UK and the US, where the term "ton" differs slightly. The British use the long ton, where 1 "ton" equals 1,016 kilograms, while in the United States, 1 "ton" is equal to 907.2 kilograms. Therefore, when specifically referring to these units, it is necessary to specify whether it's a short ton or a long ton to avoid overloading or under-loading, as the former causes financial losses and the latter can damage business relationships and even lead to commercial disputes.

Furthermore, attention should be paid to the translation of collective measures. There are two main differences between English and Chinese in this regard. First, there is a difference in the usage of numbers. Many quantities expressed in plural in English are translated into singular form in Chinese. For example, "a pair of pliers" is translated as "一把钳子" rather than "一副". Additionally, English collective measure words are more specific, specialized, and stronger. Examples include "a troop of soldiers" "a murder of crows" "a pride of lions" "a herd of cows" "a flock of geese" and "a litter of kittens". In Chinese, these are generally referred to as "一群" (a group).

(2) English and Chinese classifiers correspond one-to-one.

In Chinese, most classifiers have corresponding nouns in English, so in many cases, they can be translated directly. Some measure words have exact equivalents as well. For example:

We normally pack **each pair of socks** individually in **a polythene bag**.
我们通常将**每双袜子**独立包装在**一个塑料袋**。

Each package contains **six rolls** of bandage.
每包装有**六卷**绷带。

2.1.2 Conversion of part of speech

Conversion of part of speech is both a method of translation and a syntactic modification technique, with the latter often achieved through the former. Any part of speech can be converted under the requirement of semantic equivalence in bilingualism, changing the original syntactic structure. Therefore, conversion of part of speech significantly expands the pathway for bilingual semantic correspondence transformation. Conversion of part of speech is mainly suitable for borrowed measure words. For example, when translating phrases like "take a glance", the "have" or "take" in English means "to do, to perform". However, in Chinese, the meaning of "glance" as "to take a quick look" is not expressed as a measure word. If translated directly as "进行一扫" (to take a sweep), it would confuse readers completely. Therefore, the words "take" and "have" should be ignored, and the nominal measure word in the source text should be changed to a verb. In addition, this often involves the use of word addition to add the corresponding classifiers in the Chinese translation. Following this principle, "take a glance" is translated as "扫了一眼". For example:

    have a quarrel   争吵一番
    take a break   休息一下

3. Translation of multiples in English

Multiples are widely used in English, but the structure and usage differ significantly between English and Chinese. For example, native speakers often say "to increase by three times", while Chinese can have two different translations: "increased to four times" or "increased by three times". In other words, when expressing multiples in Chinese, sometimes the cardinal number is included and sometimes it is not. On the contrary, in English, regardless of increase or decrease, the multiple always includes the cardinal number. This can easily lead to confusion regarding the usage of words like "了" and "到". Additionally, in English, one might say "three times as many as that of last year", while in Chinese, the comparative structure can be omitted and expressed directly as "three times that of last year". In conclusion, when translating multiples, it is important to be cautious and precise in order to ensure accuracy.

3.1 Expressions of multiples

The key characteristic of expressing multiples in English is to first mention the "multiple" and then the subject or object being compared. In general, there are two sentence patterns used in English to express multiples: comparative and superlative. When translating the comparative pattern, it is rendered as "n times" (where n is the number indicating the multiple in the sentence). On the other hand, when translating the superlative pattern, it is rendered as "increased/decreased by $n-1$ times".

(1) Comparative degree of the same level represents multiples.

a. n + times + as + adjective + as. For example:

1) Our total output of the chemical fertilizer this year is approximately **three times as great as** that of last year.

今年的化肥总产量大约**是**去年的**三倍**。(或：今年的粮食产量比去年多两倍左右。)

2) I am **twice as old as** he.

我的年纪**是**他的**两倍**。

3) He earns **twice as much as** he used to.

他比往常**多赚一倍**的钱。

4) She studies **three times as hard as** I.

她用功的程度**是**我的**三倍**。

5) The warehouse under construction is **five folds as large as** the old one.

正在建造的仓库大小**是**旧仓库的**五倍**。

b. n + times + the + noun + of. For example:

1) The earth is **49 times the size of** the moon.

地球的体积是月球的**四十九倍**。

2) This river is **three times the depth of** that one.

这条河的深度是那条河的**三倍**。

3) The registered capital of the pharmaceutical company reached one billion yuan, **4 times the number of** which we had expected.

该药物公司的注册资本达10亿人民币，比我们预期**高了三倍**。

(2) Comparative degree of different levels represents multiples.

a. It contains almost **three times more** iron **than** aluminum.

其中含铁量比铝**高两倍**。

b. The prime cost will be **two times larger**.

主要成本将**超出一倍**。

c. This kind of plastic film is **twice thinner than** that one

这种塑料薄膜的厚度只有那种塑料薄膜的**三分之一**。

d. The plastic container is **five times lighter than** that glass one.

这个塑料容器的重量只有玻璃容器的**六分之一**。

3.2 Translation of increasing multiples

(1) Words indicating increase + multiples.

Verbs indicating increase include increase, rise, grow, raise, exceed, etc. They are combined with multiples in three forms: "n + times", compound words composed of numerals and "fold", and "by a factor of + n".

a. The dairy products we consume this year **expands two times**.

我们今年消耗的奶制品**增加了两倍**。

b. The total volume of state purchase in the first quarter **rose by 5.2 percent**, compared with the same period of last year.

和去年同期相比，国家第一季度的总采购量**增长了5.2%**。

c. Housing price is expected to continue to soar, finally reaching **120 percent of** that of August.

预计房价还会继续飞涨，最终达到8月份房价的**120%**。

d. Total government revenue reached 5.13 trillion yuan in 2007, **a 171% increase** over 2002.

全国财政收入在2007年达到5.13万亿美元，比2002年**增长171%**。

e. During that period the actualized EU investment in China **increased by more than 3 folds**, with nearly 20,000 European businesses now established in China。

在此期间欧盟在中国的实际投资**增长了三倍多**，现在在中国建立的欧洲企业已有近20 000家。

(2) Words indicating multiple.

In English, verbs that express multiplicative meanings include: double (两倍), triple (三倍), quadruple (四倍), quintuple (五倍), and so on. For example:

a. The two countries are scheduled to sign a long term agreement Tuesday, which is expected to **double** the trade between them.

两国计划于星期二签订一项长期协定，预计该协定将使两国的贸易额**增加一倍**。

b. Terminal Three will **double** the capacity of existing one.

三号航站楼将**是**现有航站楼容量的**两倍**。

c. The world population is **doubling** every 35 years.

世界人口的数量每隔35年就**翻番**。

d. Europe's biggest information technology service firm Atos Origin aims to **quadruple** its business in China over the next two years.

欧洲最大的信息服务公司 Atos Origin 计划在未来两年将其在华业务**增至四倍**。

(3) Words that express additive meanings + by a factor of + a number.

This structure indicates the multiple achieved after an increase, and can be translated as "increased by a factor of $n-1$" or "is $n-1$ times as (long, high, wide, etc.) as...". For example:

a. One night on the moon is **longer than** that on the earth **by a factor of 14**.

月球上的一个黑夜比地球上的一个黑夜**长十三倍**。

b. The weight of any object on the earth is **heavier than** that of on the moon **by a factor of about 6**.

地球上的物体重量比月球上的物体重量**约重五倍**。

c. The GDP per capital of this county has **increased by a factor of two** since 1978.

自1978年以来,这个县的人均国民生产总值已经**增长了两倍**。

(4) Translation of larger multiples.

Finally, it should be noted that when the multiple is significantly larger, it is advisable to take the whole number to create a sense of entirety. For example:

a. Kuwait oil wells yield nearly **500 times more than** U. S. wells.

科威特油井的产油量是美国油井的近**五百倍**。

b. The size of the sun is **a million times than that of** the earth.

太阳的体积是地球的**一百万倍**。

3.3 Methods of expressing decreased multiples

There are generally two ways to express the decrease of multiples in English: one is "reduced by n times", and the other is "reduced to n times". However, Chinese does not express it in the same way. The former is expressed in the form of "reduced to $n+1$" or "reduced by $n+1$" (when $n \leqslant 9$); the latter is expressed in the form of "reduced to $1/n$" (when n is an integer) or "reduced by $n/n-1$" (when $n \leqslant 10$).

The common structures for expressing decreased multiples are described as follows.

(1) Words indicating a decrease + multiplier.

The expression of decreased multiples in English is similar to the structure used for indicating increased multiples. It is customary to use words indicating a decrease (such as decrease, shrink, drop, decline, etc.) followed by a numeral to indicate the decreased quantity. For example:

a. 180 **decreased** by 90 is 90.

180 **减去** 90 等于 90。

b. The cost **decreased by** 40%.

成本**下降了** 40%。

c. This new process used **35% less** fuel.

这种工艺**节省了 35%** 的燃料。

d. Revenues from fiat rolled steel and other products **declined by 31%** to $17.6million compared to the fourth quarter of 2006.

来自轧制扁钢及其他产品的收入较 2006 年第四季度**下降了 31%**，达到 17 600 000 美元。

e. "Six Sigma" will require US to **reduce** defect rates **10 fold**—about 84 percent per year for five consecutive years—an enormous task.

"六西格玛"将要求美国把不合格率**降低至原来的十分之一**，连续五年每年降低大约 84%，这是个**艰巨**的任务。

It is worth noting that in Chinese, when discussing reduction or decrease by a certain amount, we often do not use multipliers but rather prefer to use fractions.

f. The administrative expenditure this year has **decreased by two times** as against that of 2002.

行政管理开支比 2002 年**降低了三分之二**。

g. If the radius **is halved**, the flow rate is **reduced by a factor of 16**.

如果把半径减半，则流速就下降十六分之一。

h. Due to the economic recession our sales volume is **2 times as small as** that of last year.

由于经济不景气，我们的销售额是去年的**二分之一**。

i. The principal advantage of the innovation is **a three fold reduction** in production cost.

该革新的主要优点是成本**减少了三分之二**。

When dealing with decimals, it is important to convert them into fractions.

j. The error probability of the equipment was **reduced by 2.5 times** through technical innovation.

通过技术革新该设备误差概率**降低了五分之二**。

(2) Words indicating a decrease + by a factor of + multiplier.

For example:

a. The personnel expenditure this year has **decreased by a factor of three** as against that of 2008.

今年的人力资源开支比2008年**降低了三分之二**。

b. The enterprise management expenditure this year has **decreased by three times** as against that of 2002.

该企业今年的行政管理开支比2002年**降低了三分之二**。

c. The principal advantage is **a fourfold reduction** in volume.

主要优点是体积缩小了四分之三。

4. Attention to expressions and translation of numbers

In English, numbers are not only translated but also written in specific formats. The general forms of writing English numbers are as follows:

(1) One-digit numbers are written in English numerals, while two digits or more are written in Arabic numerals. For example:

The budget for the **1,568** km track is about **270** billion yuan.

这个总长1 568千米的轨道预算资金为2 700亿元。

(2) In the same sentence, when two numbers appear, the numeral format should be consistent. For example:

In the report, they analyzed **230** cases of quality discrepancy in the last **5** years。

报告中他们分析了过去五年230例质量异议。

(3) Hyphens are used between digits. For example:

Japan has been China's main technology exporter in recent years: **one-fifth** of China's imposed technologies and **one-sixth** of China's imposed high technologies are from Japan.

日本近年来一直是中国的主要技术出口国：五分之一的中国进口技术以及六分之一的中国进口高科技来自日本。

（4）Add "and" after the whole number when dealing with mixed fractions. For example：

In the world of men's fashion, the shrinking of the tie from a **three and three-fourths** inch width to around **three and one-fourth** inch counts as monumental news.

在男性时尚界，领带幅宽从三又四分之三英寸（1 英寸 = 2.54 厘米）缩减到三又四分之一英寸便算作重大新闻。

（5）A number with four or more digits is written using commas to separate every three digits in American notation. For example：

A Corporation, an environmental monitoring firm, announced today that sales for the third quarter totaled US **$2,274,885**, down 36% from US **$3,569,338** for the same period of the previous year.

A 公司，一家环境监测企业，今天宣布其第三季度销售总额为 2 274 885 美元，较去年同期的 3 569 338 美元下降了 36%。

（6）Hyphenate the numbers from 21 to 99 with a hyphen. When fractions modify nouns, use hyphens to connect the words in the fraction. Such as, "thirty-five" "three-fifth" "one half" and "three-fifth majority". For example：

Twenty-one firms are to bid for a power engineering construction project in Southeast China.

21 家企业将为中国东南部的电力工程修建项目投标。

（7）Arabic numerals are not used at the beginning of the sentence. For example, "包装内随附 20 份操作指南" should be translated into "Twenty copies of the operation instructions are enclosed in the package" instead of "20 copies of the operation instructions are enclosed in the package".

（8）When writing decimal fractions, we need to add 0 before the decimal point. In English, the decimal point is read as "point", and 0 is read as "zero". The digits after the decimal point are read separately. When writing a decimal fraction, we must add 0 before the decimal point. For example, 0.32 should not be written as just ".32".

Section 4

Techniques and Methods of Sentence Translation

English texts vary in style, with complex sentence structures and a high frequency of long sentences. These characteristics pose many difficulties for translators. However, the English language has a feature called "syntactic unity", meaning that regardless of length or complexity, sentences are composed of basic elements. Translators first need to identify the main structure of a sentence and clarify its subject, predicate, and object. They then analyze the functions of subordinate clauses and phrases, as well as other elements like fixed collocations and insertions. Finally, they organize the translation according to the characteristics and expressions of Chinese to ensure a correct understanding of the sentence. In this discussion, we will focus on the translation techniques for passive voice, relative clauses, and adverbial clauses.

Ⅰ. Passive Voice

Passive voice is widely used in English. It is used when the active agent is unnecessary, undisclosed, unknown, or when it is needed to maintain coherence in the context. Although Chinese also has passive voice, its usage is much more limited. In English, passive voice sentences can often be translated into active voice sentences in Chinese, but there are also cases where the passive voice can be retained.

1. Conversion to active voice

In some cases, it is possible to change the voice and transform the original passive voice into positive voice to make the translation clear and easy to understand.

a. A contingency plan against bankruptcy was hastily drawn up.

防止破产倒闭的应急计划很快就制订出来了。

b. The special challenge that advertising presents can be illustrated by a statement made by the president of a major advertising agency in New York.

纽约一家主要广告公司的总裁所做的陈述,可以阐释当前广告业所面临的特殊困难。(原文中被动语态译为主动结构,原文中的主语在译文中作宾语。)

c. This Contract is made by and between the Buyer and the Seller, whereby the Buyer agrees to buy and the Seller agrees to sell the under mentioned commodity according to the terms and conditions stipulated below.

买卖双方同意按下列条款买卖下述商品,并签订本合同。

2. The passive voice

When translating from English to Chinese, the passive voice remains unchanged and is retained in its original form. However, translators often need to add certain prepositions in Chinese between the subject and the verb to indicate passivity. Such as"被……""给……""受……""让……""为……所……""遭……". For example:

a. Competition in business is regarded to be a means to earn money.

商业竞争被认为是一种挣钱手段。

b. Although Americans today are likely to think that Alger's stories are too good to be true, they continue to be inspired by the idea of earning wealth and success as an entrepreneur who makes it on his own.

尽管今天美国人有可能认为阿尔杰的故事好得令人难以置信,但是他们却依然为那种自力更生赢得财富和成功的企业家精神所鼓舞。

3. Conversion to subjectless sentences

a. Your early confirmation would be greatly appreciated.

万分感谢您能早日给予确认。

b. On the whole such a conclusion can be drawn with a certain degree of confidence, but only if the child can be assumed to have had the same attitude towards the test as the other with whom he is being compared, and only if he was not punished by lack of relevant information which they possessed.

总的来说，得出这种结论是有一定程度把握的，但必须具备两个条件：能够假定这个孩子对测试的态度和与他比较的另一个孩子的态度相同；他也没有因为缺乏别的孩子已掌握的有关知识而被扣分。

c. Great efforts should be made to inform young people especially the dreadful consequences of taking up the habit.

应该尽最大努力告知年轻人吸烟的危害，特别是吸烟上瘾后的可怕后果。

The three examples use the passive voice, where there is no explicit mention of the doer of the action. When translating them, it is possible to translate them to Chinese sentences without subjects.

4. "... be done" structures

Sometimes, for various reasons, the agent of the verb in English passive sentences is omitted, creating the "be done" structure. If it is translated by transforming it into the active voice, it becomes the "do..." structure. In such cases, it is often necessary to add a general subject, such as "we" "people" "everyone" "someone" etc., or translate it into a subjectless sentence in Chinese.

a. The daily closing balance per account shall be checked against actual cash on hand.

Version A：每日终了，我们应结出账面余额，并与实际库存核对。

Version B：每日终了，应结出账面余额，并与实际库存核对。

The English sentence uses the passive voice, without an agent being mentioned in the sentence. When translating, we can add a general subject "we" at the beginning of the sentence, as in Version A. Alternatively, it can be translated into a subject-less sentence in Chinese, as in Version B.

b. It is essentially stressed that the Buyers are requested to sign and return the duplicate of this Contract within 3 days from the date of receipt. In the event of failure to do this, the Sellers reserve the right to cancel the Contact.

必须强调：买方应于收到本合同之日起3日内签字并返还合同的副本，如买方不这样做，卖方保留取消合同的权利。

In short, a key focus in English translation is to correctly understand and translate compound sentences. To achieve this, it is crucial to accurately analyze the sentence structure of the source text and understand the differences in structure, word order, and voice between English and Chinese. To effectively handle the complex grammatical relationships and inherent logical connections between sentence components, continuous exploration is required in the field of business translation practice.

II. Translation of attributive clauses

In English, attributive clauses can be divided into restrictive and non-restrictive clauses. Generally, they appear after the noun they modify. The main difference between restrictive and non-restrictive attributive clauses lies in the degree of restriction they convey. However, in Chinese, the adjective usually comes before the noun it modifies, and there is no distinction in terms of restriction. Therefore, the distinction between restrictive and non-restrictive clauses is not so significant in translation. English commonly employs structurally complex attributive clauses, while in Chinese, modifiers should be concise. Thus, when translating attributive clauses, it is important to consider the expression habits of Chinese. If the attributive clause in English is too long, whether restrictive or non-restrictive, it is not suitable to be translated as an adjective in Chinese and should be dealt with using other methods. In English, when a single word functions as an adjective, it is usually placed before the head noun, except for a few cases. However, longer adjectives such as phrases, prepositional phrases, or clauses are generally placed after the head noun. Based on the understanding of these differences between English and Chinese, the following are several translation methods suitable for business sentences.

1. Preposition

This method involves placing the attributive clause before the noun it modifies in Chinese translation, using the particle "的" to connect them. Since the purpose of an attributive clause is to modify the noun, in translation, shorter attributive clauses are usually translated as prepositional phrases with "的", placed before the noun being modified. In business translation practice, we have found that the prepositional method is more suitable for translating structurally and conceptually simple restrictive attributive clauses. Some shorter descriptive non-restrictive attributive clauses can also be translated using the prepositional method, but it is not as common as with restrictive attributive clauses. For example:

a. The role of selling in our society is to identify and provide the goods and services that will satisfy the needs and wants of the consumers.

销售在社会中的作用就是识别并提供那些能够满足消费者需求的商品和服务。

In this sentence, the restrictive attributive clause "that will satisfy the needs and wants of the consumers" is used to modify the head noun "goods and services". This attributive clause is relatively short, so when translating, we often move it before the antecedent to conform to the expression habits of Chinese.

b. In an urban culture, where mobility is valued, and land is not an issue, female talents are more emphasized.

Version A：在现代城市人的观念中，价值就是流动性，与土地无关，人们更加注重的是女性的才能。

Version B：在重视流动性且土地不成为其问题的城市文化中，女性的才能更受重视。

Here, "where mobility is valued, and land is not an issue" in this sentence is a non-restrictive attributive clause. Non-restrictive attributive clauses are usually translated in two ways: either as a prepositional phrase placed before the noun it modifies or as a separate subordinate clause or sentence. Version A uses the latter approach, translating in the order of the original English sentence, which may make the intended meaning unclear. On the other hand, Version B translates it as a "的" structure placed before the noun, which better conforms to the expression habits of Chinese.

2. Postposition

In English to Chinese translation, the attributive clause is placed after the antecedent and translated as a coordinate clause. The structure of attributive clauses in English is often complex. If it is placed before the antecedent in Chinese translation, the attributive clause may appear bulky and unclear in exposition. In such cases, the attributive clause can be placed after the antecedent and translated as a coordinate clause, repeating or omitting the meaning represented by the relative pronoun. Sometimes, it can even become an independent sentence that is separated from the main clause.

a. The importer can sell the goods to a new buyer while they are being carried by means of negotiable shipping documents which are very convenient for use.

Version A: 进口商可以通过使用起来非常方便的可转让的运输单据将货物在运输途中卖给新的卖方。

Version B: 进口商可以通过可转让的运输单据将货物在运输途中卖给新的卖方，这类可转让单据用起来非常方便。

In Version A, the restrictive attributive clause introduced by "which" is placed before the antecedent, which appears cumbersome and awkward. On the other hand, Version B adopts a postposition method, repeating the antecedent "negotiable shipping documents", making the translation clear in meaning.

b. The fact that these early entrepreneurs built great industries out of very little made them seem to millions of Americans like the heroes of the early frontier days who went into the vast wilderness of the United States and turned the forests into farms, villages, and small cities.

这些早期的企业家几乎白手起家却创造了宏大的产业，在千百万美国人看来，他们恰如早期拓荒时代的英雄，走进美国一望无际的荒野，将森林变成了农场、村庄和小城镇。

In this sentence, the restrictive attributive clause "who went into the vast wilderness of the United States and turned the forests into farms, villages, and small cities" is used to modify its antecedent "heroes of the early frontier days". The attributive clause is quite long, and if translated by preposition, the translation would be cumbersome and difficult to understand. In this case, the attributive clause can be separated from the pronoun "who" and translated as a coordinating clause, omitting the antecedent, resulting in a concise and clear translation.

c. The strong influence of the success stories of the early entrepreneurs on the masses of Americans can be found in the great popularity of the novels of Alger, which were published in late nineteenth and early twentieth century America.

阿尔杰的小说大受欢迎，我们可以从中发现早期企业家的成功故事对美国大众所产生的强烈影响。这些小说于19世纪末20世纪初在美国发行。

In this sentence, the non-restrictive attributive clause "which were published in late nineteenth and early twentieth century America" modifies the noun phrase "the novels of Alger". The translation adopts a post-modification approach, separating the attributive clause from the main clause. The attributive clause restates the antecedent and becomes an independent sentence.

d. China's patriarchy is a feudal holdover, scholars say, where land equals power. Male children inherited land.

Version A：学者们说，中国的男权统治是一种土地就是权力的封建残余。土地是由男孩继承的。

Version B：学者们说，中国的男权统治是一种封建残余，在封建社会，土地就是权力，而土地是由男孩继承的。

Although the non-restrictive attributive clause is not long, the word "where" in this sentence refers to "China's patriarchy". If we use preposition method in translation, such as version A, it would limit the referent too narrowly. On the other hand, version B does not simply repeat the antecedent, but translates it as "feudal society", which is consistent with the original meaning.

3. Fusion

Fusion refers to the combination of the main clause and the attributive clause into a single sentence, with the attributive clause translated as the predicate of the main clause. Since restrictive attributive clauses are closely related to the main clause, the fusion method is often used to translate restrictive attributive clauses, especially in sentence patterns with "there be" structures containing attributive clauses.

a. We are a nation that has a government—not the other way around.

我们这个国家有一个政府，而不是倒过来，政府有一个国家。

b. Still, Hyundai Motor Company's executives returned home with growing fears that their Chinese rivals are closing the technological and design gap with Republic of Korea—a development that could be disastrous for the company.

然而，现代汽车的高管回到韩国后，越来越担心中国竞争对手正在科技和设计方面缩小与韩国的差距，对该公司而言，这种发展可能是灾难性的。

Both of the above examples contain restrictive attributive clauses. The main clause and the attributive clause are closely related, but the emphasis is on the attributive clause. When translating, the subject is rendered as a noun phrase, and the attributive clause is translated as the predicate part with the omission of the relative pronoun "that", forming a subject-predicate structure.

c. Most of the staff, who have hand signals spelling "welcome" printed on the back of their T-shirts, used to spend their days shut off from the public in special workshops for the handicapped, making things like jewellery or packaging.

大多数工作人员在T恤衫后背上印有表示"欢迎"的手势,他们过去过着与公众隔绝的日子,在为残疾人开设的特殊车间里生产珠宝之类的东西或负责包装。

The translation of the non-restrictive attributive clause in this example also uses the fusion method. The translation merges the subject of the main clause and the non-restrictive attributive clause together, and reorganizes them into a sentence.

4. Paraphrasing

a. An automatic production line is excellent for the automotive industry where thousands of identical parts are produced.

自动生产线非常适用于汽车工业,因为那里要生产成千上万个同样的零件。

In this sentence, "An automatic production line is excellent for the automotive industry" is the main clause, and "where thousands of identical parts are produced" is a restrictive attributive clause. From a grammatical perspective, this attributive clause modifies the preceding antecedent "the automotive industry". However, from a logical perspective, there is a cause-effect relationship between the attributive clause and the main clause. The translation renders the attributive clause into a causal adverbial clause, clearly indicating the logical relationship between the sentences.

b. I think it will grow even on non-irrigated land where there is a forest belt.

我想即使在没有灌溉的土地上,只要有一条树林带,它还是会生长的。

c. The two sides were edging toward an improvement of relation that in time could be capped by a high-level American visit to Moscow, perhaps even a presidential visit.

双方一步一步朝改善关系的方向前进,以便一旦时机成熟,就可以有一位美国高层人士访问莫斯科,也许甚至是总统亲自出访。

The attributive clause, which contains the purpose of improving the relationship between the parties, is translated as a purpose adverbial clause.

d. Efforts to bring industrial development to what was a backward agricultural area caused a population boom and a shortage of housing, which local builders tried to meet with cheap, jerry-built homes, or by adding extra floors to existing houses.

要给原本落后的这个农业区域带来工业发展的努力造成人口激增和住房短缺。因此,为满足需要,当地建房者千方百计地用廉价劣质建材盖房子,或在现有住房上添加楼层。

The attributive clause, which serves as an adverbial clause indicating the result, is translated as a result adverbial clause.

e. Any worker who dirties or who soils a wall with his hands or feet is docked a day's pay.

Version A:任何脏兮兮或者用手脚弄脏了墙壁的工人扣薪一天。

Version B:任何职工,若服装不整洁,或用手脚污损了墙壁,就扣薪一天。

Comparing the two versions above, it is not difficult to find that if this attributive clause is translated into a conditional adverbial clause, it would better match the way it is expressed in English.

f. Electronic computers, which have many advantages, cannot carry out creative work or replace men.

尽管电子计算机有许多优点,但是它们不能进行创造性工作,也不能代替人。

The attributive clause has the function of a concessive adverbial clause, so it is translated as a concessive adverbial clause.

It can be seen from this that the expression of language is flexible. Attributive clauses in English should be handled flexibly based on the writing style, content of the source text, and the inherent logical relationship of the context. When translating a sentence, especially when there are significant differences in grammatical and semantic structures between the source language and the target language, it often requires analysis, transformation, and restructuring. The ideal translation result is that during the process of restructuring, the information in both languages can generate a shared semantic structure, achieve conceptual equivalence, and ultimately make readers of the translation respond to the information in a manner similar to readers of the source text.

Ⅲ. Translation of Adverbial Clauses

Adverbial clauses in English can express various meanings such as the time, place, reason, condition, concession, manner, comparison, purpose, and result. Adverbial clauses with different meanings are introduced by different subordinating conjunctions. The position of adverbial clauses is different in English and Chinese. In English, the adverbial clause generally comes at the end of a sentence after the object, that is, subject + verb + object + adverbial clause. However, it sometimes appears at the beginning of a sentence as well. In Chinese, the position of adverbials is relatively fixed. Adverbials in Chinese often come between the subject and the verb, that is, subject + adverbial + verb + object, or for emphasis, adverbials are also often placed before the subject. Therefore, when translating from English to Chinese, we should follow the expression habits of Chinese and adjust the word order accordingly, without being overly constrained by the word order and structure of the source text. For example:

a. You may also need resumes and appropriate cover letters if you decide to send out unsolicited applications to the companies you have discovered in your initial search.

你如果决定向那些首次搜寻中所发现的公司主动投寄求职信的话,也许还需要简历和相应的自荐信。

In this sentence, "if" introduces a conditional adverbial clause, and the translation places the conditional adverbial clause between the subject and the verb.

b. When the levels reached 6 percent the crew members would become mentally confused, unable to take measures to preserve their lives.

当含量达到6%时,飞船上的人员将会神经错乱,无法采取保护自己生命的措施。

In the version, the temporal adverbial clause is placed at the beginning of the sentence.

c. The Greeks assumed that the structure of language had some connections with the process of thought, which took root in Europe long before people realized how diverse languages could be.

Version A: 希腊人认为,语言结构与思维过程之间存在某种联系。这个观点早在人们认识到语言的千差万别之前,就已在欧洲扎根了。

Version B: 希腊人认为,语言结构与思维过程之间存在某种联系。这个观点在人们充分意识到语言是多么的形态万千之前,早就在欧洲扎根了。

In English, the adverbial clause "long before people realized how diverse languages could be" has been translated into a time adverbial phrase in Chinese. Version A sounds more natural and is more in line with Chinese expression habits compared to version B.

d. The policies open to developing countries are more limited than for industrialized nations because the proper economies respond less to changing conditions and administrative control.

由于贫穷国家的经济对形势变化的适应能力差一些,政府对这种经济的控制作用也小一些,所以发展中国家所能采取的政策相比工业化国家就更有局限性。

In the translated sentence, the causal adverbial clause is placed at the beginning of the sentence.

e. Electricity is such a part of our everyday lives and so much taken for granted nowadays that we rarely think twice when we switch on the light or turn on the radio.

电已成为我们日常生活中如此寻常的一部分,而且现在人们认为电是理所当然的事,所以我们在开灯或开收音机时,就很少再去想一想电是怎么来的。

The adverbial clause of result in the translated sentence is placed at the end, consistent with the order of the source text.

f. The first two must be equal for all who are being compared, if any comparison in terms of intelligence is to be made.

如果要从智力方面进行任何比较的话,那么对所有被比较者来说,前两个因素必须是一致的。

The conditional adverbial clause is placed at the beginning of the translated sentence in the target text.

g. Television is one of the means by which these feelings are created and conveyed—and perhaps never before has it served so much to connect different peoples and nations as in the recent events in Europe.

Version A：电视是引发和传递这些感受的手段之一——在欧洲近来发生的事件中，它把不同的民族和国家连接到一起，其作用之大，或许前所未有。

Version B：电视是引发并传达这些情绪的方式之一，在加强不同民族和国家间的联系方面，或许它从未像在近来欧洲事务中那样起过如此大的作用。

In English, after the dash comes an inverted sentence. The normal word order is "perhaps it has never served so much to... as in... ", which is a comparative adverbial clause. The part that is repeated from the main clause is omitted after "as", namely "it has served to connect different peoples and nations". According to the meaning, it can be translated as "Its role has never been so significant before".

h. Therefore, although technical advances in food production and processing will perhaps be needed to ensure food availability, meeting food needs will depend much more on equalizing economic power among the various segments of populations within the developing countries themselves.

因此，尽管也许需要粮食生产和加工方面的技术进步来确保粮食的供给，但是满足粮食需求更多的要取决于使发展中国家内部的人口各阶层具有同等的经济实力。

In the version, the concessive adverbial clause is placed at the beginning of the sentence.

Section 5

Techniques and Methods of Discourse Translation

I. Definition of Discourse Translation

Discourse translation refers to the process of transferring the content, meaning, and style of a text or spoken discourse from one language to another. It involves not only the literal translation of individual words and sentences but also the preservation of the discourse's overall coherence, structure, and intended message. Discourse translation focuses on capturing the essence of the original discourse and conveying it effectively in the target language.

II. Characteristics of Discourse Translation

1. Cultural appropriateness

Discourse translation considers the cultural context of both the source and target languages. It involves adapting the discourse to ensure it is appropriate for the cultural background, norms, and values of the target language audience.

2. Idiomatic expression

Discourse translation aims to use idiomatic expressions that are natural and commonly understood in the target language. This helps to maintain the flow and fluency of the translation and ensures it resonates with the target language readers or listeners.

3. Coherence and cohesion

Discourse translation focuses on maintaining coherence and cohesion within the translated text. It ensures that the logical relationships, connections, and flow between sentences, paragraphs, and ideas are not lost in translation.

4. Style and register

Discourse translation takes into account the stylistic choices made by the author. It strives to capture and reproduce the author's tone, register, and rhetorical devices in the target language to have the intended effect on the audience.

Message Adaptation: Discourse translation may involve adapting the message to suit the target language audience's preferences, customs, and cultural sensitivities. This could include adjusting examples, references, or even rewriting certain sections to ensure the intended message is effectively communicated.

5. Contextual understanding

Discourse translation requires a comprehensive understanding of the source discourse, including its thematic focus, structure, and intended audience. Translators must analyze and interpret not only the literal meaning but also implicit information and underlying intentions.

6. Proofreading and revision

Discourse translation requires thorough proofreading and editing to ensure accuracy, clarity, and appropriateness. It may involve revisions in the translation to address any issues or improve the overall quality of the final translated discourse.

Discourse translation is a complex and nuanced task that goes beyond word-for-word translation. It requires linguistic skills, cultural awareness, and the ability to convey the intended message in a manner that resonates with the target language audience.

III. Translation Techniques and Methods

1. Comprehensive understanding of the source discourse

To ensure a comprehensive understanding of the source discourse, translators need to consider various factors. Firstly, they must grasp the overall theme and structure of the discourse, identifying the main ideas and supporting details. This involves analyzing the discourse's organization, such as the introduction, body, and conclusion, along with any logical or thematic progression.

Furthermore, translators should pay attention to the language style and rhetorical devices employed in the source discourse. This includes recognizing the tone, register, and figurative language used by the author. By understanding the style, translators can effectively reproduce it in the target language, maintaining the intended impact on the audience.

Identifying important details within the discourse is crucial. Translators need to discern the key points, arguments, and examples that contribute to the overall message. This involves extracting relevant information while considering the context, as some details may be implicitly conveyed or interconnected with other parts of the text.

Understanding the context is essential for accurate discourse translation. It requires recognizing the relationships between different elements in the source discourse, such as cause and effect, comparisons, or references to other texts or events. This contextual understanding helps translators accurately convey the intended meaning and avoid misinterpretation.

In summary, to fully understand the source discourse, translators must delve into its main theme, structural organization, language style, rhetorical devices, important details, and the surrounding context. By considering these elements, translators can ensure a faithful and effective transfer of the discourse's content and meaning to the target language readers.

2. Consideration of the target language readers' background and context

It is crucial to consider the background and context of the target language readers when it comes to effective communication. In order to do so, the following aspects should be taken into consideration.

(1) Study of the target language readers' culture, habits, and values.

It is essential to conduct thorough research on the target audience's cultural background, customs, and values. This includes understanding their social conventions, polite language usage, and cultural taboos. By gaining insight into their cultural nuances, we can ensure that the translated content is culturally relevant and sensible. This will help establish a connection with readers and enable them to understand and resonate with the ideas and concepts being conveyed.

(2) Integration of the target language context to select appropriate vocabulary and expressions.

In order to accurately convey the intended meaning, it is important to consider the context of the target language. This may involve selecting suitable idiomatic phrases, adjusting sentence structures, and ensuring clarity and coherence to align with the target language readers' preferred expressions. By incorporating the appropriate vocabulary and expressions, we can make the translation more natural and relatable to the target audience.

(3) Rewriting or reorganizing sentences to align with target language idiomatic expressions.

Idiomatic expressions vary across languages, and what may be idiomatic in one language may not make sense in another. Therefore, it is necessary to rewrite or reorganize sentences to adapt to the target language's idiomatic expressions. This ensures that the translated content sounds native and resonates with the target audience. By paying attention to these subtleties, we can facilitate effective communication and understanding between the source language discourse and the target language readers.

In summary, considering the target language readers' background and context involves studying their culture, habits, and values, integrating the target language context to select appropriate vocabulary and expressions, as well as rewriting or reorganizing sentences to align with target language idiomatic expressions. By taking these aspects into account, we can provide translations that are not only linguistically accurate but also culturally relevant to the target audience.

3. Maintaining text coherence and cohesion

Maintaining text coherence and cohesion is essential to ensure effective communication and convey the author's intentions accurately. To achieve this, the following strategies can be employed:

(1) Understanding the information structure and logical relationships of the discourse.

To maintain coherence, it is crucial to grasp the hierarchical structure and logical connections within a text. This involves identifying the main ideas, supporting details, and the overall flow of information. By understanding how different elements relate to each other, it becomes easier to present information in a coherent and organized manner.

(2) Using appropriate conjunctions and transitional words.

Using conjunctions and transitional words helps establish logical relationships between sentences and paragraphs. Words such as "however" "therefore" or "furthermore" indicate contrasts, cause and effect relationships, or additional supporting information. They facilitate smooth transitions between ideas, ensuring the text flows seamlessly and readers can follow the logical progression of the author's argument.

(3) Maintaining the rhythm and pacing of the discourse.

A well-crafted text maintains a rhythm and pacing that engages readers. This involves using varied sentence structures and lengths to create a balanced and harmonious flow. Short and concise sentences convey important information effectively, while longer sentences with complex structures can provide elaboration and nuance. By carefully managing the rhythm and pacing, the author's intended meaning can be accurately conveyed and the readers' attention sustained.

(4) Ensuring coherence with cohesive devices.

Cohesive devices, such as pronouns, referencing words, and lexical repetition, play a crucial role in maintaining coherence. These devices connect ideas and refer back to previously mentioned information. Pronouns like "it" or "this" refer to nouns mentioned earlier, and repetition of key terms or phrases reinforces the connection between ideas. By using cohesive devices appropriately, the text becomes more coherent and cohesive, allowing readers to easily follow the flow of the discourse.

In conclusion, maintaining text coherence and cohesion involves understanding the structural and logical relationships within a discourse, using appropriate conjunctions and transitional words, maintaining a rhythm and pacing that engage readers, and ensuring coherence with cohesive devices. By employing these strategies, the text can effectively convey the author's intentions and provide a seamless reading experience for the audience.

4. Flexible handling of semantics and cultural differences

Flexible handling of semantics and cultural differences is essential in translation to accurately convey the multiple meanings and implied information. While translating, it is crucial to pay attention to the polysemy of words and convey implicit messages effectively. Additionally, when dealing with cultural metaphors and allusions in the discourse, it is necessary to transform them appropriately to ensure comprehension for target language readers. Adjusting the discourse style and rhetorical devices moderately also contributes to better understanding of the audience.

To address the issue of polysemy, translators must carefully analyze the context and select the most suitable translation based on the intended meaning. This involves considering the nuances and connotations of words, avoiding potential ambiguity, and providing clarity to the target readers. By understanding the implied information in the source language text, translators can ensure that the translated version conveys the same intended message.

Cultural metaphors and allusions pose a challenge due to their context-specific nature. Translators must strike a balance between preserving the cultural significance and adapting them to the target language and culture. This requires comprehensive knowledge of both cultures to make informed decisions about the choice of equivalent metaphors or symbols. Transforming the cultural references into something familiar or explaining them within the text can aid in bridging the cultural gap and ensuring comprehension.

In terms of the discourse style and rhetorical devices, translators should be flexible in adapting to the target language's conventions. While maintaining the essence and tone of the source text, they need to adjust the style and rhetorical devices appropriately. This ensures that the translated text not only conveys the intended message but also engages the target language readers effectively. Translators can employ techniques such as adjusting sentence structures, modifying idiomatic expressions, or utilizing appropriate rhetorical devices to achieve this goal.

In conclusion, flexible handling of semantics and cultural differences in translation involves addressing word polysemy, conveying implicit information, transforming cultural metaphors and allusions, and adjusting the discourse style and rhetorical devices. By carefully considering these aspects, translators can ensure the target language readers' comprehension while maintaining the essence and intended meaning of the source text.

Chapter 4

Practical Application of English Translation

Section 1

Business English Translation

With the rapid development of China's foreign trade economy, business English has become a bridge for communication between companies in trade, and business English translation has become an important task in trading. Communicative Translation Theory meets these requirements and is widely applied in business English translation, achieving better translation results. This section analyzes the basic content of Communicative Translation Theory, the characteristics of business English translation, and the applicability of Communicative Translation Theory, and explains the application direction of Communicative Translation Theory in business English translation.

Ⅰ. Overview of Communicative Translation Theory

Renowned British translation educator Peter Newmark proposed the terms "semantic translation" and "communicative translation" in 1981, and classified texts into information-oriented, expressive, and appellative categories, emphasizing the importance of being faithful to the original work when translating. Newmark's theory of Semantic Translation mainly focuses on reproducing the author's thought process, paying more attention to the content of the translation, and using concise sentences to express the words, phrases, etc. in the source text. In contrast, Communicative Translation Theory emphasizes that the register of translation should be consistent with the target text, placing greater emphasis on the effect of translation. Communicative Translation Theory is generally based on paragraphs in translation and regards the target language as the translation center, focusing on readers' comprehension and reactions to the translation, and primarily ensuring that readers can read the genuine and objective information from the source text.

According to Peter Newmark, different methods are chosen in translation based on the nature of texts. Literary texts such as novels and letters that can reflect the author and the text itself belong to expressive texts. Some texts mainly aim to express the content, convey related information and knowledge, and these types of texts belong to informative texts. This type of texts requires standardized content and writing formats and can be applied in most fields. Appellative texts mainly aim to elicit corresponding feedback from readers and establish a close connection between readers and the author, such as guidebooks. Peter Newmark believes that semantic translation is more suitable for expressive texts, while communicative translation is more suitable for informative texts and appellative texts.

II. The Application of Communicative Translation Theory in Business English Translation

1. Adjustment for cultural differences among countries

The process of economic globalization has brought tremendous opportunities and challenges to countries around the world. Due to regional differences, there are significant disparities in terms of national cultures, customs, and habits. This leads to cultural differences among countries. The purpose of Communicative Translation Theory is to facilitate communication and understanding between different cultures through translation. In communicative translation, it is not just a simple conversion of one language into another, but ensuring accurate conveyance of information and cultural adaptation. Through communicative translation, people can overcome language and cultural barriers, enhance communication between different cultures and promote the development of intercultural communication. Therefore, in an environment with significant cultural differences between East and West, translators need to understand and grasp the national cultures of different countries, and use appropriate language to facilitate equal information exchange of national cultures. In practical English applications, it is common for the same word to have different meanings in different cultural contexts. For example, in China, rabbits symbolize cute animals, and the "White Rabbit" candy named after rabbits is highly popular among Chinese. However, in Australia, rabbits are not welcomed as they can damage grasslands and compete with livestock for food, negatively impacting local agriculture. Australians consider rabbits to be pests. When translating the Chinese "White Rabbit" candy brand, it cannot be directly translated as "White Rabbit", for it would have a significant impact on the brand.

2. Ensuring semantic equivalence between target and source texts

Communicative Translation Theory states that the purpose of translation is to accurately convey the information from the source text. All translation works must serve the overall translation effect. The fundamental requirement of business English translation is to maintain the equivalence of information between the translated text and the source text, achieving equivalent information transfer. In such cases, translators need to handle specific information according to cultural differences and different contexts. In real-life business English translation, many translators directly translate words, resulting in the information expressed by the original words and the translated words being non-equivalent, leading to numerous errors. For example, in China, many "国家二级企业" have been translated as "State Second-class Enterprise" in English. However, in English, "second-class" implies a decrease in quality, which not only affects the company's image but also has a negative impact on its expansion and development. It would be better to translate the term as "State-level II Enterprise". Therefore, in business English translation, translators must take responsibility for their work, preventing unfavorable consequences.

3. Requirement for accurate and precise choice of words

Business English translation is a professional technical activity that directly affects a company's economic interests. Therefore, translators must use words rigorously and accurately in business English translation. The superficial meaning must be accurate, and the deep meaning must also be conveyed accurately. If there are many instances of literal translation without the guidance of corresponding business knowledge, the intended meaning of the source text may not be accurately expressed, leading to unintended contradictions. For example, in daily life, we often translate "白酒" directly as "white wine". At first glance, our translation seems correct. However, in English, "wine" generally refers to alcoholic beverages made from fruits, such as apple wine, etc. When "wine" is used without any modifiers, it specifically refers to grape wine. This difference in meaning leads to errors in translation.

Ⅲ. The Application of Communicative Translation Theory in Business English Translation

1. The literal translation in business English

Business English translation is generally divided into three parts: direct translation, paraphrase, and adaptation. The application of Communicative Translation theory in Business English translation does not deny the status of semantic translation in Business English translation. The application of Communicative Translation Theory in direct translation fully demonstrates this point. Direct translation in Business English can be divided into two types. One type is literal translation, which translates based on the syntax and vocabulary structure of the source text without special adjustments. In many words, there is a consensus between Chinese and Western cultures, and the expressions of words are consistent. For example, we often mention "好好学习，天天向上", and its literal translation is "Good good study, day day up". This type of translation fully expresses the educational consciousness of both Chinese and Western cultures. Another type is phonetic translation, which means translating English words into Chinese based on their pronunciation. The application of this type of translation is quite common, such as "model" can be directly translated as "模特" and "salon" can be directly translated as "沙龙". This translation method is a widespread phenomenon. The direct application of Communicative Translation Theory is simple and easy to understand, widely accepted by both parties involved, and provides a better communication atmosphere, incorporating the linguistic flavor of the home country as well as the language style of the other country, which promotes communication and cooperation between both countries.

2. The liberal translation in Business English translation

By understanding the inherent meaning of the source text, content can be expressed vividly to achieve the transmission of information. This translation method is paraphrase, one of applications of Communicative Translation Theory in Business English translation. English and Chinese have many similar expression styles. For example, metaphorical expressions are frequently used in English as well. If metaphors in the English text are translated directly, it cannot achieve a good translation effect and hinders normal communication and interaction. For example, the phrase "He was born with a silver spoon in his mouth" cannot be translated literally as "他出生的时候嘴里含着银匙", which is obviously illogical. This translation does not convey the profound meaning of the sentence. However, the paraphrase application of Communicative Translation Theory can use the technique of metaphorical association and translation to truly understand the intended meaning of the source text. In reality, "a person born with a silver spoon in his mouth" indicates that he is relatively wealthy from birth. In normal expressions, there may be texts with unclear pronunciation or expression. We can use the theory of Communicative Translation to make reasonable adjustments, which can achieve better results in Business English translation.

3. Transcription in Business English translation

In Business English translation, the application and expression of direct translation and paraphrase based on Communicative Translation Theory are relatively straightforward and easy to understand. However, transcription requires translators to have strong professional skills and profound cultural knowledge to fully express the meaning of the source text. Translating the text literally or metaphorically is not sufficient for adaptation; it is necessary to transform the objects described in the source text into something else and make more adjustments to achieve communication and interaction between cultures. Compared to direct translation or paraphrase, adaptation is much more challenging. For example, the Forbidden City (紫禁城) in China is a representative cultural heritage and a well-known tourist destination, beloved by both Chinese and foreign visitors. However, in English, it is translated as

"Forbidden City". This translation method is neither a literal translation because the purple color is not translated, nor a paraphrase because if it were a paraphrase, it should have no connection with the literal expression of the text, but in fact, they are connected. Therefore, the translation adopts an adaptation approach to fully describe the Forbidden City. The application of Communicative Translation Theory can describe one thing by transforming it into another thing, as well as convert static and dynamic elements, ultimately achieving the transmission of information and the perception of ideas.

Section 2

Translation of College English Test

The translation section of the College English Test Band 4 has been adjusted from single sentence translation to paragraph translation, which requires higher skills from candidates. This section analyzes the application of several commonly used translation strategies in this type of question based on candidates' needs.

Ⅰ. Literal Translation and Liberal Translation

It is difficult to determine which is superior or inferior between literal translation and free translation. Literal translation is faithful to the original content and conforms to the original structure. Liberal translation, based on the faithful representation of the source content, breaks free from the structure of the original text, making the translation conform to the norms of the target language. Of course, "literal translation" does not mean "word-for-word translation", and "liberal translation" does not mean "incoherent translation". In the process of translation, we often need to combine both strategies. For example:

很多年轻人想要通过旅行体验不同的文化,丰富知识、拓宽视野。(December,2014)

Many young people want to experience different cultures, enrich their knowledge, and broaden their horizon through travel.

The source text contains three parallel structures of verb-object, which are neatly organized. In the translation, the same structure is used to convey the meaning of the source text while preserving its structure. For another example:

该比例在所有核国家中居第30位,几乎是最低的。(December,2014)

The proportion ranks 30th among all countries possessing nuclear energy, which is almost the lowest.

"核国家" in the source text is not directly translated, but rather translated as "countries possessing nuclear energy" to convey a more accurate and standardized meaning.

There's a demo about paragraph translation in College English Test Band 4, December, 2023.

在中国农历中,立秋(Start of Autumn)意味着夏天的结束和秋天的开始。立秋带来的首先是天气的变化,气温逐渐下降。人们看到树叶开始变黄飘落时,知道秋天已经来临,这就是所谓的"一叶知秋"。但此时酷热的天气并未完全结束,高温通常还会持续一段时间,被称为"秋老虎"。立秋对农民意义重大,这时各种秋季作物迅速生长、开始成熟,收获的季节即将到来。

Start of Autumn signifies the end of summer and the beginning of autumn in the Chinese lunar calendar. Firstly, Start of Autumn brings the change of weather, with the temperature gradually decreasing. When people see that leaves are turning yellow and falling, they realize that autumn has arrived, which is the so-called "knowing the autumn has arrived through the falling of one leaf". However, the heat doesn't entirely end at this moment. it usually lasts for a while, which is called "Autumn Tiger". Start of Autumn means a lot to farmers because at this time all kinds of autumn crops grow rapidly and begin to mature, and the season of harvest is coming.

Ⅱ. Conversion of Part of Speech

English and Chinese languages have many differences in grammar, expression, and other aspects, resulting in different usage and habits concerning word classes. To make the translation conform to English expression conventions, we need to flexibly employ strategies for word class transformation to complete the translation.

For example:

大熊猫是一种温顺的动物,长着独特的黑白皮毛。(December,2014)

The giant panda is a kind of docile animal with unique black and white fur.

Compared to English, verbs are more frequently used in Chinese, and there is no change in person or tense, nor a distinction between predicate and non-predicate verbs. When translating, we need to transform Chinese verbs into other word classes according to English conventions. In this example, the translated text uses "is" as the predicate verb, and "长着" is translated as "with", which is more in line with English expression conventions.

Ⅲ. Voice Transformation

Chinese sentences focus on meaning and function; grammar is implicit, and its grammatical markers, such as tense, voice, and mood, are all included within the sentence and need to be determined. In English, on the other hand, form is emphasized, and there are clear markers for tense, voice, and mood. For example:

中国南方大多种植水稻。(December, 2015)

Rice is grown in most areas of southern China.

Although the subject is missing in the original sentence, the meaning can still be conveyed. When translating from Chinese to English, we need to focus on the form. Using "rice" as the subject in the translation is in line with English expression habits.

Ⅳ. Rearrangement of Word Order

In Chinese, the position of adverbials is more flexible, while in English, it is more fixed and generally placed at the end of the sentence. For example, "中国其他地区的著名景点和历史名胜" is translated as "the famous scenic spots and historical resorts in other parts of China". Another example:

在中外游客眼中,这个古镇被视为爱情和浪漫的天堂。(December, 2015)

This ancient town is regarded as the paradise of love and romance in the eyes of both Chinese and foreign visitors.

From the perspective of verbs, Chinese narrates events according to the chronological order of actions, which is different in English.

中国结……经过数百年不断的改进,已经成为一种优雅多彩的艺术和工艺。(December,2013)

The Chinese knot,... has become an elegant and colorful art and craft through centuries of continuous improvement.

Section 3

Translation of Subjunctive Mood in Business English Translation

Business English is an important branch of contemporary English and serves as the universal official language in international trade. Polite expressions in business English are particularly important in business activities and are increasingly valued by learners. Business English covers a wide range of areas, including finance, insurance, contracts, marketing, and foreign trade, involving various rights and obligations. When using business English, it is important to pay attention to the precision and accuracy of its language. The appropriate use of the subjunctive mood can create a favorable business environment, establish a harmonious negotiation atmosphere, leave a good impression on the other party's behavior, and accelerate the process of trade between both sides, ultimately achieving the desired goals. Besides, in business English, the subjunctive mood is usually formed by "should + do". Within the context of business contracts, "should" typically does not convey the intention of the subject of the sentence, but rather states specific provisions and requirements. It signifies a mandatory obligation to assume responsibility or fulfill obligations, indicating that "this clause carries the instructive and obligatory nature stipulated by law". The application of the subjunctive mood ensures that the contract text is both polite and courteous while having legal effect.

Ⅰ. Definition and Usage of the Subjunctive Mood

1. Definition of the subjunctive mood

Subjunctive mood refers to a verb form that expresses the speaker's attitude or viewpoint towards an action, event, or state. English has three moods: indicative, imperative, and subjunctive. The subjunctive mood is used when the speaker expresses something contrary to the facts, highly unlikely to occur, or subjective wishes, requests, or suggestions.

2. Usage of the subjunctive mood

First, the subjunctive mood is used in unreal conditional sentences, where the verb forms in both the main clause and the subordinate clause are generally fixed. There are several specific types:

(1) Subjunctive mood in situations contrary to the present reality, expressing situations that are opposite to the facts or do not exist at all at the time of speaking. For example: If I were you, I would take full advantage of this opportunity. (如果我是你，我会充分利用这个机会。)

(2) Subjunctive mood in situations contrary to the past reality, expressing situations that were opposite to past facts. For example: If the company had enough funds, it would not have gone bankrupt. (The fact is that due to insufficient funds, the company has already gone bankrupt.)

(3) Subjunctive mood in situations contrary to the future reality, expressing subjective speculation about future situations that may be opposite to reality or highly unlikely to occur. For example: If it should be fine tomorrow, we would climb mountain. (如果明天天气好，我们就去爬山。)

Second, the subjunctive mood is used in subject clauses. "It" serves as the formal subject. The sentence pattern is "It is necessary/essential/important/significant/natural/advisable/vital/urgent/strange that + should + infinitive verb form". For example: It is necessary that you should sign the contract in time.

Third, the subjunctive mood is used in object clauses following verbs that express suggestions, commands, and requests, as well as in apposition to nouns. These verbs include advise (advice), propose (proposal), suggest (suggestion), order, ask, require(requirement), etc. For example:

I suggest that we should hold a meeting next week. (我建议我们下星期应该举行会议。)

Another example: I make a proposal that we should get more people attend the conference.(我建议我们应该让更多的人参加会议。)

Ⅱ. Translation Principles of Subjunctive Mood in Business English

Business English is a form of English used in business transactions, applied in various international business activities and workplaces. Appropriate expressions in business English can create a harmonious and cordial atmosphere and contribute to reaching agreements. To some extent, business English is a comprehensive application of professional knowledge and language use in a business context. Professionalism, colloquialism, and practicality are the prominent features of Business English. When using the subjunctive mood in Business English, it is important to pay attention to its essential characteristics, and the translation process should adhere to the following principles.

1. Principle of accuracy

Business English is characterized by precise and standardized wording with concise and accurate language. Therefore, during the translation process, efforts should be made to ensure accuracy. The translation of sentences containing the subjunctive mood also requires understanding the source text correctly and grasping the grammatical structure of the sentence. This requires a thorough understanding of the expression of the subjunctive mood, its usage, and pragmatic functions. For example:

Should the sellers be unable to cover insurance and open L\C at once, the buyers' loss would be born by the sellers. (如卖方不能及时保险和开具信用证, 买方一切损失由卖方负责。)

In this case, it can be determined that it is an omitted conditional sentence with "if". By recognizing the grammatical structure of the sentence correctly, the translation of this sentence containing the subjunctive mood can be accurately rendered. Additionally, attention should be paid to correctly translate specialized terms such as "L/C" (letter of credit) "The sellers" "The buyers" and "cover" (insurance) in order to accurately and correctly translate this sentence with the subjunctive mood.

2. Principle of practicality.

Business English belongs to the practical writing, and its content and readers have strong purposes, so the style should be formal and the wording should be precise. There is no need to use a lot of fancy rhetoric to enhance the effectiveness of writing. Generally, concise and understandably formal language is sufficient. In writing, the author should clarify his own attitude and avoid using ambiguous words, otherwise, it may affect the original purpose of expression.

For example, when expressing a hope for a reply, in the closing of a letter a fixed expression is commonly used: "We would appreciate if you could send us your reply".

In long-term international trade communication, some practical and concise fixed sentence patterns have been widely accepted and used by foreign trade practitioners. However, overly rigid and complex formal communication can make the other party feel disrespected and undervalued.

3. Principle of politeness

Since Chinese does not have the subjunctive mood, when translating sentences with subjunctive mood in business English, attention should be paid to the use of politeness principle. The translation should appear polite and implicit in order to avoid unnecessary conflicts and contradictions. For example:

We leave the insurance arrangement to you, but we wish that you could have the goods covered against all risks. (保险事宜交由贵方安排, 但希望贵方能为该货物保一切险。)

In this example, the use of the verb's subjunctive mood greatly softens the tone of communication between parties in business negotiations. When translating, it is important to consider the other party's face and use polite and explicit language strategies to achieve the desired communicative effect and facilitate the final transaction.

Ⅲ. The Application of Subjunctive Mood in Business English

The subjunctive mood, as an important rhetorical device, is widely used in various forms of communication in Business English, such as business letters, contracts, and negotiations, effectively facilitating normal business activities.

1. The application of subjunctive mood in business letters

In business letters, using a declarative tone to make suggestions may appear too definite and absolute, causing the recipient to feel resentful or disgusted. However, the subjunctive mood can make the speaker's tone more polite and courteous, making it easier for the recipient to accept the writer's viewpoint and further communicate. Therefore, the subjunctive mood is often used to express suggestions and ideas in a more tactful manner, with verbs such as should, would, could, might + do. For example:

(1) We would prefer an alternation of payment terms and a discount of 5% in your price. (我们希望选择一种支付方式并以贵方价格5%的折扣成交。)

(2) We prefer an alternation of payment terms and a discount of 5% in your price. (我们宁愿选择一种支付方式并以贵方价格5%的折扣成交。)

In the above examples, the use of the subjunctive mood in the first sentence creates a more polite and tactful tone compared to the second sentence, enhancing effective communication.

2. The application of subjunctive mood in business contracts

Business contracts are legally binding documents that formalize agreements between parties, characterized by a formal and precise language style. The use of the subjunctive mood can alleviate tense and serious atmospheres.

Example 1:

(1) It is required that both parties should abide by the terms and conditions of the contract. (要求双方都应遵守该合同条款。)

(2) We require that both parties should abide by the terms and conditions of the contract. (我们要求双方都应遵守该合同条款。)

Example 2:

(1) It is necessary that one party should inform another party in advance. (一方有必要提前通知另一方。)

(2) One party should inform another party in advance. (一方应该要提前通知

另一方。)

In the above examples, the first sentence uses the passive voice in the subjunctive mood, while the second sentence uses the active voice. Converting active sentences into passive sentences with the subjunctive mood accurately conveys the intention and is more easily acceptable, whereas active sentences may convey a sense of command.

3. The application of subjunctive mood in business negotiations

In international business negotiations, there are significant cultural, religious, and customary differences between different countries. To avoid misunderstanding during communication, the subjunctive mood is often employed. For example:

If you could make a concession, we would order more commodities. (如果贵方能做出让步,我方将会订更多的货物。)

In the above example, when one party cannot accept the conditions proposed by the other party due to various factors, a blunt and straightforward refusal can lead to a deadlock in negotiations and potentially jeopardize future cooperation. Using the subjunctive mood in a more tactful manner helps ease tension and facilitates smooth negotiations.

Business English, due to its practical nature, is widely used in business activities. The subjunctive mood, as an important rhetorical device, not only eases the atmosphere of conversation but also promotes pleasant and harmonious communication between individuals. In response to ever-changing market situations and consideration of the customs and habits of the other party's country, the use of the subjunctive mood allows for explicit and polite expressions while conveying the true intention. As users of Business English, it is important to recognize and analyze the polite expressions, understand their characteristics, and master their specific application in practice, which is of great practical significance in using Business English correctly in business activities.

Section 4

Translation of English Advertisement

The continuous development of economic globalization and market internationalization has made advertising ubiquitous and an important way for many businesses, enterprises, and consumers to learn about product information. To gain a foothold in fierce competition, it is necessary to fully demonstrate the advantages of products, and product. Advertising is the preferred choice for companies. Advertising designers need to mobilize all language resources to fully express the goals of the advertisements, enabling consumers and others to have a deep understanding of the products. Therefore, almost all rhetorical devices are used in English advertisements. Based on this, teachers should focus on updating educational concepts, improving teaching methods, and further enhancing college students' translation skills in English. This section takes the current situation of college English translation teaching practice as a starting point, explores the application of metaphorical rhetoric and its translation methods in English advertisements.

Ⅰ. Characteristics of English Advertisements

1. Vocabulary characteristics

English advertisements use a rich and vibrant vocabulary that is influential and strives for conciseness while still maintaining linguistic distinctiveness and individuality. Usually, English advertisements use precise words to convey product information, allowing readers to understand at a glance and leave a lasting impression. For example, "Just do it" and "Good to the last drop".

2. Grammatical characteristics

English advertisements demonstrate the use of various grammar features. Simple sentences are predominant, while compound sentences are less common. Imperative sentences are also frequently used, and sometimes ellipsis is employed to enhance the effectiveness of advertising. For example, the simple sentence: "Take time to indulge". The imperative sentence: "Obey your thirst". The ellipsis: "Always with you".

3. Rhetorical characteristics

The use of rhetorical devices enhances the creativity and impact of advertisements. As a promotional language, advertisements often employ a variety of rhetorical devices. In particular, the use of metaphorical techniques enhances the linguistic power of advertising, making the rhythm stronger, stimulating readers' imaginative thinking, emphasizing the content of the advertisements, and making them captivating. For example, "Ask for more!" and "Start ahead.".

Ⅱ. The Usage of Metaphor in English Advertisements

Metaphor is a figure of speech in which a word or phrase is used to compare two different things, such as "the curtain of night". The term "metaphor" contains the meaning of "across". Metaphors involve two elements: the metaphorical subject and the vehicle. Metaphor is a pragmatic phenomenon that can only be determined within a specific cultural context or linguistic context. Its basic usage involves using words or phrases that describe one thing to metaphorically represent another. English advertisements frequently employ various rhetorical devices to achieve the best advertising effects.

1. Analogizing personal attributes

Analogizing personal attributes involves connecting the relevant characteristics of one thing and making a comparison to highlight the superiority of a product. For example: "Toyota moves forward as your partner." This advertisement personifies Toyota products, metaphorically representing them as companions in our lives. "Toyota cars" are the subject, while "partner" is the vehicle. By comparing Toyota cars to companions, the advertisement demonstrates the significance of Toyota cars in our lives. It subtly uses metaphor to express the excellence and quality of Toyota products. Companions are an indispensable part of people's lives, and by using the attributes of companions to showcase the superiority of the product, the advertisement conveys to readers that when choosing a car, Toyota is the first choice. Another example is: "Breakfast without orange juice is like a day without sunshine. " In this advertisement, "orange juice" is the subject, and "a day without sunshine" is the vehicle. It metaphorically compares a breakfast without orange juice to a day without sunshine. The advertisement cleverly utilizes the rhetorical device of metaphor to emphasize the importance of orange juice in breakfast. Days with sunshine are universally liked and desired, and by using the concept of sunny days, the advertisement vividly portrays the importance of orange juice and guides readers to perceive it as an essential choice for breakfast.

2. Highlighting expertise and advantages

Highlighting the specific features or advantages of something to showcase the superiority of the advertised product is a common application of metaphor. For example, "Made in paradise" and "The taste of paradise". These two advertisements share a common characteristic: they employ the technique of value metaphor by associating the advertised product with something as valuable as "paradise". This effectively showcases the limitless value of the product. At the same time, by utilizing people's beliefs and knowledge about "paradise", the advertisements fully promote the product. The use of terms like "paradise" in the advertisements adds a concept of "prestige", aiming to elevate the status and value of the goods through metaphor, generating a favorable impression among readers and creating a desire and demand for the advertised product—truly reflecting its value.

III. Translation of Metaphors in English Advertisements

The translation of implicit metaphors in English advertisements greatly affects their effectiveness. The best translation method is to skillfully translate the implicit metaphors in English advertisements, bringing out the vivid and wonderful effects of the metaphors. Generally, there are three translation methods for implicit metaphors in

English advertisements: literal translation, liberal translation, and dynamic translation. The specific method to be used depends on the nature of the advertisement.

1. Literal translation

Literal translation is a widely used method in English advertisement translation. It treats sentences in English advertisements as basic units, translating them word by word while preserving the original sentence structure and rhetorical devices according to the context of the advertisement, thus reproducing the original content. Literal translation requires language that is plain and easy to understand, accurately conveying the meaning of the advertisement. For example: "Our eyebrow pencils are as soft as petals." The advertisement employs the rhetorical device of metaphor by comparing the product to soft petals. The metaphor is appropriate and subtle, making readers unconsciously develop a sense of tenderness and desire to purchase the product.

2. Liberal translation

The purpose of liberal translation is to make the translation more vivid and flavorful. When literal translation fails to capture the essence and flavor of the original advertisement or sounds awkward and difficult to understand, the translator needs to change the sentence structure or rhetorical devices, use words and phrases that are similar in meaning to the original ones, and reorganize and clarify the expression to convey the essence and spirit of the source text. For example: 城乡路万千，路路有航天。——航天汽车

The translation: East, west, Hangtian is the best.

In this example, "East, west, Hangtian is the best" is cited from an American norm "East or west, home is the best", and it is easy to remember. From the example we can see that the two sentences have got totally different structures. If we translate the advertising slogan directly, the translation version would be too long and we also have to further explain what is "路万千" and "路路". The receptors may still not fully understand the message behind it. However, the translation, which has nothing to do with the original one in terms of form, successfully conveys the idea of the original version: no matter where you go, Hangtian brand is the best car you have ever used.

From the example we can see that, we have to pay more attention on the content except for the form, only in this way can the successful translation version be fulfilled.

3. Dynamic translation

Dynamic translation is a method that combines literal and free translation, allowing the expression of the advertisement's essence to be vividly conveyed. In dynamic translation, the choice of translation method is based on sentences, words, and the context, while remaining faithful to the source text. The same word or phrase may have different meanings in different advertisements, so it may require literal translation, free translation, or dynamic translation. Therefore, translators need to apply the correct method to ensure the accuracy of the translation. For example: "... Blessed by year-round good weather, Spain is a magnet for sun worship and holiday makers..."(西班牙一年四季气候宜人,是太阳崇拜者和度假者向往的地方。) The translation of this advertisement uses a combination of literal and free translation. The implicit metaphor is transformed into an explicit metaphor, conveying the meaning of comparison and showcasing the beauty of Spain, thus attracting readers. By metaphorically comparing Spain to a magnet, it signifies the country's strong appeal and its ability to attract numerous tourists. Through reading this advertisement, people feel the desire to travel to Spain.

The translation of metaphors in advertisements emphasizes the art of language, the art of form, and the art of rhetoric, and through accurate translation, it expresses the implied meaning of the metaphors. The rhetoric and form in English advertisements not only depend on the remarkable effects of rhetorical devices but also on the accuracy of their translation. The use of metaphors as rhetorical devices, when done vividly and cleverly, can be memorable. Therefore, when translating English advertisements, translators need to fully understand the advertised products, choose appropriate translation methods based on this understanding, reproduce the linguistic characteristics of the original advertisements, and showcase the charm of the advertisements. In conclusion, teachers should focus on updating their educational perspectives, improving teaching methods, and further enhancing the English translation skills of college students.

Section 5

Translation of Chinese Cultural Classics

In this section, the translation of Chinese cultural classics will be mainly focused on. For the convenience of discussion, the term "Chinese cultural classics" in this section mainly refers to classic literary works. Chinese classic literary works encompass many works that possess profound cultural connotations and historical significance, such as poems in the Tang Dynasty, *The Dream of the Red Mansion*, etc. These works not only hold an important position in the history of Chinese literature but also reflect the life, customs, and values of ancient Chinese society. The translation of these classic works plays a significant role in promoting cultural exchange and understanding between China and the West.

I. Discussions on Literary Translation

Literary works are a kind of art created in language. What we demand of them is not merely the recording of concepts and incidents. Besides these, they should possess artistic images which are attractive to the readers. In other words, the reader must have a strong feeling towards the characters' thought and behaviour through the artistic images portrayed in the literary works. Literary translation is to reproduce the original artistic images in another language so that readers of the translation may be inspired, moved and aesthetically entertained in the same way as those who read the original. However, there are still some different views and discussions on whether literary works can be translated.

1. Translatability of literary works

It is universally acknowledged that every writer has a literary style and that his style is reflected in his writing. As everybody knows, both Li Bai (李白) and Du Fu (杜甫) were great poets of the Tang Dynasty in China, but their literary styles are different. Li's is elegant and forceful whereas Du's profound and thoughtful. It is required that the translator should realize the author's process of artistic creation, grasp the spirit of the original, find the most appropriate confirmation in his own thought, feeling and experience, and reproduce fully and correctly the content and form of the original in a literary language suited to the original style. The main task of literary translation lies in the faithful reproduction of the spirit and features of the original, such as creative artistic translation is quite necessary.

Therefore, many support the view that literary works are translatable. They argue that, although there may be some difficulties in the translation process, with appropriate translation techniques and methods, the core emotions and meanings of literary works can still be conveyed in other languages. They see translation as a way of cross-cultural communication that can promote understanding and communication between different cultures.

2. Untranslatability of literary works

However, there are still quite a few who believe that literary works are expressions of culture, with unique language, emotions, and artistic styles, making it a challenge to accurately reproduce them in other languages. This perspective suggests that elements such as the flavor, rhythm, and vocabulary choices in literary works are difficult to perfectly be conveyed in translation, thus they consider literary works cannot be fully translated. Besides they consider the original literary style untranslatable.

For example, when it comes to Tang poetry, a traditional form of Chinese literature, translation also presents challenges. Tang poetry conveys complex thoughts and emotions by using concise language, while also by incorporating cultural, historical, and societal backgrounds. When translating Tang poetry, translators not only need to understand the original meaning but also consider how to preserve the poetry's rhythm and beauty. Translators often strike a balance between literal and artistic translation, aiming to retain the original meaning while striving to give the poetry some artistic value in the target language.

In conclusion, while the translation of literary works faces challenges, with proper translation strategies and techniques, the core essence and emotions of literary works can still be conveyed to other languages and cultures.

Ⅱ. Principles of Literary Translation

(1) **Faithfulness**: Translators should understand that "faithfulness" is nuanced and not merely mechanical. They ought to consider the entire text, both the original and translated versions, and adeptly maintain fidelity to the essence of the source material without resorting to a rigid, formulaic approach.

(2) **Coherence**: In literary translation, a significant emphasis is placed on "coherence". When faced with a conflict between "faithfulness" and "coherence", priority is usually given to ensuring the text flows smoothly and cohesively.

(3) **Balancing "faithfulness" and "expressiveness"**: To navigate the tensions between "faithfulness" and "expressiveness", translators should consider three key factors. Firstly, they should take the purpose of the translated work and the target audience into consideration. Secondly, they should analyze the genre and unique characteristics of the source text. Lastly, they should take into account the broader context, encompassing the linguistic environment of both the source and translated texts. In essence, "faithfulness" in literary translation refers to honoring the spirit of the source material, while "expressiveness" involves capturing the intended impact of the translation.

(4) **Reproduction**: Literary translation is to reproduce the original artistic images in another language. A high degree of creativity is essential in the art of literary translation. Literary translators should possess a high level of reproduction.

(5) **Cultivating literary prowess**: Enhancing literary translation skills necessitates continual improvement in literary cultivation. This encompasses not only the mastery of vocabulary, sentence structure and expression but also the development of a distinct "literary temperament" and infusion of literary flair into the

translation. Therefore, translators should consistently strive to elevate their literary acumen.

III. Appreciation of Translated Literary Works

1. Appreciation of different translations of *The Dream of the Red Mansion*

The Dream of the Red Mansion is considered as one of the most outstanding works in Chinese classical literature. It has a history of over two hundred years, during which it has been translated into foreign languages several times. Currently, there are multiple foreign language versions and abridged versions, among which two translations have had significant influence. One is *The Dream of the Red Mansion* translated by Yang Xianyi and his wife Gladys Yang (referred to as the Yang's version), and the other is *The Story of the Stone* co-translated by David Hawkes and John Minford (referred to as the Hawkes' version). Translating a monumental masterpiece like *The Dream of the Red Mansion*, which represents Chinese culture, into English faces numerous difficulties, particularly in terms of cultural nuances. As linguist and translation theorist Eugene Nida pointed out, "If two cultures are closely related but their languages differ greatly, the translator should engage in significant formal transformations in the translation. In such cases, a similar culture can often provide a series of corresponding expressions in terms of content. Compared to situations where both language and culture differ, the translation difficulties are correspondingly much more. In fact, cultural differences present much more complex issues for translators than language differences" (Nida, 1964). Given the challenges brought about by cultural aspects, both Chinese and Western translation theorists have attempted to propose theoretical guiding principles. In China, translation practitioners have always adhered to three principles by Yan Fu, namely, "faithfulness, expressiveness and elegance". In the West, the main guiding principles include Nida's "Theory of Equivalence Translation", as well as Peter Newmark's theories of "communicative translation" and "semantic translation". In fact, these translation theories share theoretical consistency—all of them recognize that "faithfulness" as the primary principle is correct, as it is determined by the essence of translation. "Faithfulness" is the foundation followed by expressiveness, ensuring that the translated text fulfills the same functions as the source text, that is, to convey the same meaning to the readers of the translated text as the readers of the source text. Finally, based on "faithfulness" and "expressiveness", full considerations should be given to the acceptability of the translated text to its readers. In Newmark's words, this is "communicative translation", and in Yan Fu's words, it is "elegance".

The following will provide a comparative analysis of the principles adopted by the two translations of *The Dream of the Red Mansion* in terms of conveying different cultural background information.

Chapter three of *The Dream of the Red Mansion* describes the scene where Lin Daiyu enters the Rongguo Mansion and is adopted by Grandmother Jia. Although it is not lengthy, this chapter covers a wide range of cultural aspects, including titles, religion, customs, architecture, utensils, clothing, arts, poetry and so on. These cultural elements often carry a strong "ethnic flavor". Therefore, "faithfulness" becomes crucial here, meaning that the translator should "convey the accurate meaning of the source text as much as possible" in the translation, aiming to reproduce the charm of the original work and display the cultural characteristics in the source text. For example:

a. ……"况且这通身的气派，竟不像老祖宗的外孙女，竟是个嫡亲的孙女，怨不得老祖宗天天口头心头一时不忘"……

Yang's version: "Her whole air is so distinguished! She doesn't take after her father, son-in-law of our Old Ancestress, but looks more like a Chia. No wonder our Old Ancestress couldn't put you out of her mind and was forever talking or thinking about you."

Hawkes' version: "And everything about her so distingue! She doesn't take after your side of the family, Grannie. She's more like Jia."

In novels, specific words like titles and appellations often carry rich connotations and cultural significance. It is challenging to translate them into English with precise and comprehensive meanings. In Hawkes' version, "Grannie" is used as a reference, which can be considered equivalent in terms of addressing someone elderly. However, there is a significant difference in connotation between the source text and

Chapter 4　Practical Application of English Translation

the translation. In the source text, Wang Xifeng refers to Grandmother Jia as "老祖宗"(Old Ancestress) to both show respect and emphasize her high status in the Jia family. Therefore, "老祖宗"(Old Ancestress) does not simply mean "grandmother" in the general sense but carries a specific meaning. In this regard, Hawkes' translation of "老祖宗"(Old Ancestress) as "Grannie" does not fully capture the connotations of the source text. On the other hand, Yang translates "老祖宗" literally as "Old Ancestress", which not only conveys the meaning of respect and authority that Grandmother Lady Dowager holds in the Jia family but also preserves the cultural significance of the source text. It can be considered a more faithful rendition.

b. 贾母正面榻上独坐，两边四张空椅，熙凤忙拉了黛玉在左边第一张椅子上坐了，黛玉十分推让。

> Yangs' version: The Lady Dowager was seated alone on a couch at the head of the table with two empty chairs on each side, Hsi-feng took Tai-yu by the hand to make her sit in the first place on the left, but she persistently declined the honour.
>
> Hawkes' version: The table at which Grandmother Jia presided, seated alone on a coach, had two empty chairs on either side, Xi-feng tried to seat Dai-yu in the one on the left nearer to her grandmother—an honour which she strenuously resisted.

Both translations can be considered to accurately convey the information of the source text. Upon careful comparison, Yang's translation can be seen as aiming for absolute faithfulness to the source work, even to the point of achieving a word-for-word equivalent translation. While this approach is faithful, it may not read idiomatically in English. "Faithfulness" is, of course, a crucial aspect of translation and holds great importance. However, if a translator is overly focused on semantic translation, tightly adhering to the source text and prioritizing absolute faithfulness, it may actually hinder the achievement of a faithful translation. On the other hand, Hawkes' translation spontaneously provides words without extensive crafting and cleverly enables readers to grasp the customs and etiquette of feudal society in China. It is a faithful and communicative translation.

Translation is more than simply transferring words from one language to another;

it is an aesthetic endeavor that requires the translator to transform the source text into a translated version while considering their own aesthetic experience. It also involves a transformation of ways of thinking. This transformation goes beyond a simple word-for-word correspondence, emphasizing the use of our own ways of thinking to convey the essence of the source text. At the same time, efforts are made to stay consistent with the source text in style to ensure that the conveyed information is in line with the original one. The ultimate goal is to accurately reproduce the aesthetic experience conveyed by the source text. Additionally, the translator strives to maintain consistency in style with the source text, aiming to accurately reproduce its aesthetic experience.

The Dream of the Red Mansion is widely regarded as a representative novel that provides readers with an aesthetic experience. Its literary language is intricate and refined, showcasing the pinnacle of ancient Chinese fictional art. However, when translating such a work, it is particularly challenging to preserve its unique language style. Nonetheless, both translations mentioned earlier demonstrate the translators' profound artistic understanding and cultivation by successfully maintaining stylistic equivalence.

Fuzziness is an inherent aspect of human language. Nevertheless, the degree of fuzziness varies across languages due to differences in cultural backgrounds, social life, and customs. However, these differences do not impede translation between different languages. Let's take the following sentences as an example.

c. 两弯似蹙非蹙罥烟眉，一双似喜非喜含情目。态生两靥之愁，娇袭一身之病。泪光点点，娇喘微微。闲静时如姣花照水，行动处似弱柳扶风。心较比干多一窍，病如西子胜三分。

Yang's version: Her dusky arched eyebrows ere knitted and yer not frowning, her speaking eyes held both merriment and sorrow; her very frailty had charm. Her eyes sparkled with tears, her breath was soft and faint. In response she was like a lovely flower mirrored in the water; in motion, a pliant willow swaying in the wind. She looked more sensitive than Pikan [1], more delicate than Hsi Shih [2].

1. A prince noted for his great intelligence at the end of the Shang Dynasty.

2. A famous beauty of the ancient kingdom of Yueh.

Hawkes' version: Her mist-wreathed brows at the first seemed to frown, yet were not frowning;

Her passionate eyes at first seemed to smile, yer were not merry;

Habit had given a melancholy cast to her tender face;

Nature had bestowed a sickly constitution on her delicate frame.

Often the eyes swam with glistening tears;

Often the breath came in gentle gasps;

In stillness she made one think of a graceful flower reflected in the water;

In motion she called to mind tender willow shoots caressed by the wind,

She had more chambers in her heart than the martyred Bi Gan;

And suffered a tithe more pain in it than the beautiful Xi shi.

This passage depicts the ethereal beauty and melancholic nature of Lin Daiyu when she is first encountered by Jia Baoyu. It makes use of a variety of poetic descriptions, such as "罥烟眉"(eyebrows like wisps of smoke), "含情目"(eyes filled with tenderness), "两靥之愁"(cheeks marked by sorrow), "一身之病" (fragile and delicate physique), "泪光点点"(teardrops shimmering), "娇喘微微" (gentle sighs), "姣花照水"(flowers mirroring upon the water), "弱柳扶风" (willow branches swaying in the breeze) and so on. Moreover, it incorporates several hedges like "seems" "not" "like", etc. Hawkes' translation delves into the profound significance of the original text and employs language that captures the elusive beauty in a more idiomatic English manner. In Hawkes translation, the following words each have their corresponding translations: "似蹙非蹙" —at the first seemed to frown, yet were not frowning; "似喜非喜" —at first seemed to smile, yet were not merry; "罥烟眉" —her mist-wreathed brows; "含情目" —her passionate eyes; "两靥之愁" —a melancholy cast to her tender face; "一身之病" —a sickly constitution on her delicate frame; "泪光点点"—often the eyes swam with glistening tears; "娇喘微微"—often the breath came in gentle gasps. In this way, the language style corresponds to the original text style. Besides, when translating "闲静时如姣花照水, 行动处似弱柳扶风", Hawkes translated it as "she made one think of a graceful flower reflected in the water; she called to mind tender willow shoots caressed by the wind", evoking the readers' imagination of the beauty of Daiyu, which is both vivid and poetic. On the contrary, the English translation by Yang is inferior in terms of language. For example, "罥烟眉" and "含情目" are respectively translated as "her dusky arched eyebrows" and "her speaking eyes", while "态生两靥之愁, 娇袭一身之病" is translated as "her very frailty had charm". Yang translation uses plain language that doesn't quite align with the source text, thereby missing out on the poetic and visual beauty it carries.

2. Appreciation of translated Chinese poems

Concerning the problem of translating poems, "Absolute equivalence in translation is never possible. But effective translating can be accomplished". Poems call for the beauty in form, sound and meaning. Since the main task of poetry translation lies in the faithful reproduction of the spirit and features of the original, such creative artistic translation is quite necessary. Thus, a translator of poems should not be satisfied with the mere conveying of the ideas in the original, but must strive for the reproduction of the original beauty. For examples:

静 夜 思

［唐］李白

床前明月光,
疑是地上霜。
举头望明月,
低头思故乡。

NIGHT THOUGHTS

Li Bai

I wake, and moonbeams play around my bed,

Glittering like hoar-frost to my wandering eyes;

Up towards the glorious moon I raised my head,

Then lay me down and thoughts of home arise.

tr. by Herbert A. Giles

IN THE QUIET NIGHT

Li Bai

So bright a gleam on the foot my bed——

Could there have been a frost already?

Lifting myself to look, I found that it was moonlight,

Sinking back again, I thought suddenly of home.

tr. by Witter Bynner

STILL NIGHT'S MUSE

Li Bai

Afront the bed the Luna beams bright,

Wearing a look of seemingly rime white.

Eyes upcast toward the Luna,

Eyes downcast, engenders my nostalgia.

tr. by Huang Long

Compared with the translations by Giles and Bynner, Huang Long's translation obviously excels in terms of structure, melody, and word choice. The original poem consists of four lines with five syllables each, totaling 20 syllables. Giles' translation has four lines with 10, 12, 11 and 10 syllables, totaling 43 syllables; Bynner's translation has four lines with 10, 9, 13 and 12 syllables, totaling up to 44 syllables. In contrast, Huang Long's translation has 37 syllables in four lines, making it closer to the source text. On the other hand, Huang Long's translation effectively handles the issue of rhyme, such as "bright" with "white", "eyes upcast" with "eyes downcast", which achieves the same effect as the source text. More importantly, Huang Long's choice of words maintains the formality and literary style of the source text, such as "luna" "rime" and "nostalgia", which are all formal literary or poetic terms; while Giles and Bynner opts for common words like "moon" "frost" and "thought of home". As a result, Huang Long's translation appears more elegant, with a more classical style and a stronger flavor of ancient poetry, whereas Giles and Bynner's translations seem plain in comparison. This difference is closely related to the choice of words and their level of formality.

From the above examples, it can be seen that the translation of Chinese classical poetry has strict requirements for word choice, namely, accurate semantics, appropriate language style, harmonious sound and rhyme. Only when these three aspects are achieved can it be considered the best choice of words. However, most translators often neglect certain aspects when choosing words. If two of the aspects mentioned above mentioned above can be considered, it is already commendable, and it is extremely rare to achieve all three. Huang Long's translation pays great attention to the careful consideration and understanding of word choice, demonstrating exceptional craftsmanship and achieving results that are almost identical to the source text. For example:

回乡偶书

贺知章

少小离家老大回,

乡音无改鬓毛衰;

儿童相见不相识,

笑问"客从何处来?"

COMING HOME
He Zhizhang

I left home young. I return old,
Speaking as then, but with hair grown thin;
And my children, meeting, do not know me.
They smile and say: "Stranger, where do you come from?"

tr. by Witter Bynner

Lv Shuxiang points out: "Whether the Chinese characters '儿童' refer to the children in the family or those in the village, it seems that 'the children' may be used in either case. Besides this, the translation tallies with the original and reads like a very fine poem."

Lv speaks highly of the translation of this poem in the form of free verse. His comments are objective and just for the following reasons.

(1) The translation in the main retains the beauty in meaning.

(2) It also consists of four lines which are even as a whole judged from the number of accented syllables, which shows that the translation has taken the beauty in form into consideration.

(3) It has a fluent natural rhythm, reads smoothly and sounds pleasant to the ear, which means that it is full of beauty in sound.

Riming, of course, is an essential element of the beauty in sound in a rhymed poem but the natural rhythm a constituent too. And what's more, the simple and plain style of the original has got reproduced in the translation.

Ⅳ. Strategies to Deal with Fuzziness in Literary Works

Literary works, especially poetry and fiction indeed hold pivotal positions in Chinese culture, bearing not only a wealth of historical and cultural information but also reflecting the unique aesthetic emotions and artistic styles of the authors. During the creation of literary works, the authors often employ fuzzy languages, so fuzziness is frequently discovered in literary works. It is fuzziness that brings a unique artistic charm and fuzzy beauty to literary works. Fuzziness, as an inherent feature of natural language, runs through the whole process of human being's cognition. Fuzziness mainly stems from linguistic fuzziness; however, linguistic mainly lies in the semantic level. Therefore, when doing translation, translators are supposed to take semantic fuzziness seriously. In the semantic level, translators need to change the linguistic form to translate fuzzy terms. That is to say, fuzzy terms can be changed into precise terms and vice versa. But whether these terms are seemingly fuzzy or precise, they must equally contain fuzzy senses. Therefore, the translators need to deal with fuzziness both in Chinese and English literary works translation. Here are three techniques to deal with fuzziness while doing translations.

1. Translation from fuzziness to fuzziness

This technique is to render fuzzy terms in the source language into fuzzy terms in the target language. It works in the cases when the translator can find an equivalent in the target language of the word in the source language. Although there are differences between English and Chinese, there are still some same or similar expressions by coincidence as are usually vivid and easy to comprehend. The similarities between the two languages make it possible to employ this convenient and useful approach This technique provides a plain and familiar translation for Chinese readers. As a widely used technique, it is popular with translators in that it achieves equivalence both in content and form to the largest extent. However, due to the difference of languages and cultures, translators still come across two different translation circumstances when using this technique.

(1) The first way is to translate fuzzy terms in source language into its direct equivalents in the target language. This way can be used only when there are same expressions both in English and Chinese. Examples are as follows.

a. The old man was thin and gaunt with deep wrinkles in the back of his neck. (E. Hemingway, *The Old Man and the Sea*)

老头后颈上凝聚着很深的皱纹，显得又瘦又憔悴。

In this sentence, there are three fuzzy words, namely, "thin" "gaunt" and "deep", they are translated into their fuzzy equivalents "瘦" "憔悴" and "深".

b. 这是未庄赛神的晚上。这晚上照例有一台戏，戏台左近，也照例有许多的赌摊。做戏的锣鼓，在阿Q耳朵里仿佛在十里之外。（鲁迅《阿Q正传》）

On that particular evening, Weizhuang was holding festivals in honour of its gods and, as the custom, a dramatic performance was being offered. Near the stage were the customary and numerous gambling tables. The racket of the gongs of the play seemed to be ten Chinese miles away from Ah Q's ears.

There are several fuzzy words in the source text, such as "晚上" "近" "许多", etc. It is quite proper for the translator to render them as evening, near, and numerous, which are also fuzzy words.

c. 曲曲折折的荷塘上面，弥望的是田田的叶子。叶子出水很高，像亭亭的舞女的裙。层层的叶子中间，零星地点缀着些白花，有袅娜地开着的，有羞涩地打着朵儿的；正如一粒粒的明珠，又如碧天里的星星，又如刚出浴的美人。微风过处，送来缕缕清香，仿佛远处高楼上渺茫的歌声似的。（朱自清《荷塘月色》）

All over this winding stretch of water, what meets the eye is a silken field of leaves, reaching rather high above the surface, like the skirts of dancing girls in all their grace. Here and there, layers of leaves are dotted with white lotus blossoms, some in demure bloom, others in shy bud, like scattering pearls, or twinkling stars, or beauties just out of the bath. A breeze stirs, sending over breaths of fragrance, like faint singing drifting from a distant building.

In the source text, there are many fuzzy words, such as "高" and "美人" etc. They are translated into their fuzzy equivalents which are faithful to the source text.

d. 两岸的豆麦和河底的水草所发散出来的清香，夹杂在水气中扑面的吹来；月色便朦胧在这水气里。淡黑的起伏的连山，仿佛是踊跃的铁的兽脊似的，都远远地向船尾跑去了，但我却还以为船慢。他们换了四回手，渐望见依稀的赵庄，而且似乎听到歌吹了，还有几点火，料想便是戏台，但或者也许是渔火。

那声音大概是横笛，宛转，悠扬，使我的心也沉静，然而又自失起来，觉得要和他弥散在含着豆麦蕴藻之香的夜气里。（鲁迅《社戏》）

The scent of beans, wheat and water-weeds wafted towards us through the mist, and the moonlight shone faintly through it. Distant grey hills, undulating like the backs of some leaping iron beasts, seemed to be racing past the stern of our boat; but I still felt our progress was slow. When the oarsmen had changed shifts four times, we began to make out the faint outline of Chaochuang and to catch the sound of singing and music. There were several lights too, which we guessed must be on the stage unless they were fishermen's lights.

The music was probably fluting. Eddying round and round and up and down, it soothed me and set me dreaming at the same time, till I felt as though I was about to drift far away with it through the night air heavy with the scent of beans, wheat and river-weeds.

Since the author was sitting on the boat, and the background is the night, it is obvious that he couldn't completely see the things on each bank clearly. Thus, the author employed a series of fuzzy words, and which can be found their equivalents in English.

e. 庭院深深深几许,

杨柳堆烟,

帘幕无重数。(欧阳修《蝶恋花·庭院深深深几许》)

Deep, deep the courtyard where he is, so deep,

It's veiled by smokelike willows heap on heap,

By curtain on curtain and screen on screen. (许渊冲, 1990: 62)

f. 花明月暗笼轻雾, 今宵好向郎边去。(李煜《菩萨蛮·花明月暗笼轻雾》)

Bright flowers bathed in thin mist and dim moonlight,

'Tis best time to steal out to see my love tonight. (许渊冲, 1990: 78)

g. 深院静, 小庭空。(李煜《捣练子令·深院静》)

Deep garden still,

Small courtyard void. (许渊冲, 1990: 96)

h. 宝髻松松挽就, 铅华淡淡妆成。(司马光《西江月·宝髻松松挽就》)

Loosely she has done up her hair;

Thinly she has powered her face. (许渊冲, 1990: 154)

(2) In most cases, the fuzzy terms in the source language cannot be directly turned into their equivalents. That is to say, they should be changed into another fuzzy terms, but they are not equivalent in the literal meaning. In different contexts, the translator should choose different words, which would be more appropriate and accurate in that a rigid equivalent would violate the faithfulness to the original meaning. Whether a word is well chosen affects greatly the accuracy of expression. However, to have a proper choice of a word is easier said than done. Let's take the word "good" as an example. In most cases, "good" will be interpreted into other fuzzy words in Chinese.

In W. Thackery's *Vanity Fair*, there exists one sentence with "good", but they are rendered differently into Chinese. The sentence follows like this:

a. ... Yet, as it sometimes happens that a person departs his life, who is really deserving of the praises the stone-cutter carves over his bones, who is a good Christian, a good parent, child, wife or husband; who actually does have a disconsolate family to morn his loss.

不过,我们偶然也有几个死人当得起石匠刻在他们朽骨上的好话。真的是虔诚的教徒、慈爱的父母、孝顺的儿女、贤良的妻子、尽职的丈夫,他们家里的人也的确哀思绵绵地追悼他们。

Suppose the fuzzy word "good" is rendered as "好" in Chinese, then the version might be like this:真的是好教徒、好父母、好子女、好妻子、好丈夫。If so, the version would be dull without any literary quality. In this sentence, "good" is respectively translated into "虔诚的""慈爱的""尽职的""孝顺的" and "贤良的", by which the advantage of receptor language has been brought into full play and unnecessary repetition is avoided. This turns out to be the most effective way in translating such kind of words, especially when used repeatedly in the same text. Furthermore, as Feng Qinghua once pointed out that, as for what is "好教徒、好父母、好子女、好妻子、好丈夫", different people may have different judgments, therefore, they would have different understandings and expressions of "好" in the above-mentioned five phrases.

b. 中国的男人,本来大半都可以做圣贤,可惜全被女人毁掉了。……秦……虽然史无明文,我们也假定他因为女人,大约未必十分错;而董卓可是的确给貂蝉害死了。(鲁迅《阿Q正传》)

Of the males of the species in China, more than half are capable of becoming saints and men of virtue, but it is regrettable that they are ruined by women, ... as for Qin – although history does not state clearly why it fell, if we assume that its downfall was due to a woman, we may not be far from the truth; but Dong Zhuo's death was surely brought about by Diao Chan.

In the source text, there are three hedges in the sentence "大约未必十分错", the translator rendered it as "we may not be far from the truth". Obviously, "大约" is not translated, and "未必" and "十分" only find their fuzzy equivalents in the source text.

In other words, a word in Chinese has a lot of equivalent synonyms in English under different circumstances, there would be different translations. "千" and "万" in Chinese idioms or sentences has always been used to convey fuzzy information of quantity. We can find many in Tang Poetry and Song Ci (a kind of literary style, which was popular in Song Dynasty in China). However, there's no exact equivalents of these words in English. Therefore, there are various ways to reproduce "千" and "万". Although these translations vary, they all convey fuzzy meanings of "千" and "万". Thus, this technique makes it possible to translate poems for it provides a great many lively and appropriate translations. The examples are as follows.

a. 此地一为别，孤蓬万里征。(李白《送友人》)

Here we must make separation,

And go out through a thousand miles of dead grass. (Ezra Pound)

b. 天台四万八千丈，对此欲倒东南倾。(李白《梦游天姥吟留别》)

While Sky-Terrace, four hundred and eighty thousand feet high,

Staggers southeastward before it. (阿成，杨宪益等. 2001：57—63)

c. 梅落繁枝千万片，犹自多情，学雪随风转。(冯延巳《鹊踏枝·梅落繁枝千万片》)

Thousands of petals fall from the mume trees

Reluctantly and whirl like snow in the breeze. (许渊冲，1990：56)

d. 念去去，千里烟波，暮霭沉沉楚天阔。(柳永《雨霖铃·寒蝉凄切》)

On miles and miles of misty waves where sail the ships,

And evening clouds hang low in boundless Southern skies. (许渊冲，1990：104—105)

e. 黄河远上白云间，一片孤城万仞山。(王之涣《凉州词》)

The Yellow River reaches high beyond the clouds;

Amid the massive mountains lies the solitary silver of a town.

(张庭琛，2006：112—113)

f. 欲穷千里目，更上一层楼。(王之涣《登鹳雀楼》)

You can enjoy a grander sight

By climbing to a greater height. (张庭琛，2006：114)

g. 千山鸟飞绝，万径人踪灭。(柳宗元《江雪》)

A hundred mountains and no birds,

A thousand paths without a foot print.(黄国文,2006:212)

In this version, it uses figures to translate the figures "千" and "万", however, "千" and "万" are reduced into "a hundred" and "a thousand". And in the example a, b and c, "万" also finds another versions in the form of figures, that is "a thousand", "four hundred and eighty thousand" and "thousands of". In other examples, other fuzzy words are employed to translate "千" and "万" in different collocations. In example d and f, "千里" refers to a long distance.

Besides, some colour words cannot find their exact equivalents in the target text. The reasons are: First, different languages have quite different words for expressing colours and each language has a unique segmentation of the spectrum. Second, different languages have different colour words, which are not always equivalent to each other. Third, in different languages, the words expressing different hues of the same colour may vary. Fourth, when facing the same colour the same person may use different words to express it in different situations, and people speaking different languages may use different colour words. Therefore, in translation, we should also note that different languages have different words for colours, and those words do not always correspond to each other. For example, when we look at the word "blue" in English, we think of "蓝色" in Chinese. But when "blue" is used to refer to someone's face, we would change it a little bit. Sometimes, we even choose to use another colour according to people's habits of the target text. Thus, when translating this sentence "His face turned blue with fear", we cannot say "他的脸吓得发蓝了". Instead, we use "发青""发灰" or "发紫" according to the idiomatic expressions in Chinese. More typical examples appear when we turn "green with envy" from English into Chinese, in which we do not say "眼绿", but "眼红". Similarly, in Chinese we have "红茶" instead of "黑茶" for English "black tea". In *The Dream of the Red Mansion*, there's a passage describing the display of the room, in which there are several color words.

The passage goes like this:

原来王夫人时常居坐宴息,亦不在这正室,只在这正室东边的三间耳房内,于是老嬷嬷引黛玉进东房门来。临窗大炕上铺着猩红洋罽,正面设着大红金钱蟒靠背，石青金钱蟒引枕，秋香色金钱蟒大条褥。两边设一对梅花式洋漆小几。左边几上文王鼎匙箸香盒；右边几上汝窑美人觚，觚内插着时鲜花卉，并茗碗痰盒等物。地下面西一溜四张椅上，都搭着银红撒花椅搭，底下四副脚踏。椅之两边，也有一对高几，几上茗碗瓶花具备。其余陈设，自不必细说。（曹雪芹，高鹗《红楼梦》第三回）

Yang's version: Since Lady Wang seldom sat in this main hall but used three rooms in the east side for relaxation, the nurse led Daiyu there. The large kang by the window was covered with a scarlet foreign rug. In the middle were red back-rests and turquoise bolsters, both with dragon-design medallions, and a long greenish yellow mattress also with dragon medallions. At each side stood a low table of foreign lacquer in the shape of plum-blossom. On the left-hand table were a tripod, spoons, chopsticks and an incense container, on the right one, a slender-waisted porcelain vase from the Ruzhou Kiln containing flowers then in season, as well as tea-bowls and a spittoon. Below the kang facing the west wall were four armchairs, their covers of bright red dotted with pink flowers, and with four footstools beneath them. On either side were two tables set out with teacups and vases of flowers. The rest of the room need not be described in detail.

In a word, this technique is practical and mostly preferred in the case of fuzzy word translation since it might achieve equivalence both in meaning and form. In the process of translation, after a thorough analysis of the original syntax and the general idea of the source text, choice of words becomes the determining factor in a good translation, for an adequate translation is based on weighing words carefully and polishing sentences meticulously. Thus a translator needs to make his or her version be in harmony with the original in diction in choice of words so as to achieve equivalence both in form and meaning.

2. Translation from fuzziness to precision

This technique means to render fuzzy terms in source language into precise ones in the target language. When doing translations, the translators cannot avoid coming across some fuzzy and abstract words. Although the translators can easily understand the meanings conveyed by these abstract words, they cannot find an equivalent in the target language. In order to keep the translated versions smooth and faithful to the context, translators tend to substitute the abstract and fuzzy words, that is to say, to make abstract concrete and to make fuzzy precise. Take the following sentence as an example:

There is more to their life than political and social and economic problems, more than transient everydayness.

他们的生活远不止那些政治的、社会的和经济的问题,远不止一时的柴米油盐的问题。

In Chinese, there's no equivalent of the fuzzy and abstract word "everydayness". In order to convey the pragmatic meaning and reproduce informative function of the original text, the translator adopts the technique of translating fuzziness into precision. The word "everydayness" makes people think of its associative meaning, namely, the daily necessities of life. To render "everydayness" into "柴米油盐" conforms to Chinese people's thinking mode. We Chinese are good at thinking in images and tend to use seemingly specific expressions to convey fuzzy senses. Thus, it might be much better to specify the word and use a plain and precise word to substitute the fuzzy word.

Here are some other examples.

a. 王夫人道:"……没有对证,赵姨娘那里肯认账。事情又大,闹出来,外面也不雅,等他自作自受,少不得要自己败露的。"(曹雪芹,高鹗《红楼梦》第八十一回)

Yang's version:... observed lady Wang:"... But without her evidence, how are we to get Concubine Zhao to confess? And if such a scandal got out, our reputation would suffer. We'd better give her rope to hang herself—she's bound to give herself away one of these days."

b. 然而竟未发现对方在钩心斗角的同时,还做了不少幕后工作。(罗广斌,杨益言《红岩》第六章)

While each had been trying to put spokes in the other's wheels, he had failed to discover that Li Jigang had surreptitiously done a good deal of work.

c. 还有点美中不足的地方,早晨给车夫们摆饭的时节,祥子几乎和人打起来。(老舍《骆驼祥子》第十四回)

Another fly in the ointment was that Xiangzi has nearly got into a fight that morning when the rickshaw pullers were having their feast.

Though these vivid and concrete translations differ from the form of the original fuzziness, they reproduce the original meaning vividly and appropriately.

3. Translation from precision to fuzziness

Sometimes translators should make use of fuzzy terms to translate precise terms. Precise terms in one language are usually superficially specific while containing fuzzy senses. So translators are supposed to delve into their semantic appearance and dig out the deep connotation in the first place. Thus, context should be taken into consideration.

Some examples are in the following:

a. She loved him too well not to detect from the deepened line between his eyes and a score of minute signs that he had received an unexpected blow. (A. Cronin *The Citadel*)

她深深爱着他，能轻易地从眉宇间那变深的纹路和许多别的琐细形迹上瞧出来，丈夫受到了一个意外的打击。

According to the literal meaning, "a score of" means "二十来种" in Chinese. However, "a score of" is a fixed expression in English, meaning "a lot of". Thus, if we render it into "二十来种", seemingly precise, is not proper. So the fuzzy term "许多" is employed and thus quite well expresses the meaning. Therefore, when determining the meaning of the words, the translator needs to consider the words used with the key words he or she is to focus on. That is, the translator needs to take the direct language context into consideration.

b. ... She too was a determined woman in her different way, and she measured Madam Defarge with her eyes, every inch.

她也是一个很有决断，个性鲜明的女人。这时，她张大眼睛，把达伐奇太太从上到下，仔仔细细地打量了一番。

In English, "inch" refers to the measure of length equal to 2.54cm or one twelfth of a foot, it means "英寸" in Chinese. In Chinese, however, we do not have such kind of measurement and "every inch" is a fixed expression, meaning entirely or completely. Thus, it cannot be translated into "每一英寸". Thus, in determining the meaning of words or idioms, the translator must not only look at the syntagmatic contexts but also the cultural contexts, for "the cultural contexts of words" are the keys to understanding the meaning of texts.

As for translating Chinese into English, there also exists such kind of phenomenon. For example:

c. 欲别牵郎衣,

郎今到何处?

不恨归来迟,

莫向临邛去。(孟郊《古别离》)

You wish to go, and get your robe I hold,

"Where are you going—tell me, dear—today?

Your late returning does not anger me,

But that another steals your heart away."

This is a poem depicting the departing scene of a pair of lover. It describes the girl's psychology vividly. While translating this poem, the greatest difficulty lies in the understanding and expressing of the last line. "莫向临邛去" stems from an allusion. It is said that Sima Xiangru fell in love with Zhuo Wenjun when he was traveling in Linlai County, a county of southwestern Sichuan Province of China, which was called Linqiong (临邛) in Han Dynasty. Thus, "临邛" here doesn't refer to the place, but to find a new lover. Even in China, many readers are unfamiliar with the allusion, not to mention the foreign readers, thus it is the "kernel" in the course of translation. Just as Nida pointed out that a dynamic translation must fit the receptor language and culture in order to make the translated message intelligible and natural to the target language receptors, who are unaccustomed to the source language and culture. Therefore, the translator render it into "that another steals your heart away". Not only does it convey the fuzzy meaning of the source text, but also conforms to the English reader's language habits. Therefore, in the process of translation, cultural context should be taken into consideration as well, for we need to consider the cultural factors when deciding the meaning of the words.

For example, "友谊" in Chinese usually means friendship between friends, however, in the following sentence, it means differently. "他一气之下,看破红尘, 遁入深山,索性在一个小庙里削了发,不多久,有人说他和山麓的尼姑发生

了友谊，沸沸扬扬，流言蜚语，愈传愈盛。"As we know, in the feudal days, a man should not touch the hand of a woman in giving or accepting anything, let alone build up "友谊" between a monk and a nun. In this specific context, the meaning of "友谊" thus turns naturally into flirtation or flirtatious behaviour (or flirting with each other) between the monk and the nun as it is conditioned by the direct context.

Other examples are as follows:

d. "怕嚷啊，当初别贪便宜呀！你是了味啦，叫我一个人背黑锅，……"（老舍《骆驼祥子》）

"If you are afraid of my making a noise you shouldn't have put one over on me in the first place! You got what you wanted and now you expect me to take the consequences all on my own..."

"背黑锅" is an idiom in Chinese, meaning "take the consequence" in English. The writer merges the colloquial vernacularism naturally into the context so as to reinforce the expressiveness of utterances. In translation, we should dig out the connotation of the idiom"背黑锅", and reproduce its meaning. Although the local color in the original, of course, largely lost, it apparently retains in the translation most of what is in the source text and meanwhile presents no difficulty in understanding the translation. Since "背黑锅" bears the cultural color in the original, the cultural color should be retained or revealed as much as possible in the target language. In Chinese we have many such kind of idioms, hence, as a literary translator, in the course of translation, he should have put the term in specific social and cultural set.

The three techniques discussed here just offer a reference to translators. No matter which technique is employed, the final goal is to achieve equivalence as closely and naturally as possible.

Section 6

Translation of Chinese Political Documents

This chapter focuses on the basic principles of translating Chinese political documents, systematically analyzes different translation strategies for Chinese political documents, and emphasizes the flexible application of diverse translation strategies while faithfully conveying the original semantic content.

Ⅰ. Basic Translating Philosophy and Principles

When translating Chinese political documents, it should be based on the fundamental purpose of conveying information from Chinese to English, emphasizing cross-cultural communication awareness and adhering to the principles of faithfulness to the source text and readers' acceptance.

1. Cross-cultural communication awareness

Cross-cultural communication generally refers to the process of communication and interaction between people with different cultural backgrounds in specific contexts. The specific process and actual effects of cross-cultural communication are influenced by various factors such as culture, language, society, and psychology. It is a dynamic process of mutual contact, understanding, and gradual integration among all parties involved in the communication. In order to achieve successful cross-cultural communication, we should uphold the cultural view of civilization exchange, possess rich cross-cultural knowledge, and have proficient language communication skills.

As a cross-linguistic and cross-cultural information exchange activity, translation is a typical cross-cultural communication behavior. Therefore, effective translation communication depends on the mutual understanding and respect between the involved parties, so as to ensure that the connotations and characteristics of the source text are fully understood or accepted by the readers of the translated text. Cultural confidence is a fundamental requirement for the dissemination of Chinese culture in the new era. It emphasizes adhering to the Chinese cultural standpoint, fully respecting, inheriting, and promoting Chinese excellent traditional culture, advocating the learning and rational reference of outstanding foreign cultures, keeping pace with the times, grasping the direction of cultural development, and demonstrating the style and demeanor of Chinese culture. In short, introducing China to the world truthfully and comprehensively, assisting the global dissemination of Chinese culture and discourse, strengthening international communication capabilities, and enhancing China's cultural soft power are the cross-cultural communication concepts that Chinese translation should adhere to.

2. Accuracy and faithfulness

Chinese political documents is the official authoritative documents of Communist Party of China and Chinese government, which reflects the country's major political principles and serves as an important platform for China's international communication and a key carrier for showcasing China's image. Therefore, the translation of Chinese political literature for foreign readers is a special practice of external publicity. It is an important component of the Party and the government's efforts to convey China's voice, enhance the national image, and engage in international exchanges. It is crucial to emphasize the accurate understanding and faithful conveyance of the ideas and content of the source text, while also considering the expectations and reactions of the international readership.

To begin with, given the uniqueness of Chinese political documents in terms of text type, thematic content, publishing institutes, and social influence, the principle of translation should ensure an accurate and systematic understanding of the core content of the source text. It should objectively and comprehensively reproduce the ideas and intent of the source text, so that the original purpose of the text can be presented truthfully and completely to the readers of the translated text.

Besides, considering the uniqueness of Chinese political documents in terms of ideological system and language expressions, translation should take into account the differences in language, culture, and thinking between Chinese and English. It should emphasize the actual reception by the readers of the translated text and adopt flexible and diverse translation strategies to ensure that the main ideas of the source text can be effectively understood by the readers of the translated text. It is important to note that due to the political sensitivity of political documents and the historical nature of specific translation schemes, adjustments to translation strategies regarding readers' reception should also be carefully considered. Consistency with historical translations should be maintained for key concepts based on specific circumstances.

In conclusion, faithfully conveying the ideas and content of the source text is the fundamental principle of translating Chinese political literature for foreign audiences. Meanwhile, considering the differences in language and culture between China and foreign countries, especially the reading habits and psychological expectations of foreign audiences, achieving "mutual understanding between Chinese and foreign cultures" is the guiding principle of translating Chinese political documents for foreign readers. By balancing the accuracy and integrity of the original ideas with the readability and acceptability of the translated text, it ensures the translation quality of Chinese political literature and enhances the effectiveness of China's political discourse in foreign communications.

Ⅱ. Strategies for Translating Chinese Political Documents

1. Semantic equivalence

Semantic equivalence, also known as corresponding translation strategy, refers to the situation where the meanings of words in the source text are the same as those in the target text, maintaining basic correspondence in terms of inherent semantics and pragmatic meanings. In such cases, it is possible to consider using corresponding expressions in the target language in order to convey the semantic content of the original words. For example:

低碳发展 low-carbon development

供给侧结构性改革 supply-side structural reform

经济全球化 economic globalization

生态红线 ecological red lines

资源配置 resource allocation

Some concepts in Chinese political literature are composed of multiple words, characterized by a unique style and deep semantics, forming a specific terminological expression. In certain cases, there is no equivalent expressions in the target language for these specific concepts, but each word in the concept can be directly translated. As a result, the overall translation of these concepts generates a sense of "estrangement", aiming to emphasize the characteristics of the original words and maintain the connotation of the original concept. When translating, the differences in word order between the source text and the target text need to be taken into account. For example:

爱国统一战线 patriotic united front

社会主义核心价值观 the core socialist values

中国特色社会主义 socialism with Chinese characteristics

Chinese political documents often employ metaphors or colloquial language to express specific semantics. They have a unique style and distinctive semantics. In specific contexts, it is advisable to retain the linguistic features of the source text's vocabulary in order to vividly convey the original ideas. This can also be classified as a corresponding translation strategy. For example:

a. 坚定不移"打虎""拍蝇""猎狐"。

We have taken firm action to "take out tigers" "swat flies" and "hunt down foxes".

b. 巡视利剑作用彰显,实现中央和省级党委巡视全覆盖。

Disciplinary inspections have cut like a blade through corruption and misconduct; they have covered every Party committee in all departments at the central and provincial levels.

c. 坚持照镜子、正衣冠、洗洗澡、治治病的要求,开展党的群众路线教育实践活动和"三严三实"专题教育。

We have committed to "examining ourselves in the mirror, tidying our attire, taking a bath, and treating our ailments", launched activities to see members command and act on the Party's mass line, and initiated a campaign for the observance of the Thee Guidelines for Ethical Behavior and Three Basic Rules of Conduct.

d. 我反复讲,鞋子合不合脚,只有穿的人才知道。中国特色社会主义制度好不好、优越不优越,中国人民最清楚,也最有发言权。

I have often said that only the wearer of the shoes knows if they fit or not. The Chinese people know best whether the Chinese socialist system suits the country or not.

It should be emphasized that the connotation of specific words and their context should be carefully considered, and various translation strategies should be comprehensively applied to effectively convey the core meaning of the source text.

2. Semantic interpretation

Semantic interpretation refers to an explanatory translation strategy in which the corresponding expressions of the source text do not have a direct correspondence in the target language. This occurs when there is a difference or conflict in meaning between the words or when the semantic meaning of the source text is specific and not suitable for direct conversion into an equivalent expression in the target language. In such cases, it is necessary to provide explanations or elucidate the specific content or ideas of the source text, making the connotation of the original words more explicit and facilitating understanding for readers of the target language.

a. 小康社会。

"小康社会"是具有鲜明中国特色的时政话语,主要指经济富裕、政治民主、文化繁荣、社会公平、生态良好,需要根据具体语境作具体说明。

The concept of "Well-off society" is a political discourse with distinctive Chinese characteristics, primarily referring to a state of moderate prosperity characterized by economic affluence, political democracy, cultural prosperity, social equity and good ecology, which needs to be explained according to specific context.

决胜全面建成小康社会

to secure a decisive victory in building a moderately prosperous society in all respects

b. "三农"。

①"三农"指农业、农村和农民,要根据具体语境加以说明。

"Three rural issues" refer to agriculture, rural areas, and farmers, which need to be explained based on specific contexts.

②新时代"三农"工作必须围绕农业农村现代化这个总目标来推进。

The work on agriculture, rural areas and rural people in the new era must focus on the general goal of modernizing agriculture and rural areas.

③培养造就一支懂农业、爱农村、爱农民的"三农"工作队伍。

We will train professional rural service personnel who have a good knowledge of agriculture, love our rural areas, and care about rural people.

Semantic interpretation can also involve adjusting the nature of words, which is known as word class conversion. It involves expressing the semantic meaning of the original words using words with different properties.

④当前,世界多极化、经济全球化、文化多样化、社会信息化深入发展,人类社会充满希望。

The world today is moving towards multi-polarity and becoming more economically globalized, culturally diverse, and IT-driven. All this offers hope to humanity.

In this sentence, there is a continuous occurrence of an abstract Chinese noun "化". It is inappropriate to simply translate it into corresponding English abstract noun. Instead, it can be transformed into noun, gerund, adjective, etc., while considering the specific meanings of the word.

3. Semantic fusion

Semantic fusion refers to a method of condensing and expressing the core meaning of words or phrases in the source text when their semantic content is not obvious or when there is repetition in the form or meaning. It is a concise way to represent the semantic essence. Semantic fusion can be used for translating Chinese abstract nouns within certain categories, as well as for simplifying repetitive expressions in Chinese, known as "synonymous repetition".

(1) Abstract nouns within certain categories.

a. 要加强对全会精神贯彻落实情况的监督检查。

We will strengthen our supervision of the implementation of these decisions.

The word "情况" in this sentence does not hold any actual meaning and doesn't need to be translated accordingly. It can be directly expressed as "落实" in terms of semantics.

b. 我国稳定解决了十几亿人的温饱问题。

China has effectively addressed the food and clothing needs of over a billion people.

In this sentence, the word "问题" doesn't carry any substantial meaning. The translation should focus on conveying the semantic content of "being well-fed and clothed".

(2) Repetitive expressions in Chinese.

a. 在激烈的国际竞争中，惟创新者进，惟创新者强，惟创新者胜。

Against the backdrop of international competition, only those who innovate can make progress, grow stronger and prevail.

In this sentence, "创新者" appears continuously, but its emphasis is more on the actions and results. Therefore, in the translation, it is not necessary to repeat it.

b. 世界每时每刻都在发生变化，中国也每时每刻都在发生变化。

The world is changing with every second, every moment; and China, too, is changing with every second, every moment.

In this sentence, the repetition of "每时每刻都在发生变化" emphasizes that China, just like the rest of the world, is experiencing rapid changes constantly. To reflect the emphasis in the source text, the repetition can be expressed in the translation.

4. Semantic substitution

Semantic substitution refers to the use of similar words or phrases in the target language that may not directly correspond to the semantic meaning of the words or phrases in the source text. This technique allows for the full presentation of the original content and ideas in translation.

a. 改革全面发力、多点突破、纵深推进。

We have taken moves across the board, achieved breakthroughs in many areas, and made further progress in reform.

In this sentence, "全面" or "多点" can be expressed as comprehensive, in all areas, in all aspects, all-round, and other corresponding English words to convey the same semantic meaning as the source text.

b. 脱贫攻坚战取得决定性进展，六千多万贫困人口稳定脱贫，贫困发生率从百分之十点二下降到百分之四以下。

Decisive progress has been made in the fight against poverty: More than 60 million people have been lifted out of poverty, and the poverty headcount ratio has dropped from 10.2 percent to less than 4 percent.

In this sentence, "贫困发生率" can be translated into English as "poverty headcount ratio" or "poverty incidence" as commonly used expressions. If translated as "poverty occurrence rate", it would be considered Chinese-style English.

5. Contextualization of words

Contextualization of words refers to the richness of semantic meanings in the source text, where the specific reference and connotations vary in different contexts. It also takes into account the differences in semantic scope between the source text and translated words, requiring a corresponding expression in the target language with specific words. Take "强国" as an example:

人才强国战略

the strategy on developing a quality workforce

建设制造强国

to build China into a manufacturer of quality

加快建设人才强国

to step up efforts to make China a talent-strong country

推进贸易强国建设

to turn China into a trader of quality

推进体育强国建设

to build China into a country strong in sport

实现农业大国向农业强国跨越

to transform China from a country with high agricultural output to one with a leading edge in agriculture

为建设科技强国、质量强国、航天强国、网络强国、交通强国、数字中国、智慧社会提供有力支撑

to provide powerful support for building China's strength in science and technology, product quality, aerospace, cyberspace, and transport, and for building a digital China and a smart society

6. "Small words, big translation"

"Small words, big translation" refers to the use of common and simplified words to convey the unique or complex semantics of the source text. It means expressing the significant aspect of the source text through a "small" translation approach, such as using structures that include verbs like "do" "work" "make" "take" etc., to elaborate on the main ideas in the source text.

a. 保持政治定力，坚持实干兴邦，始终坚持和发展中国特色社会主义。

We must maintain our political orientation, do the good solid work that sees our country thrive, and continue to uphold and develop socialism with Chinese characteristics.

b. 全党要坚定信心、奋发有为，让中国特色社会主义展现出更加强大的生命力！

Our entire Party should develop unshakable confidence, work hard and work well to see socialism with Chinese characteristics display even stronger vitality.

c. 深化金融体制改革，增强金融服务实体经济能力，提高直接融资比重，促进多层次资本市场健康发展。

We will deepen institutional reform in the financial sector, make it better serve the real economy, increase the proportion of direct financing, and promote the healthy development of a multi-level capital market.

Section 7

Translation of Chinese Culture

Chinese culture, especially traditional Chinese culture, as one of the oldest and most complex cultures in the world, has a significant impact on global cultural exchange and academic development. With the deepening of globalization, translating Chinese culture into other languages has become particularly important, as it not only promotes the international dissemination of culture but also enhances cross-cultural understanding and respect. However, this process is full of challenges, especially regarding how to handle culture-specific elements and ensure the accurate transmission of information. This section aims to explore the main challenges in the process of translating Chinese culture, viable translation strategies, and analyze their practical applications through specific examples.

Ⅰ. The Features of Chinese Culture

The features of traditional Chinese culture lies in its profound historical accumulation, unique values, rich cultural forms, and the pursuit of a harmonious society. Here is a specific analysis of its uniqueness.

1. Value concepts

To begin with, Chinese culture emphasizes benevolence as the core, focusing on people-oriented thought, which prioritizes the interests of the people. Integrity and justice is another feature of Chinese Culture. Integrity serves as the basic norm for social interaction, while justice represents the embodiment of social fairness and moral standards. Besides, in Chinese culture, people pursue harmony and great unity. Chinese culture pursues social harmony and advocates the ideal of "Great Unity", which envisions a world without war where everyone is equal.

2. Traditional virtues

Traditional Chinese culture, with its profound historical roots and unique moral values, significantly influences the way of life for its people. Among the core virtues deeply ingrained in this culture are the principles of unceasing self-improvement, respect for work and collective spirit, and filial piety along with family love. These traditional virtues not only shape individual behavior but also contribute to the harmonious fabric of society at large.

The notion of unceasing self-improvement encourages individuals to always strive for betterment and personal growth, reflecting a lifelong commitment to learning and self-cultivation. This ethos is closely tied to the Confucian ideal of personal development as a path to contributing positively to society.

Moreover, respect for work and collective spirit highlights the importance of dignity in labor and the value of collaboration. Therefore, every job is honored, and teamwork is essential for achieving common goals and fostering a strong sense of community and shared responsibility among members of society.

Filial piety and family love form the cornerstone of Chinese family ethics. Filial piety encompasses more than just obedience; it involves deep respect for elders and ancestors, providing care and support when needed. The concept of family extends beyond the nuclear unit, creating a broad network of mutual care and affection that reinforces societal cohesion.

These traditional virtues continue to guide contemporary Chinese society, offering a framework for ethical behavior and social interaction that bridges the gap between ancient wisdom and modern life. They serve as a testament to the enduring legacy of Chinese culture, promoting individual excellence while simultaneously encouraging harmony within the family and the community at large.

3. Humanistic spirit

The humanistic spirit that permeates traditional Chinese culture emphasizes the pursuit of moral excellence and benevolent actions, encouraging individuals to not only aspire to be better but also to do good in their daily lives. This ethical framework is deeply entrenched in Confucian teachings, where the cultivation of virtue and the practice of kindness are considered essential for personal development and social harmony.

Chinese culture places great emphasis on the practical application of knowledge, believing that theories must be translated into action. This approach encourages individuals to use their understanding of cultural precepts and moral lessons to intervene in real-world situations, addressing practical challenges with wisdom and insight. It's about applying intellectual insights to concrete problems, ensuring that learning is not merely an abstract exercise but a tool for creating positive change.

This humanistic philosophy underscores the importance of balancing individual aspirations with communal well-being. It promotes the idea that each person has the potential to make a difference, inspiring a proactive attitude towards resolving issues and improving society.

In essence, the humanistic spirit of Chinese culture, with its focus on moral uprightness and pragmatic wisdom, fosters an environment where people are encouraged to live ethically, act benevolently, and engage actively in the betterment of themselves and their communities. This tradition continues to influence modern society and individual conduct, providing a timeless guide for navigating the complexities of human interaction and societal development.

4. Cultural diversity and integration

The cultural diversity and integration of Chinese culture reflect a dynamic interplay between maintaining indigenous traits and embracing external influences. This harmonious coexistence is evident in China's historical willingness to absorb and fuse the essence of other cultures while preserving its own distinctiveness. Pragmatically, this cultural openness has facilitated effective communication and exchange with foreign cultures, leading to the evolution of new cultural forms that are both distinctly Chinese and resonant with global audiences. Such interactions have not only enriched Chinese culture but also contributed to a broader humanistic spirit that transcends geographical and cultural boundaries. Through this process of integration and exchange, Chinese culture continues to thrive and impact the world stage, demonstrating the enduring power of diversity and unity in the global tapestry of humanity.

Overall, the uniqueness of traditional Chinese culture is not only reflected in its rich content and profound value concepts but also in its pursuit of a harmonious society, respect for tradition and innovation, and an open and inclusive cultural attitude. These unique features give Chinese culture significant global influence and value, contributing importantly to the development of cultural diversity worldwide.

II. Difficulties in Translation of Chinese Culture

Chinese culture boasts a rich history and diverse artistic forms, many of which are unique, such as Chinese poetry, calligraphy and Peking opera. The translation of these cultural forms is not merely a linguistic transformation but also a conveyance of cultural essence. Translators often encounter difficulties in finding equivalent expressions, bridging significant cultural background differences, and understanding local dialects, all of which greatly increase the complexity of translation. The challenges of translating Chinese culture are reflected in the following aspects.

1. Difficulties in finding equivalent expressions

Many unique Chinese cultural elements and concepts have no direct counterparts in English, such as the term "道" (Dao) in Daoist philosophy. Translators must strive to create translations that are both faithful to the source text and understandable to the foreign readers. This often requires adopting interpretative translation strategies, which not only raise the difficulty of translation but also demand higher levels of cultural understanding and creativity from the translator.

2. Cultural background differences

Many Chinese customs, festivals and etiquette are deeply rooted in specific historical and cultural contexts. It can be quite challenging for foreign readers unfamiliar with these backgrounds to understand such cultural phenomena. Translators need to convey not only the superficial textual information but also bridge the gap between different cultures, enabling readers to get rid of cultural barriers and appreciate the essence and charm of the culture.

3. The intricacies of local dialects

China's vast geographical expanse is home to numerous dialects that differ in phonetics, vocabulary, and even grammatical structures. How to accurately convey the special flavor and local features of the dialects to standard Mandarin readers or foreign audiences poses a significant challenge. When dealing with dialects, translators often need to balance preserving the original flair with ensuring clarity, testing not only their translation skills but also their cultural sensitivity.

In conclusion, the uniqueness and diversity of Chinese culture provide rich material for translation work but also present considerable challenges. Translators must overcome linguistic barriers and bridge cultural differences, attempting to build communication bridges between different cultures.

Ⅲ. The Application of Translation Theories in Chinese Cultural Translation

The Dynamic Equivalence Theory emphasizes that the experience of target language readers should be similar to that of source language readers, requiring translators to be faithful to the original text while also considering the acceptability of the target culture. Foreignization and domestication are two fundamental translation strategies. The former emphasizes preserving the characteristics of the source language culture, while the latter focuses on making the translation conform to the habits of the target language culture. In practical translation, translators need to flexibly apply these theories based on the characteristics of the text and the purpose of translation.

1. Dynamic Equivalence Theory and its application

The Dynamic Equivalence Theory, proposed by Eugene A. Nida, emphasizes that translation should produce an effect that is "the closest natural equivalent" to the original text, focusing on the recipient's response. This theory posits that the experience of target language readers should be similar to that of source language readers, requiring translators not only to be faithful to the original message but also to consider the acceptability and cultural background of the target culture. In the practice of Chinese cultural translation, applying the Dynamic Equivalence Theory means that translators need to maintain the style of the original text while ensuring that the translation is natural, fluent, and easy to be understood in the target language culture. The application of Dynamic Equivalence Theory is particularly important in the translation of Chinese culture. Taking Chinese poetry as an example. The artistic conception, rhythm, and subtlety are the soul of the poem. Translators must not only convey the direct meaning of the words but also transmit the emotions and artistic conception behind the poem, which requires translators to have a high level of language cultivation and profound cultural understanding. For instance, when translating Tang poetry, translators can choose expressions in the target language that evoke similar emotions or add annotations to explain the cultural background and meaning of the original text, thus enabling target language readers to experience the text in a manner similar to that of the source language readers.

2. Foreignization and domestication

Foreignization refers to the preservation of the source language culture's characteristics during the translation process, allowing target language readers to experience exotic flavors; whereas domestication focuses on making the translated work conform to the habits of the target language culture to enhance readability. These two strategies are particularly important when dealing with texts that have profound cultural backgrounds. In Chinese cultural translation, employing a foreignization strategy can showcase the uniqueness of Chinese culture, but excessive foreignization may lead to difficulty in understanding for target readers; conversely, excessive domestication may result in the loss of the original flavor of Chinese culture. Therefore, translators must flexibly apply these two strategies based on the characteristics of the text and the purpose of translation. In specific translation practices, the choice between foreignization and domestication strategies should be flexibly adjusted according to the characteristics and purpose of the translation. For texts filled with rich Chinese elements, such as Peking opera scripts or classical literary works, adopting a foreignization strategy can help preserve the original cultural characteristics. For example, classic roles in Peking opera such as "Sheng" "Dan" "Jing" and "Mo" can be translated through transliteration accompanied by annotations to maintain their cultural uniqueness. However, considering the acceptability of target language readers, certain details or phrases might need to be treated with domestication to facilitate better understanding. For instance, idioms or colloquialisms can be translated into equivalent expressions in the target language instead of being literally translated, to ensure the accurate conveyance of meaning.

In summary, in the practice of Chinese cultural translation, the effective application of dynamic equivalence theory, foreignization, and domestication strategies provides significant methodological support for overcoming cultural and linguistic barriers in translation. By flexibly employing these theories and strategies, translators can not only convey the profound essence of Chinese culture more faithfully but also promote exchange and understanding between different cultures. Therefore, for translators engaged in Chinese cultural translation, mastering these theories and strategies and enhancing their cross-cultural communication skills are indispensable tasks.

Ⅳ. Strategies and Techniques of Chinese Cultural Translation

In order to effectively handle cultural differences in translation, translators can adopt various strategies such as domestication and foreignization. Additionally, mastering some practical techniques, like in-depth research into Chinese culture and history, as well as developing sensitivity to the differences between Chinese and English languages, are also key to improving translation quality.

1. Domestication

The domestication translation strategy, also known as "localization", involves adjusting the source text to conform to the cultural and linguistic norms of the target language. This approach aims to make the translated text feel natural and familiar to the target audience, often by replacing unfamiliar cultural elements with familiar ones from the target culture. For example:

只有各国行天下大道，和睦相处，合作共赢，繁荣才能持久，安全才有保障。

Only when all countries pursue the cause of common good, live in harmony, and engage in cooperation for mutual benefit will there be sustained prosperity and guaranteed security.

In this translation, the phrase "行天下大道" comes from *Mencius · Teng Wen Gong Xia*, which means "walking on the grandest path in the world". Here, "道" means a great path or road. Instead of translating "道" literally as "road" or "path", the translator used a domestication strategy, converting "行天下大道" into "pursue the cause of common good". It means "to pursue an endeavor with shared interests", turning Chinese-specific vocabulary into expressions that Western readers can easily understand, accurately conveying the original text's meaning. For another example, "先立后破" is translated as "build the new before discarding the old". Here, "先立后破" means creating new things after breaking the old fixed patterns. Instead of translating it literally, the translator employed a domestication strategy, rendering it as "build the new before discarding the old", which precisely conveys the original meaning in a simple and understandable way.

In summary, the domestication translation strategy seeks to bridge the cultural gap by making the translation fit comfortably within the target culture, even if it means altering some aspects of the source text.

2. Foreignization

Foreignization is a translation strategy that was introduced by the American scholar Lawrence Venuti in his work *The Translator's Invisibility*. This strategy involves retaining the foreignness or otherness of the source text, including its cultural and linguistic peculiarities, so that the translated text reminds readers of its origins in another culture.

For example:

a. 万物并育而不相害, 道并行而不相悖。

All living things may grow side by side without harming one another, and different roads may run in parallel without interfering with one another.

This sentence "万物并育而不相害, 道并行而不相悖" comes from *The Book of Rites · The Doctrine of the Mean*, meaning that all things under heaven can develop together without harming each other, and various codes of conduct can operate simultaneously without contradicting each other. In this sentence, the translator adopted an foreignization translation strategy, where "道" was not translated as "code of conduct" based on its meaning rather than translated it as "roads" based on its literal meaning. However, this does not hinder Western readers' understanding. On the contrary, it adds a more vivid imagery, allowing them to better grasp the profound meaning and appreciate the extensive depth of Chinese culture.

b. 民为邦本。

Regarding the people as the foundation of the state.

This is an important aspect of Confucian political thought, originating from *Shang Shu · The Song of Five Sons*, where "邦" means state and the people are the foundation of the state. Here, the translator has translated it based on its literal meaning, adopting an foreignization translation strategy, which not only makes it understandable for Western readers but also promotes Chinese culture.

c. 前途光明，任重道远。

Our future is bright, but we still have a long way to go.

The Chinese "任重道远" comes from *The Analects · Tai Bo*, meaning the responsibility is significant, and the journey is long. "任" refers to responsibility, "道" refers to the journey. In this sentence, the translator adopted a foreignization translation strategy, where "任重道远" was translated as "We still have a long way to go", indicating there is still a long road ahead. "任重" was not translated, which is correct because it does not affect the conveyance of the original meaning and the understanding of Western readers. Adding it would make it more cumbersome as "The task is heavy and we still have a long way to go".

3. The combination of domestication and foreignization

In translation, it is essential to combine the strategies of domestication and foreignization. Domestication refers to closely integrating the cultural connotations of the source language with the target language to make the translation more accessible to the target language readers. On the other hand, foreignization involves retaining the cultural characteristics and habits of the source language to more faithfully reflect the features of the source language. In the actual translation process, the flexible combination of these two strategies can better convey the cultural connotations of the original text, ensuring that the translation not only conforms to the idiomatic usage of the target language but also preserves the distinctiveness of the original text.

Here's an example of how this strategy might be applied:

他山之石,可以攻玉。

Domestication translation: Experience from others can help improve oneself.

Foreignization translation: Stones from other hills can also polish jade.

Combination of domestication and foreignization: Just as stones from other hills can also polish jade, experiences from others can help improve ourselves.

In this example, the combination strategy maintains the original metaphor from the Chinese proverb while also providing a more accessible interpretation for readers who may not be familiar with the cultural context. More examples are as follows:

a. 他吃过的盐比你走过的路还多。

Domestication translation: He has more experience than you've had hot dinners.

Foreignization translation: The salt he has eaten is more than the roads you have walked.

Combination of domestication and foreignization: The salt he has eaten is more than the roads you have walked—in terms of experience, he's had more hot dinners than you.

In this translation, both "吃过的盐" (salt eaten) and "走过的路" (roads walked) are metaphors for the extent of one's experience. The foreignized translation retains the direct metaphors from the original, while the domesticated version switches to a commonly used expression in English. The combined translation not only conveys the meaning of the source text but also provides a familiar expression for readers, which make it more readable.

b. 他的名字是"麻烦"的代名词。

Domestication translation: His name has become synonymous with "trouble".

Foreignization translation: His name is the synonym of "mafan".

Combination of domestication and foreignization: His name has become synonymous with "mafan", literally meaning "trouble".

If the Chinese phrase "麻烦" is directly translated into "mafan", it might be difficult for non-Chinese speakers to understand. The domesticated version replaces it with the English equivalent "trouble" for clarity. The combined translation offers both the direct translation and an explanation, preserving the uniqueness of source texts while making the translated text accessible.

c. 他喜欢做老好人。

Domestication translation: He likes to play the good Samaritan.

Foreignization translation: He likes to be an old good person.

Combination of domestication and foreignization: He likes to be an old good person, essentially playing the good Samaritan.

The term "老好人" has a specific connotation in Chinese culture, referring to someone who often helps others, sometimes at their own expense. The foreignized translation keeps the original phrasing, but it may not be easily understood by foreign readers. The domesticated version uses the well-known image of the "good Samaritan" to clarify the meaning. The combined translation shows both the literal translation and introduces a western idiom to help readers understand better.

Through these examples, we can see that Chinese cultural characteristic words are very diverse, including four-character idioms, proverbs, distinctive political terms, and some words that are not so easy to translate. This not only requires the translator to have a deep understanding of Chinese culture, but also to be familiar with standard English expressions and have an understanding of English-spoken countries' culture. When translating Chinese cultural characteristic words, we need to clarify the purpose of translation, whether it is to make Western readers understand or to promote Chinese culture, and then choose the translation strategy. The "domestication" and "foreignization" translation strategies are not mutually exclusive, they each have their own advantages and can be used in combination. Regardless of which translation strategy we choose, we should make full use of their respective advantages.

V. Appreciation of Chinese Cultural Translation

The art of translation has always been a fascinating topic for linguists and cultural enthusiasts alike. It involves not only the transfer of words from one language to another but also the understanding and interpretation of cultural nuances, traditions, and customs. In this section, we will delve into the appreciation of Chinese cultural translation, focusing on traditional festivals such as the Lantern Festival (元宵节), the Double Seventh Festival (七夕节), and so on.

China, with its rich history and diverse culture, offers a plenty of unique festivals that are deeply rooted in its social fabric. These festivals are not only celebrations of seasonal changes or historical events but also reflect the values, beliefs, and aspirations of the Chinese people. As such, they serve as windows into the country's cultural identity and provide valuable insights into its societal norms and practices.

However, translating these cultural elements can be challenging due to the complexities involved in conveying their meanings and significance accurately. The task requires not only proficiency in both languages but also a deep understanding of the cultural contexts in which these festivals are celebrated. This is where the appreciation of Chinese cultural translation comes into play.

In this section, we will explore how translators navigate the delicate balance between maintaining faithfulness to the source text and adapting it to suit the target readers' cultural expectations. We will examine how the translators try to overcome potential obstacles and ensure that the essence of these festivals is preserved in translation.

Through our analysis, we aim to shed light on the intricate process of translating cultural elements and highlight the importance of cultural sensitivity in achieving effective cross-cultural communication. By appreciating the efforts made by translators to bridge cultural gaps, we can gain a deeper understanding of China's rich tapestry of traditions and foster greater appreciation for the diversity of human cultures.

春 节

春节是中国最具特色的重要传统节日，标志着中国农历新年的开始。节日活动从除夕一直持续到正月十五元宵节。春节是家人团圆的节日。在外地工作的人，都会不远千里回到家里和父母团聚。[1]在除夕之夜，一家人聚在一起包饺子，吃年夜饭，即团圆饭。[2]晚上12点左右，家家燃放烟花爆竹，辞旧迎新，希望送走不幸、迎来好运。[3]春节第一天，大家互相拜年，送上最美好的祝愿。春节期间，家家户户都会贴春联、贴年画，还会举行丰富多彩的活动，如敲锣、打鼓、踩高跷、舞龙舞狮等。

The Spring Festival

The Spring Festival is the most characteristic and important traditional Chinese festival, marking the beginning of the Chinese New Year. The festivities last from Chinese New Year's Eve to the Lantern Festival on the 15th day of the first lunar month. The Spring Festival is a time for family reunions. People working away from home will travel a long distance to come back to join their parents. On New Year's Eve, the whole family gets together, making dumplings and enjoying the meal of the Eve, or family reunion dinner. Around 12 o'clock at night, every family sets off fireworks and firecrackers to greet the new days and send off the old ones, hoping to cast away bad luck and bring forth good luck. On the first day of the Spring Festival, people pay New Year's calls, giving best wishes to one another. During the Spring Festival, every household will paste up Spring Festival couplets and Chinese New Year pictures. There are various activities, such as drum beating, gong striking, stilt walking, and dragon and lion dances.

There are some analysis about the translation of the Spring Festival.

(1) The phrase "不远千里" in this sentence is intended to convey the idea of "traveling a long distance" rather than a literal "thousand li", so it is not directly translated as "travel a thousand li", but instead as "travel a long distance". This kind of transformation from imagery to abstraction is a common technique in Chinese to English translation. "和父母团聚" is translated as "join their parents", and the English verb "join" is used appropriately, avoiding a literal translation and resulting in a concise and natural translation.

(2) This sentence uses coordinated structures and contains three verbs: "聚" (gather), "包" (make dumplings), and "吃" (eat). The translation regards "一家人聚在一起" as the main part, and then explains what they do together afterwards. It uses two parallel participle phrases "making dumplings" and "enjoying the meal of the Eve" as adverbial phrases to demonstrate the clear organization of main and subordinate elements.

(3) This sentence contains three distinct phrases. The translation treats "燃放烟花爆竹" as the main part and translates the subsequent "辞旧迎新" as a purpose clause. The final phrase "希望送走不幸，迎来好运" is rendered as a participial phrase introduced by "hoping", resulting in a compact structure and clear logic.

元宵节

农历正月十五元宵节是中国的传统节日。[1]元宵节又称灯节或上元节,是春节后的第一个重要节日,标志着春节的结束。[2]农历的第一个月称为元月,古人称夜为"宵",而元月十五晚上又是一年中第一个月圆之夜,所以称正月十五为元宵节。[3]元宵节的习俗在全国各地不尽相同,其中赏花灯、猜灯谜、吃元宵是几项最常见的民间习俗。很多地方举办元宵节灯会,会上设计各异的灯笼吸引人们前来观赏。吃元宵是元宵节的另一项重要内容。[4]据说,吃元宵的习俗起源于汉代,唐宋时期开始流行。元宵有"团圆"之意,因此吃元宵喻示着家庭团圆、和谐幸福。如今,元宵已成为人们的日常饮食之一,在超市一年四季都可以买到。[5]

The Yuanxiao Festival

The Yuanxiao Festival in China is a traditional festival celebrated on the 15th day of the first month on the lunar calendar. The festival, also known as the Lantern Festival or the Shangyuan Festival, is the first important festival after the Spring Festival, marking the end of the latter. The first month of the lunar calendar is called the yuan month, and in ancient times, the night was called *xiao* in Chinese. The 15th day of the yuan month sees the first full moon of the lunar year. Therefore, the day is called the Yuanxiao Festival. Although customs of the festival vary from region to region, the most common ones include seeing lantern exhibits, trying to solve riddles written on lanterns, and eating yuanxiao. In many places lantern fairs are held on this day, attracting people to come and see the lanterns of various designs. Eating yuanxiao is another important part of the festival. It is said that the custom of eating yuanxiao originated from the Han Dynasty and became popular during the Tang and Song periods. Yuanxiao has the connotation of reunion, thus eating yuanxiao signifies family reunions and a happy, harmonious family life. Nowadays, yuanxiao has become a food in peoples daily life and is available in supermarkets all year round.

There are some analysis about the translation of the Yuanxiao Festival.

(1) The translation of this sentence cleverly uses "the Yuanxiao Festival" as the subject of the sentence, followed by a specific introduction of the Lantern Festival's

date. When translating from Chinese to English, it is important to carefully choose the appropriate subject in order to arrange the word order of the translation properly.

(2) The key information in this sentence is that the Lantern Festival "是春节后的第一个重要节日(is the first important festival after the Spring Festival)". Therefore, the translation treats "又称灯节或上元节(also known as the Lantern Festival or the Feast of the First Full Moon)" as a past participle phrase to provide additional information, and treats "标志着春节的结束(marking the end of the Spring Festival)" as a present participle phrase acting as an adverbial, with the latter referring to the Spring Festival mentioned earlier to avoid repetition.

(3) This sentence is relatively long, and the translation should be divided into three separate sentences to facilitate reader understanding.

(4) In this sentence, "内容" can be understood as "activities" or "components", so it is not appropriate to translate it directly as "content". Therefore, it is translated freely as "part" with flexible translation methods. When translating from Chinese to English, it is important to pay attention to similar situations and avoid creating awkward translations or deviating from the original meaning by translating word for word.

(5) The use of the adjective "available" effectively conveys the meaning of "can be purchased".

七夕节

农历七月初七是中国的七夕节。[1]七夕节源自牛郎与织女[2]的传说。相传牛郎和织女相爱并结为夫妻,后来被王母娘娘拆散。[3]但是,王母娘娘被牛郎织女的爱情感动,因此允许他们在每年的农历七月初七相会。[4]据传,在七夕的夜晚,人们可以看到牛郎织女在银河相会。姑娘们会在这天晚上向天上的织女乞求自己能够心灵手巧,获得美满姻缘。[5]随着时代的变迁,有些习俗正在改变或消失。如今,在乡村,七夕节的一些传统活动仍然被保存下来,而在都市,人们赠送鲜花或礼物给爱人来庆祝这个节日。七夕节是中国传统节日中最具浪漫色彩的一个。很多年轻人选择在这一天结婚,以期婚姻幸福,白头偕老。

The seventh day of the seventh month on the lunar calendar is the Chinese Qixi Festival, or the Double Seventh Festival. The Qixi Festival originated from the legendary story of Niulang, a cowherd, and Zhinv, a weaving maid. Legend has it that

Niulang and Zhinv fell in love and got married, only to be separated by the Goddess of Heaven. However, she was so touched by their love for each other that she allowed them to meet on the seventh day of the seventh lunar month every year. It is said that on the night of Qixi, people can see Niulang and Zhinv meeting in the Milky Way. On this night, girls would pray to Zhinü for wisdom, good sewing skills, and a happy marriage. However, with the change of times, some customs have changed or disappeared. Today, some traditional customs of Qixi are still observed in rural areas of China, while in urban areas people send flowers or gifts to their beloved ones on this festival. The Qixi Festival is the most romantic of all traditional Chinese festivals. Many young person choose to marry on this day, hoping for a happy marriage and lifelong devoted love.

There are some analysis about the translation of the Qixi Festival.

(1) The translation of "七夕节" provides two options, one is the transliteration "the Qixi Festival", and the other is the descriptive translation "the Double Seventh Festival" to facilitate understanding for target readers.

(2) The handling of "牛郎" and "织女" is common in Chinese to English translation, using the transliterations "Niulang" and "Zhinv" first, followed by the English explanations "a cowherd" and "a weaving maid" to facilitate understanding for Western readers.

(3) "相传" is translated into the idiomatic expression "Legend has it that…" "后来被王母娘娘拆散" is translated as "only to be separated by the Goddess of Heaven" with an appropriate tone. The usage of "only to do sth." often indicates an unexpected or unpleasant result.

(4) The translation of this sentence does not stick to the original cause-and-effect relationship on the surface, flexibly using the commonly used English structure "so… that…", effectively conveying the original meaning.

(5) In this sentence, "会" indicates a past habitual action, and the translation uses "would". "乞求" actually refers to praying, so it is not suitable to use words like "beg", therefore the translation is using the structure "pray to sb. for sth."

(6) This sentence describes the urban-rural contrast, so the translation uses the word "while" to convey the contrasting meaning.

重阳节

每年的农历九月初九是中国的传统节日重阳节[1]。重阳节的起源可以追溯到战国时期，到了唐代，重阳节正式成为节日，沿袭至今。[2]在汉语中，"九九"与"久久"同音，有"长久""长寿"的含义，因此九月初九是一个值得庆贺的吉利日子。[3]重阳节的庆祝活动丰富多彩，包括登高、赏菊、佩戴茱萸、吃重阳糕、饮菊花酒等。[4]古代文人有不少贺重阳、咏菊花的诗词佳作。虽然重阳节的习俗很多，重阳节的核心文化价值始终是平安和谐，这一点两千多年来从未改变。[5] 1988 年，中国政府把每年农历的九月九日定为"老年节"，倡导全社会尊老、敬老、爱老、助老。2013 年，中国又以法律形式将其确定下来，体现了对老年人的关怀。如今，在重阳节这天，各地都会为老年人组织丰富多彩的活动，如义诊、书法展、绘画展、摄影展等。

The Chongyang Festival

The Double Ninth Festival, also called the Chongyang Festival and observed on the ninth day of the ninth lunar month, is a traditional Chinese festival. This festival dates back to the Warring States Period, and in the Tang Dynasty, it became an official festival, passed down to the present time. As double ninth is pronounced the same as "久久" in Chinese, which signifies forever and longevity, the day is considered an auspicious day worth celebrating. There are various activities to celebrate the festival, including ascending mountains, admiring the beauty of chrysanthemums, wearing the zhuyu plant, eating Chongyang cakes, and drinking chrysanthemum wine. Ancient literary figures composed many famous poems celebrating the Chongyang Festival and odes to the chrysanthemum. Despite all the different custom, of celebration, safety and harmony has remained the festival's core cultural value for over 2,000 years. In 1988, the Chinese government designated the ninth day of the ninth lunar month as the Day of Older Persons, advocating social respect, care, and help for the elderly. In 2013, China made the Day of Older Persons a legal holiday, showing the country's loving concern for the elderly people. Today various activities will be organized across the country for elderly people on the day, including offering free medical treatment and holding exhibitions of calligraphy, paintings, and photos for them.

There are some analysis about the translation of Chongyang Festival.

(1) "Chongyang Festival" and "Double Ninth Festival" are two possible translations for "重阳节", with the former being a transliteration and the latter being a meaning-based translation, which may be easier for target readers to understand.

(2) This sentence is about the origin of the Chongyang Festival. In translation, the phrase "dates back to" is used. The phrase "date from" can be also used to translate "追溯到". "沿袭至今" is translated as "passed down to the present time", which is similar to a non-restrictive clause to modify "an official festival".

(3) The first half of the translated sentence is a causal adverbial clause introduced by "as", while the second half is the main clause. When talking about the meaning of "九九", a non-restrictive relative clause introduced by "which" is used, making the sentence structure more coherent.

(4) The sentence discusses celebration activities. The phrase "activities to celebrate the festival" is used in the translation. In the sentence, "登高" means the custom of ascending mountains to view the distance, so it is translated as "ascending mountains". There is no exact corresponding English word for "茱萸", so Chinese pinyin is used in the translation accompanied by the category word "plant", which is a commonly used technique in Chinese to English translation.

(5) The two clauses of this sentence have a subtle contrastive relationship. It is quite skillfully handled in the translation by using a prepositional phrase introduced by "despite".

粽　子

粽子是端午节的传统食物。传统的粽子形似金字塔，由竹叶或芦苇叶包裹，由糯米做成。[1]传说[2]人们端午节吃粽子是为了纪念伟大诗人屈原。作为中国历史上具有鲜明文化特色的传统食物，粽子的种类繁多，口味也各不相同。在中国北方，粽子多为甜味，原料主要是糯米和红枣。而在中国南方，比如在广东，粽子多为咸味，有猪肉粽、火腿粽、咸蛋粽等。[3]虽然粽子最初是一种节日食物，但是现在一年四季都有出售。吃粽子的风俗也流传到了日本及东南亚国家。

Zongzi

Zongzi is a *traditional* Chinese food for the Duanwu Festival. Traditionally, it is a pyramid shaped dumpling made of glutinous rice wrapped in bamboo or reed leaves. According to the legend, *zongzi* was eaten on the Duanwu Festival in memory of the great poet, Qu Yuan. As a traditional food with distinctive Chinese cultural characteristics, *zongzi* comes in a great variety of types and flavors. In the north of China, *zongzi* is mostly sweet, made of glutinous rice mixed with jujube fruits. However, in the south of China, say, Guangdong Province, *zongzi* tends to be savory – the fillings vary from pork to ham to salted eggs. Although it started as a holiday food, *zongzi* is now available the whole year round. The custom of eating *zongzi* also finds its way to Japan and countries in Southeast Asia.

There are some analysis about the translation of *zongzi*.

(1) In the source text, there are three clauses, however, it was translated into one. The past participles "made of" and "wrapped in" are used, which is concise in wording.

(2) "传说" can be translated as "Legend has it that..." or "According to legend..."

(3) "比如" can be translated as "say", which is equivalent to "for example" and is often used in spoken language with a casual tone. "有猪肉粽、火腿粽、咸蛋粽等" refers to the fillings of *zongzi*, so the subject "the fillings" is used. When giving examples of *zongzi* fillings, the phrase "vary from...to..." is naturally used.

(4) "粽子最初...." can be translated as "it started as". Of course, it can also be translated as "it was originally..."

(5) "流传到" can be translated as "finds its way to", which vividly depicts the spread, surpassing common expressions like "spread to".

Of course, Chinese traditional culture is profound and extensive. We can see that translating Chinese culture is a challenging yet highly valuable process. In the future, translation teaching should pay more attention to the cultural literacy and bilingual abilities of translators, while also constantly exploring and innovating translation methods to better promote communication and understanding between different cultures.

Chapter 5

Opportunities and Challenges of English Translation Teaching in the Digital Era

In the digital era, English translation teaching faces significant influences and changes. Digitalization is characterized by the increased use of technology and the widespread availability of digital resources. This era has brought about a surge in the demand for English translation due to several factors.

Firstly, the digital age has connected people from different cultures and languages, leading to a greater need for effective communication. As businesses and individuals engage in global interactions, the demand for accurate and efficient translation services has grown exponentially.

Secondly, the Internet and digital platforms have made information accessible to a global audience. This has resulted in a higher requirement for English translation to bridge language barriers and enable the exchange of knowledge and ideas across borders.

Thirdly, the rise of E-commerce and international trade has created a need for proficient translation to facilitate seamless communication between sellers and buyers. Websites, product descriptions, and marketing materials often require professional translation to cater to diverse markets.

Furthermore, the digitization of content has expanded the scope of translation beyond traditional domains. With the growth of social media, online content creation, and multimedia platforms, there is a demand for translation in various formats, such as subtitles, captions, and localized content.

Overall, the digital era has significantly increased the demand for English translation services. This creates both opportunities and challenges for English translation teaching, which will need to adapt to this shifting landscape to empower learners with the necessary skills to meet these demands.

In this chapter, we will discuss some problems such as the opportunities and challenges of English translation teaching in digital era, the strategies of English translation teaching in digital era, the relationship between translation and technology, research on translation teaching in digital era and development of translation major, so as to bring some inspirations and thoughts to the readers.

Section 1

Opportunities of English Translation Teaching in the Digital Era

In the digital era, English translation teaching has been presented with new opportunities that have revolutionized the way translation has been taught and practiced. These opportunities can be categorized into three key aspects: access to abundant translation resources and tools, enhanced translation efficiency and accuracy, and expanded translation fields and employment prospects.

1. Access to abundant translation resources and tools

The digital age has brought an enormous wealth of translation resources, such as online dictionaries, corpora, and translation memory databases. These resources provide students with instant access to high-quality linguistic references, specialized glossaries, and comprehensive language databases, facilitating the learning process. Additionally, machine translation (MT) tools have advanced significantly, offering students valuable insights into different translation approaches and aiding them in developing their own translation strategies.

2. Enhanced translation efficiency and accuracy

With digital advancements, translation has become faster and more efficient. Computer-assisted translation (CAT) tools streamline the translation process by storing and reusing translated segments, improving consistency and reducing repetitive work. These tools enable translators to produce higher volumes of translations within shorter time-frames while maintaining quality. Moreover, machine learning and neural machine translation models have undergone major improvements, providing translators with instant suggestions and alternative translations, ultimately enhancing the overall accuracy of translations.

3. Expanded translation fields and employment prospects

The digital era has broadened the horizons of translation as an academic discipline, as well as a professional career. With the increasing demand for translation services in various industries, such as E-commerce, technology, and entertainment, translation professionals now have ample opportunities to work in specialized fields. The rise of online platforms and E-commerce has led to global connectivity, creating a need for accurate and culturally sensitive translations. Furthermore, the digital revolution has opened up freelance and remote work possibilities, enabling translators to work independently and access a global clientele.

In conclusion, the digital era has provided English translation teaching with unprecedented opportunities. These include wider access to resources and tools, improved efficiency and accuracy in translation processes, and expanded career prospects in diverse fields. Embracing these opportunities allows aspiring translators to thrive in an increasingly interconnected and digital world.

Section 2

Challenges of English Translation Teaching in the Digital Era

In the digital era, English translation teaching faces new challenges. These challenges can be categorized into three key aspects:

1. Facing competition and advancements in machine translation

The digital era has witnessed significant advancements in MT technology. With the rise of powerful neural machine translation models and online translation tools, there is increasing competition between human translators and automated systems. This challenges English translation education to emphasize the unique skills and added value that human translators bring, such as cultural understanding, creativity, and critical thinking. Moreover, students need to be aware of the limitations and potential pitfalls of machine translation in order to effectively collaborate with and utilize these tools.

2. Cultivating students' adaptability to the digital era

The digital age demands translators who can adapt to rapid evolving technologies and changing communication methods. English translation education needs to equip students with the necessary digital literacy skills and familiarity with translation software and tools. Students should be proficient in using CAT tools, terminology management systems, and other digital resources. In addition to translation skills, students need to develop problem-solving abilities to handle new challenges and complexities that emerge in the digital landscape.

3. Dealing with language and cultural differences

In the digital era, translators encounter diverse linguistic and cultural challenges.

Chapter 5 Opportunities and Challenges of English Translation Teaching in the Digital Era

In addition to language differences, nuances, idiomatic expressions, and cultural references add layers of complexity to translation tasks. English translation education should train students to navigate these challenges by promoting intercultural competence and sensitivity. Students should be encouraged to develop cultural awareness, research skills, and to adopt a contextual approach, ensuring that translations capture the intended meaning while being culturally appropriate for the target audience.

By addressing these challenges, English translation teaching can prepare students to excel in the digital era, enabling them to effectively compete with machine translation, adapt to technological advancements, and handle the complexities of language and cultural variations.

Section 3

Strategies of English Translation Teaching in the Digital Era

The digital era has revolutionized various aspects of our lives, including the field of translation. To equip students with the necessary skills and adaptability, English translation teaching needs to integrate technology, cultivate innovative thinking, and emphasize the importance of language and cultural exchange. There are three key strategies to achieve these goals.

1. Integrating technology and tools into teaching practice

To keep pace with the digital era, English translation education must incorporate technology and translation tools into teaching practices. One effective approach is to introduce CAT tools, which enhance translation efficiency and accuracy. Students should receive hands-on training to become proficient in using CAT tools and other translation softwares. Additionally, educators can utilize online resources and virtual collaboration platforms to foster interactive learning environments and provide real-time feedback. By integrating technology, students can adapt to the digital landscape and develop practical skills desired in the industry.

2. Cultivating innovative thinking

Information Retrieval Skills: In the digital era, translators need to think creatively and possess strong information retrieval skills. English translation education should encourage students to explore creative solutions, such as adapting translations for different media platforms or addressing cultural nuances. By engaging in critical thinking and problem-solving activities, students develop the ability to overcome

Chapter 5 Opportunities and Challenges of English Translation Teaching in the Digital Era

linguistic and cultural challenges effectively. Furthermore, educators should emphasize the importance of efficient information retrieval, teach students how to access and evaluate various online resources to enhance their translations. Cultivating these skills enables students to produce high-quality translations that meet the demands of the digital era.

3. Emphasizing bilingual and cultural exchange

Language and culture play integral roles in translation. English translation education should emphasize the significance of two-way language and cultural exchange. Students should have opportunities to engage with native speakers and immerse themselves in authentic language contexts through activities such as language exchanges or online communities. By doing so, students enhance their linguistic competency and cultural understanding, enabling them to accurately convey the intended meaning in translations. Furthermore, educators must foster a deep appreciation for cultural diversity, encouraging students to research and understand cultural references and idiomatic expressions. This cross-cultural competence ensures translations are culturally appropriate and resonate with the target audience.

English translation teaching in the digital era necessitates strategies that integrate technology, cultivate innovative thinking, and prioritize language and cultural exchange. By embracing these strategies, educators can empower students to excel in the dynamic field of translation, where the abilities to adapt to technology, think creatively, and promote cross-cultural understanding are essential.

Section 4

Expectations of English Translation Teaching in the Digital Era

In conclusion, the digital era has had a significant impact on English translation education, presenting both opportunities and challenges. As summarized throughout this chapter, several key points have emerged.

1. The impact of the digital era on English translation teaching

The digital era has revolutionized the field of English translation education in numerous ways. Firstly, the integration of technology and translation tools has greatly enhanced the efficiency and accuracy of translations. CAT tools and other softwares have become indispensable tools for translators, improving their productivity and the overall quality of translations. Additionally, the digital landscape has provided learners with access to abundant online resources and virtual collaboration platforms, offering interactive learning environments and real-time feedback. These technological advancements have reshaped the traditional methods of teaching and learning, emphasizing the importance of hands-on training and practical skills.

2. Emphasizing how to maximize opportunities and address challenges in the digital era

In order to fully leverage the opportunities presented by the digital era and overcome its challenges, several strategies need to be implemented. Firstly, educators should continue integrating technology and translation tools into teaching practices, ensuring that students are well-versed in their usage. This includes training students in the effective utilization of CAT tools, translation softwares, and online resources.

Chapter 5 Opportunities and Challenges of English Translation Teaching in the Digital Era

By doing so, students can adapt to the rapid evolving digital landscape and possess the necessary skills for success in the industry.

Moreover, cultivating innovative thinking is vital. English translation teaching should encourage students to think creatively and adapt their translations for different media platforms or cultural contexts. This fosters versatility and adaptability, skills that are highly valued in the digital era. Additionally, information retrieval skills must be emphasized. Students should be equipped with the ability to efficiently access and evaluate online resources to ensure the accuracy and reliability of their translations.

Last but not least, the digital era demands cross-cultural competence. English translation education should emphasize the importance of two-way language and cultural exchange. Students should have opportunities to engage with native speakers and immerse themselves in authentic language contexts. The exposure to different cultures ensures translations are not only accurate, but also culturally appropriate.

By implementing these strategies, English translation teaching can harness the opportunities presented by the digital era, while effectively addressing the challenges it brings. This will empower students to excel in the ever-changing landscape of translation, be equipped with the necessary skills to adapt to technology, think innovatively, and promote cross-cultural understanding.

In conclusion, English translation teaching must continually evolve to meet the demands of the digital era, integrate technology, cultivate innovative thinking, and prioritize cross-cultural competence. By doing so, educators can equip students with the skills and adaptability required to succeed in the dynamic field of translation.

Section 5

Translation and Technology

From the previous discussion, we have seen that in the digital era, technological advancements have brought unprecedented opportunities and challenges to English translation teaching, and have also presented us with a promising expectations for English translation teaching in the digital era. It can be said that the relationship among science, technology and translation is inseparable. Technological progress has driven the development of translation tools, while also providing more data and methodology for translation research. Therefore, it is necessary to further explore the relationship between technology and translation.

Ⅰ. An Overview of Translation and Technology

According to the definition provided by the International Organization for Standardization in Translation Services—Requirements for Translation Services issued by British Standards Institution in 2015, translation technology consists of a series of tools used by human translators, revisors, reviewers, and other related personnel to assist them in their work. These tools include:

1) Content management systems;

2) Writing systems;

3) Desktop publishing(tools);

4) Word processing software;

5) Translation management systems;

6) Translation memory tools and CAT tools;

Chapter 5 Opportunities and Challenges of English Translation Teaching in the Digital Era

7) Quality assurance tools;

8) Revising tools;

9) Localization tools;

10) MT tools;

11) Terminology management systems;

12) Project management software;

13) Speech recognition software.

These translation technology tools are broadly used and cover a relatively wide range, the classification of these tools is based on the primary function of each type of tool. In the actual use of these tools, a particular function of one type may be used to replace another. In a narrow sense, translation technology tools refer to those directly related to human translators, namely CAT tools and MT tools, which are also the first two concepts people might think of when discussing translation technology. Computer-aided translation refers to the process where the computer provides auxiliary services for the human translation, and human being is the main translator. The extent of the assistance depends on human beings. Computer-aided translation is a "human-translating, machine-assisting" behavior, whereas machine translation is a "machine-translating, human-assisting" or "machine-translating" behavior.

Based of the development of machine translation, there are primarily two types: rule-based machine translation (RBMT) and statistical machine translation (SMT). rule-based machine translation is the earliest proposed form of machine translation technology, which dominated the field in the 1970s and 1980s. This method requires related softwares to perform linguistic analysis on the source language text before converting it into the target language based on an existing rule base. For those source sentences that conform to linguistic rules, this method usually yields satisfactory translation results. However, for sentences that do not follow these rules, the quality of the translation is less reliable. Since languages are always dynamic, creating a comprehensive rule base is crucial for this approach. The problem is that we can never exhaust all the variations in a language, which is where the difficulty of rule-based machine translation lies.

Statistical machine translation begins in the 1990s and is more widely used currently. In this method, the related software acquires linguistic knowledge from a corpus and then use that acquired knowledge for subsequent translations. The more linguistic knowledge the related software acquires, the more mature the translation results is. The following items need to be taken into consideration when using statistical machine translation: (1) the size of the corpus. Larger corpora yield better results, especially if they contain many high-quality sentence pairs; (2) whether the corpus is categorized by specific domains; (3) the designing level of the translation engine. Modern machine translation has entered the era of neural machine translation, but it still relies on the use of highly-precised corpora. The limitation of statistical machine translation is that it lacks linguistic knowledge during the translation process, which means it may fail to account for certain special linguistic phenomena due to insufficient or flawed corpus data, thus affecfing translation accuracy. Therefore, machine translation often requires post-editing(PE) to enhance the quality of the target text.

As a translation technology, CAT appeared later than MT, but its emergence is closely related to MT.

Ⅱ. The Integrated Development History of Translation Technology

The integration of MT and CAT is a natural progression. The reasons are as follows: currently, MT still requires PE. Only after editing can the translated text meet higher translation standards, which is the process of machine translation editing. On the other hand, CAT adopts a "human-translating, machine-assisting" model, where with the aid of sufficient corpora, the translation produced by the computer only needs appropriate editing by translators to achieve a high-quality version. Here, the translator' role also embodies an editing action.

Early in the 21st century, scholars predicted that an integrated CAT system combining both CAT and MT would emerge in the future, sharing a bilingual parallel corpus. This prediction was quickly realized when the 2009 version of SDL Trados Studio integrated Google's machine translation engine right into the system.

Chapter 5 Opportunities and Challenges of English Translation Teaching in the Digital Era

III. The Interrelationship between Translation and Technology

Translation technology was born out of translation, and translation has become more vibrant thanks to the development of translation technology. Whether acknowledged it or not, it is a fact that translation technology has begun to change, or, to a certain extent, has already changed translation. In the digital era, translation is no longer an individual activity but one with collective characteristics. This is reflected in aspects such as the production of target texts, the application of corpora, the management of translation projects and the setup of translation workflows. The translation determines the starting point of translation technology, but the influence of future translation activities on the development of translation technology will diminish. In rule-based machine translation, the technology considered by human beings is limited to the textual level; in statistical machine translation, the focus is on corpora, and the improvement in translation quality is very significant; after the emergence of neural machine translation, translation software is like the human brain, learning from corpora, leading to a leap in translation quality.

To accurately define the interrelationship between translation and technology, it is first necessary to clarify the concepts of the two elements: the translation subject and the translation object. The translation subject can be a human translator, a machine, or an effective combination of both; the translation object refers to various genres of texts awaiting translation. The match of the two entirely depends on the execution of translation management. This is also why translation subjects of institutions generally adopt translation management systems.

From the evolution of translation technology, "assistance" and "replacement" are the best descriptors of its evolution. In the early stages of evolution, technology played a supporting role at most; when the quality of translations assisted by technology began to approach that of human translations, technology started to play a replacement role. So how can human translators, as primary agents of translation, play their roles effectively? Two aspects are worth noting: one is the cultivation and improvement of their own translation abilities; the other is the attention and master of translation technology. The former is an eternal topic and one of the themes of translation education; no human translator should neglect the improvement of their own translation skills due to the effective intervention of translation technology. Only by enhancing their translation abilities to the highest level and effectively applying modern translation technology can human translators always ensure their status as the main agents of translation.

In order to master translation technology, one must pay attention to its narrow and broad senses. From a narrow perspective, translators must be proficient in a specific translation technology, because without a concrete understanding of a technology, one cannot make an accurate judgment about it or the entire field of translation technology. From a broad perspective, relying on a certain translation technology is far from sufficient when performing a translation task. The development of translation technology is eternal and will experience accelerated growth. In the digital era, teachers should improve their teaching abilities and combine information technology with their teaching. Teachers should try to effectively apply translation technology to their teaching and research so that they can cultivate more qualified linguistic talents.

Section 6

The Development Trend of Translation Studies in the Digital Era

In the digital Era, technology has had a profound impact on translation and translation teaching. Research on translation teaching has become increasingly important than ever before. Therefore, it is necessary to study the trends of translation development, the sociology of the translation profession, and the rise of non-professional translation in the digital era. Educational institutions and research organizations should strengthen cooperation and conduct in-depth research on translation teaching in the digital era, exploring the best teaching models and strategies to meet the needs and challenges of the digital era.

I. Industrialization and Professionalization of Translation

Translation studies entered a period of cultural turn, during which the interdisciplinary development of translation theory was largely based on the theoretical advancements in disciplines such as literature, cultural sociology, and linguistics. During this time, researchers have attempted to uncover different aspects of translation activities, expanding the horizons of translation studies from language to culture, from meaning to function, from text to context, and from individual translators to society. Concurrently with theoretical developments, the explosive growth in market demand and rapid technological progress have also spurred the globalization, industrialization, and intelligent development of translation practices. Consequently, translation research has opened up many new fields, and traditional translation models are facing new opportunities and challenges as the frontiers of translation studies continue to expand.

In the past 20 years, with the rapid development of globalization and the further refinement of social occupational division, there has been an increasing demand for professional language services in economy, political communication, and so on. Driven by forces such as translation associations, translation companies, and relevant government agencies, translation activities have shifted from being individually or institutionally isolated to becoming market-oriented and operating on a large scale. An increasing number of professional translators have emerged; the professional division of labor in translation has become more detailed; and systems for translator education, training, and certification have matured. These phenomena are concrete manifestations of the industrialization and professionalization of the translation market.

Although the development of the translation industry and the translation job market is changing rapidly, a systematic model accepted by theoretical paradigm has not been proposed by current research. As for translation market research, translation is regarded as a product or service, and its cross-lingual and cross-cultural nature gives way to its socio-economic characteristics. Therefore, relevant translation studies also primarily seek theoretical support from the disciplines of professional sociology and industrial economics, using concepts and theoretical frameworks provided by these disciplines to deepen understanding of the translation industry or propose solutions to the existing problems in the translation market.

This section first briefly introduces descriptive studies related to the translation market, and then focuses on exploring the possibilities of applying theories from professional sociology and industrial economics to study the professionalization and industrialization of translation. Professionalization and industrialization are two sides of the same coin in the marketization process of translation. The former starts from the perspective of professional translators and falls within the category of professional sociology, studying the stages and indicators that translation must go through to elevate from a common occupation to a profession, as well as the roles and power dynamics of various parties in this process; the latter starts from the perspective of industrial development and falls within the category of industrial economics, mainly focusing on issues such as industry norms, pricing mechanism, and quality control. Although these two originate from different theoretical frameworks, both aim towards the ultimate goal of establishing order in the translation market.

II. Translation Market Description Research

Research on translation markets and the development of the translation profession is characterized by its market-orientation, especially in the early stage of industrialization, where objectively describing the market conditions as both the foundation and one of the goals of theoretical research. Therefore, many early studies focused on describing the state of the translation market, striving to objectively depict aspects such as the size of the translation market, the social status and remuneration of translators, the acceptance of translation courses and professional training, and the market recognition of translation qualifications. A representative work among these early descriptive studies is Daniel Gouadec's *Translation as a Profession*. This book provides a comprehensive and detailed portrayal of the translation job market and can almost serve as an introductory guide for professional translators. It focuses on the specific scenarios in the work of professional translators, closely examines all aspects of their work, pays attention to the translators' personal interests, and introduces in detail the characteristics of the translation profession, workflow, role division, related institutions, relevant training, and challenges brought by new industry developments. Similar literature includes Choi & Lim's overview of the current situation and issues of translation market in Republic of Korea.

Although such literature can provide practitioners with a wealth of practical information, most of the literature mainly introduce personal experiences, so they cannot provide objective research methods and theoretical guidance. In light of this, by using sociological methods, some studies have collect first-hand data from translation practitioners through questionnaires and interviews. These studies cover various aspects of the translation profession, such as using questionnaires to compare and analyze the expected remuneration, education level, professionalism, visibility, reputation, and power within the company between regular full-time translators and core company employees. Other similar surveys include studies on the translation market and the status of translators in ASEAN countries, as well as research on the status and self-awareness of translators in Malaysia.

By a detailed analysis of the Canadian Translators Association journals and recruitment advertisements, Bowker found that translators' professional qualifications lack recognition by the public, and recruiters place more emphasis on translators' education background and work experience, showing little understanding of the professional qualification certification mechanisms. Other similar studies have also confirmed from different perspectives that low professional status of translators is a global phenomenon. As a profession, which requires specialized knowledge, skills, and ethical standards, translation has not been fully recognized. The methods of questionnaires and interviews have compensated to some extent for the deficiencies of traditional experiential discourse and have been considered the best way to understand market conditions, especially the professional status of practitioners. On the basis of description, the focus of translation market research lies in understanding and analyzing the conditions of the translation market and selecting more effective theoretical perspectives to help researchers deeply understand the operational rules of the translation market and solve the problems encountered at various stages of industrialized development. The widespread use of sociological empirical research methods in the above studies also reflects the sociological nature of translation market research, indicating that some theories proposed by sociologists regarding professions and specializations can be used to examine the current state of translation industrialization.

Ⅲ. Professional Sociology Research

Professional sociology is one of the subfields of sociology, mainly focusing on a category of work with higher social status-professions. Although in China "profession" is often translated as "职业"(occupation), within the theoretical framework of professional sociology, there is a distinction between occupation and profession, and this distinction is the fundamental starting point of its research. Therefore, only by translating them respectively as "职业"(occupation) and "专业"(profession) can their differences be reflected.

Chapter 5 Opportunities and Challenges of English Translation Teaching in the Digital Era

The core of professional sociological research lies in distinguishing between the concepts of "occupation" and "profession" and analyzing the characteristics and professionalization process of professions.

1. Distinction between occupation and profession

Occupation: Typically, occupation refers to the paid work that people frequently engage in, such as translation (both written and oral).

Profession: Profession is not only a type of occupation but also requires practitioners to have formal training, high educational qualifications, specialized knowledge and skills, and enjoys higher reputation and social status. Typical professions include doctors and lawyers.

2. Characteristics of a profession

(1) Specialized knowledge and systematic theory: Professionals need to possess profound knowledge and theoretical system.

(2) Entry mechanism for the industry: Usually, the entry mechanism for the industry is based on higher education, certification, and professional training.

(3) Ethical norms and professional associations: Professionals should adhere to morals and may belong to relevant professional organizations.

(4) Higher educational level, social status, and remuneration: These are the social recognition commonly enjoyed by professionals.

3. Professionalization process

The professionalization process of translation describes the transition from simple paid work to acquiring professional status. This process involves enhancing the social status of the translation occupation, establishing industry standards and ethical norms, and potentially setting up professional certification and education training systems.

From the discussion mentioned above, it is clear that occupation refers to remunerative work that people frequently engage in, which can be further divided into categories such as translation and interpretation, which is one of the most basic occupational categories. On the other hand, a profession is first and foremost a type of occupation, but it also requires practitioners to receive formal training, possess higher education, specialized knowledge and skills, and enjoy higher reputation and social status.

In summary, all professions are occupations, but not all occupations eventually become professions; or in other words, not all individuals with jobs and stable income can be referred to as professionals. Currently, within the Chinese translation industry, discussions and researches on the professionalization of translation essentially describe the process by which translation evolves from a remunerative occupation to a profession and achieves professional status. In the theoretical framework of professional sociology, the term "专业化" (professionalization) corresponds to the English term professionalization, accurately reflecting the goal and process of elevating the status of the translation profession.

Different scholars have vastly different summaries of the characteristics of different professions, but there is still consensus among them. It is generally believed that for a profession to be recognized, it needs to have several basic characteristics: specialized knowledge and systematic theory, an industry mechanism based on higher education, qualification certification, and training, professional ethical norms, and professional association organizations, as well as practitioners with higher levels of education, social status, and salary returns.

4. Reflections on the research of sociology of translation as a profession

The early research on professional sociology primarily focused on the medical and legal professions in western countries. Gradually, its attention shifts to other professions, such as education and nursing. These studies may hold some references for research on the professionalization of translation, but there are still significant differences between the aforementioned professions and the field of translation, including industry disparities and socio-cultural backgrounds. Therefore, when examining the development of the translation profession from the perspective of professional sociology, it should be rooted in an understanding of the nature and practice of translation.

Professional status implies a certain degree of professional autonomy, meaning that professionals have the authority to determine their work content and methods. The factors affecting professional autonomy are complex, but the fundamental premise

Chapter 5 Opportunities and Challenges of English Translation Teaching in the Digital Era

lies within the profession itself: professional knowledge must be sufficiently complex and profound that amateur without specialized education may find it difficult to comprehend or master. Only by achieving this can professionals gain recognition from clients and society, which makes it possible to implement market entry systems at the policy or regulatory level. In other words, a certain degree of professional exclusivity is a prerequisite for maintaining professional status.

However, compared to the classic subjects of professional sociology in western countries, such as medicine and law, it is not hard to see that knowledge and skills required for professional translators do not unequivocally reach the level of professional exclusivity. Firstly, researches on translation competencies and translator capabilities reveal that a considerable part of the translation skills are not exclusive to the profession of translation. Sometimes, professionals who are proficient in foreign languages may be more suited for highly specialized translation tasks than those without subject expertise. Secondly, current translation vocational education is primarily skill-oriented. Although the abstract theoretical research may be helpful, it does not play a decisive role. Furthermore, under the influence of globalization, advancements in Internet technology, and national policies, bilingual and intercultural competence education is becoming increasingly widespread. This inevitably leads to societal misconceptions about the translation profession, maintai-ning a degree of openness in the translation market and adding difficulty to the implementation of industry entry mechanisms. Relevant surveys also indicate that the market has a low acceptance rate for translation qualification certifications.

As for the profession of translation, it is clearly unrealistic and may not always be beneficial to achieve a complete monopolistic control of the market, where only qualified individuals are permitted to engage in translation work. In the face of the non-professional translation boom in the digital era, we might consider incorporating non-professional translation into the hierarchy of the translation market, allowing it to form an integral part alongside other types of professional translation. Beyond vertical stratification, there are also significant differences between horizontally segmented specialties. For example, the pace of professional development in interpretation and translation is not uniform. To some extent, it can be said that interpretation is more easily to gain professional status compared to translation. As for interpretation itself, further distinctions can be made, such as conference interpretation which began to gain international recognition in the 1950s and quickly professionalized.

The factors affecting professional status are diverse. Except for the depth of professional knowledge and skills mentioned above, other factors also influence a profession's status within the social structure.

Ⅳ. Concerns and Challenges of Deprofessionalization: The Rise of Non-Professional Translation in the Digital Era

The impact of the digital era on the translation market cannot be overlooked. The evolution of online communication has transformed both translation and the organizational models of translation associations. In the digital era, the social signals that signify a translator's professional status are gradually shifting to electronic media. Consequently, the rise of outsourced translation, volunteer translation, and machine translation are often seen as elements that disrupt the order of the translation market. Initially, the development of the Internet technology may lead to disorder of translation market and low-quality translation. Therefore, translators need to establish their professional status in the digital era.

In the digital era, new media emerged and developed quickly, the advancements in Internet collaborative technology are propelling the production, dissemination and exchange of global culture towards computer-mediated communication. The globalization and networking of culture have created a massive demand for translation that cannot be met by commercial translation services alone. Supported by Internet technologies related to interaction, collaboration and distribution, a participatory network culture is thriving. The demands for translation lead to an emergence of numerous "volunteer" translators who are happy to translate without compensation. They take pleasure in translation and engage in free translation activities in their spare time. In the past, more than a decade, they have grown into an "Internet translation force" that cannot be overlooked.

Non-professional translators, based on sharing and participatory culture on the Internet, have fundamentally changed the traditional top-down cross-cultural

Chapter 5   Opportunities and Challenges of English Translation Teaching in the Digital Era

communication model initiated by patrons such as states, industry organizations, and publishers. In situations where patrons are absent or unable to meet Internet users' demands, Internet users will take an active role in cross-cultural dissemination, producing the translation products they desire and constructing their ideal language and cultural exchange models. In this sense, the Internet volunteer translators, represented by fansub groups, have brought profound changes to translation practices, especially those serving cross-cultural communication, compelling us to re-examine the roles and relationships among participants in translation. This phenomenon has attracted widespread attention from both industry and academy. There are a wide variety of terms used to describe it, such as non-professional translation, Internet translation, amateur translation, fans translation, community translation, user-generated translation, volunteer translation, participatory translation, and so on. These terms reflect different focuses of various scholars on this phenomenon. For instance, Internet translation emphasizes the distribution channel; amateur translation highlights the identity of the translator; fans translation reflects the motivation of the translators; community translation underscores the service purpose and audience.

The focus of the discussion here is on the challenges posed to the professional translation by non-professional translation, the term "non-professional translation" is primarily used. Non-professional translation refers to spontaneous, unpaid translation activities. Some scholars have pointed out that unpaid non-professional translation could disrupt the translation market, affecting job opportunities and market prices for professional translators. However, more scholars are optimistic about this trend, considering it a challenge and even an opportunity for an increasingly open and diversified translation market. The reasons are as follows.

First of all, professional translators alone cannot fully meet the market's enormous demands for translation services, and the emergence of non-professional translators effectively complement professional services. For example, due to cultural globalization, a large number of entertainment programs and films are accessible to the Internet users. They are eager to engage in global cultural communication. However, due to the various restrictions of copyright, business regulations, and national policies on the introduction of cultural products, these translation needs are not met through commercial channels. This creates a gap between supply and demand, but non-professional translators have risen to fill to some extent.

Secondly, the collaborative and sharing work mode of non-professional translation aligns with the development trends of digital era and has considerable inspirational value for the growth of the translation industry. In the digital era, non-professional translation has a significant threat to the labor market structure and poses the greatest threat to the identity and livelihood of professional translators. In the digital era, the potential issues of professional translation are increasingly highlighted. Therefore, the translation profession should reflect on and actively respond to the changes brought by this trend to have development and progress.

In addition, through a certain division of labor and cooperation, non-professional translation might bring more development opportunities for professional translators. In fact, although non-professional translators can complete certain translation tasks and may seem to replace professional translators superficially, the translation tasks they undertake are often larger in volume, lower in quality, and urgent in time, requiring the collaborative completion of a large number of translators. This necessitates the involvement of professionally educated and trained translators. Moreover, professional and non-professional translators can collaborate due to project, management, technical support, quality assurance, qualification verification, and so on.

In terms of translation teaching, although it is not yet widespread, many teachers have begun integrating online translation platforms and volunteer translation projects into translation curriculum design and teaching practice. Volunteer translation projects provide a platform for translators to exercise their skills, accumulating translation experience of engaging in professional translation work, which will help the students smoothly shift from students to professional translators. Engaging in volunteer translation while studying translation not only helps students improve their translation skills but more importantly, enhances their awareness of social services, cultivates their teamwork abilities.

When addressing these challenges, it is crucial to devise appropriate strategies in translation teaching. The teachers can fully use digital technology to design interactive and personalized teaching content. It is quite important for teachers to realize that

Chapter 5 Opportunities and Challenges of English Translation Teaching in the Digital Era

they should pay more attention to cultivate students' independent thinking and creativity. Moreover, interdisciplinary teaching methods that integrate science and technology with translation can provide students with a more comprehensive knowledge system and practical experience. The teachers should apply the latest scientific and technological achievements to their teaching practices so as to enhance the students' learning effectiveness and competitiveness.

In the digital era, it is particularly important to conduct in-depth research on translation teaching tailored to this era and to explore the most appropriate teaching models and strategies. Furthermore, the development of the translation profession needs to keep pace with the times, continuously updating curriculum design and teaching methods to meet the demands and challenges of the digital era.

In summary, English translation teaching in the digital era faces challenges but also holds tremendous opportunities. Only through scientific research and innovative teaching strategies can we better meet these challenges and provide better support for the career development of the students.

主要参考文献

1. Eugene A. Nida. *Language and Culture:Contests in Translating*[M]. Shanghai: Shanghai Foreign Language Education Press,2001.

2. Ma Huijuan. *A Study on Nida's Translation Theory*[M]. Beijing:Foreign Language Teaching and Research Press,2003.

3. Xiao Junshi. *An Approach to Translation from Chinese into English and Vice Versa*[M]. Beijing:The Commercial Press,1982.

4. Nida, E. A. ,&Charles R. Taber. *The Theory and Practice of Translation*[M]. Shanghai:Shanghai Foreign Language Education Press,2004.

5. Nida, E. A. *Language, Culture and translating*[M]. Shanghai:Shanghai Foreign Language Education Press,2003.

6. Baker, M.. *In Other Words:A Coursebook on Translation*[M]. Beijing:Foreign Language Teaching and Research Press,2000.

7. Channell, J. *Vague Language*[M]. Shanghai:Shanghai Foreign Language Education Press,2000.

8. Li Yan. *On Fuzziness in Literary translation*[M]. Shanghai:Shanghai International Studies University,2003.

9. 张培基,等. 英汉翻译教程[M]. 上海:上海外语出版社,1980.(2000重印).

10. 张培基. 英汉翻译教程[M]. 上海:上海外语出版社,2009.

11. 叶晓英,白瑞丽. 英语翻译理论多视角探究[M]. 北京:中国书籍出版社,2017.

12. 李文革. 西方翻译理论流派研究[M]. 北京:中国社会科学出版社,2004.

13. 平君. 基于应用语言学的大学英语教学模式改革研究[J]. 吉林省教育学

院学报，2018（8）：76.

14. 司显柱，曾剑平. 英汉互译教程［M］. 北京：北京大学出版社，2009.
15. 程晓堂，郑敏. 英语学习策略［M］. 北京：外语教学与研究出版社，2002.
16. 苗兴伟，秦洪武. 英汉语篇语用学研究［M］. 上海：上海外语出版社，2010.
17. 谢建国. 英语翻译［M］. 北京：机械工业出版社，2005.
18. 景志华，孙东菱. 实用英语翻译［M］. 北京：中国电力出版社，2013.
19. 曹勇宏，方青卫. 大学英语翻译理论与技巧［M］. 开封：河南大学出版社，2000.
20. 赵红军. 英语翻译基础［M］. 沈阳：东北大学出版社，2014.
21. 陈可培，边立红. 应用文体翻译教程［M］. 北京：对外经济贸易大学出版社，2012.
22. 廖国强，江丽容. 实用英汉互译理论、技巧与实践［M］. 北京：国防工业出版社，2011.
23. 赵广发，胡雅玲，薛英英，等. 英语实用文体翻译理论与实践研究［M］. 北京：中国水利水电出版社，2016.
24. 叶子南. 高级英语翻译理论与实践［M］. 4版. 北京：清华大学出版社，2020.
25. 彭萍. 实用语篇翻译：英汉双向［M］. 2版. 北京：中国宇航出版社，2022.
26. 陆巧玲，周晓玲. 网络环境下大学英语教学改革理论与实践［M］. 上海：上海交通大学出版社，2012.
27. 王成云，闫红梅. 人民日报学术文库：汉英翻译理论与实践［M］. 北京：人民日报出版社，2015.
28. 杜春雷，蒋欣. 实用商务英语函电［M］. 南京：东南大学出版社：2014.
29. 何刚强. 笔译理论与技巧［M］. 北京：外语教学与研究出版社，2009.
30. 佟磊. 英语翻译理论与技巧研究［M］. 长春：东北师范大学出版社，2017.
31. 胡伟华，等. 新编英语翻译理论与实践教程［M］. 北京：外语教学与研究出版社，2016.

32. 张维友. 英汉语词汇对比研究［M］. 上海：上海外语教育出版社，2010.

33. 武锐. 翻译理论探索［M］. 南京：东南大学出版社，2010.

34. 黄成洲，刘丽芸. 英汉翻译技巧：译者的金刚钻［M］. 西安：西北工业大学出版社，2008.

35. 谢天振. 中西翻译简史［M］. 北京：外语教学与研究出版社，2009.

36. 于元根. 二十世纪的中国语言应用研究［M］. 太原：书海出版社，1996.

37. 钟书能. 英汉翻译技巧［M］. 2版. 北京：外语教学与研究出版社，2021.

38. 廖七一. 当代英国翻译理论［M］. 武汉：湖北教育出版社，2001.

39. 宿荣江. 文化与翻译［M］. 北京：中国社会出版社，2009.

40. 王恩科，李昕，奉霞. 文化视角与翻译实践［M］. 北京：国防工业出版社，2007.

41. 张全. 全球化语境下的跨文化翻译研究［M］. 昆明：云南大学出版社，2010.

42. 王宏印. 中国文化典籍英译［M］. 北京：外语教学与研究出版社，2009.

43. 冯庆华. 实用翻译教程：英汉互译［M］. 上海：上海外语教育出版社，2001.

44. 孙友中. 高等学校外国语言文学类专业"理解当代中国"系列教材. 英语系列教材. 汉英翻译教程［M］. 北京：外语教学与研究出版社，2022.

45. 黄国文. 翻译研究的语言学探索［M］. 上海：上海外语教育出版社，2006.

46. 刘重德. 文学翻译十讲［M］. 北京：中国对外翻译出版公司，1998.

47. 周方珠. 翻译多元论［M］. 北京：中国对外翻译出版公司，2004.

48. 黄国文. 翻译研究的语言学探索［M］. 上海：上海外语教育出版社，2006.

49. 桂乾元. 翻译学导论［M］. 上海：上海外语教育出版社，2004.

50. 王东风. 国外翻译理论发展研究［M］. 北京：外语教学与研究出版社，2020.12（2024.1重印）.

51. 陈毅平，秦学信. 大学英语文化翻译教程［Z］. 北京：外语教学与研究出版社，2024.4.

52. 刘宓庆. 新编当代翻译理论［M］. 北京：中国对外翻译出版公司，2005.10.

53. 赵秋荣，葛晓华. 翻译能力研究［M］. 北京：外语教学与研究出版社，2023.4（2023.10重印）.

54. 金惠康. 跨文化交际翻译续编［M］. 北京：中国对外翻译出版公司，2003.9.

55. 杨志红. 翻译测试与评估研究［M］. 北京：外语教学与研究出版社，2019.9（2021.3重印）.

56. 陈治安，文旭，刘家荣. 模糊语言学概论［M］. 重庆：西南师范大学出版社，1997.

57. 毛荣贵. 翻译美学［M］. 上海：上海交通大学出版社，2005.

58. 许渊冲译. 唐宋词一百五十首［Z］. 北京：北京大学出版社，1990.

59. 吕叔湘. 中诗英译比录［Z］. 上海：上海外语教育出版社，1980.

60. 阿成，杨宪益，等. 唐诗：英汉对照［Z］. 北京：外文出版社，2001.

61. 伍铁平. 模糊语言学［M］. 上海：上海外语教育出版社，1999.

62. 吴海慧. 奈达功能对等视角下的商业广告语汉译英翻译［D］. 吉林财经大学，2011.